Management
By
Values

Management By Values

Management Respecting and Promoting Values

Edited by **Andrzej Herman**
Tadeusz Oleksyn
Izabela Stańczyk

Jagiellonian University Press

The book has been financed by the Jagiellonian University from the funds of the Warsaw School of Economics

REVIEWER

Prof. Krzysztof Marecki

COVER DESIGN

Marta Jaszczuk

ISBN 978-83-233-4011-9

www.wuj.pl

Jagiellonian University Press
Editorial Offices: Michałowskiego St. 9/2, 31-126 Cracow
Phone: +48 12 663 23 82, Fax: +48 12 663 23 83
Distribution: Phone: +48 12 631 01 97, Fax: +48 12 631 01 98
Cell Phone: +48 506 006 674, e-mail: sprzedaz@wuj.pl
Bank: PEKAO SA, IBAN PL 80 1240 4722 1111 0000 4856 3325

WORK AND AUTHORS

I. SURVEY RESEARCH (pages 13–155)
The authors (in alphabetical order): Andrzej Herman (ed.), Andrzej Metelski, Tadeusz Oleksyn (ed.), Grzegorz Sobiecki, Izabela Stańczyk (ed.)

II. CASE STUDIES (pages 157–234)
1. Capgemini – Values on the global market
    Authors: Tadeusz Oleksyn, Izabela Stańczyk
2. Qumak S.A. – Values in an innovative firm
    Authors: Tadeusz Oleksyn, Izabela Stańczyk
3. Five O'Clock – Values in a family firm
    Authors: Izabela Stańczyk, Tadeusz Oleksyn
4. Delphi Automotive S.A. – Drive values
    Authors: Izabela Stańczyk, Tadeusz Oleksyn

III. CHOSEN AXIOLOGICAL ISSUES (pages 235–328)
1. Contemporary economic axiology and its relations with the management of economic value
    Author: Andrzej Herman
2. Nature of values and catalogue of values in management
    Author: Tadeusz Oleksyn
3. Final reflections
    Authors: Andrzej Herman, Tadeusz Oleksyn

CONTENTS

Tadeusz Oleksyn

INTRODUCTION

The research described here is the continuation of several years of the subject matter of research on MANAGEMENT BY VALUES (MBV), which has been realized since 2012 within the framework of self-analysis by the College of Science on Entrepreneurship of SGH Warsaw that is also run with the participation of scientific and research employees from other colleges.

In the period of 2013–2014, empirical research was executed which consisted of the following:

(1) survey research, which was run in accordance with the original research tools that were prepared, tested and perfected in the third quarter of 2013, while also the copyright IT system aiding the formulation of results;

(2) case studies of enterprises of interest to researchers from the viewpoint of the level of involvement and advancement in the sphere of MBV (research run from the second quarter to the fourth quarter of 2014).

Two copyright studies are directly related to this research, namely Andrzej Herman on the issue of the axiology of economic values and the proposition of the catalogue of values by Tadeusz Oleksyn which is a modified version of a similar catalogue dating from the year 2012. Both of these works have been presented in section 3 of the herein work.

The work has been carried out within the framework of statutory research of College of Science on Entrepreneurship of SGH Warsaw (research no. KNOP/S/03/14) by the employees of the aforesaid college with the participation of Izabela Stańczyk PhD from the Faculty of Management and Social Communication of the Jagiellonian University in Cracow and Grzegorz Sobiecki PhD from the Faculty of Economics and IT of Warsaw University of Life Sciences.

The undertaking of this subject matter was the result of the conviction of both the authors, as well as the people from the management team of the Warsaw School of Economics that accepted and financed it on the premise that **management should both respect and promote values**, not only economic values, but also non-economic ones that are important for our contemporary civilization that are frequently precious and cultural heritage of many centuries. This conviction reinforces the analysis of the cause of the last global crisis that occurred in the years 2007–2008 and which still has not been overcome (in the opinion of a multitude of people), as not all the causes have ceased to exist.

Out of all the numerous techniques of management, the technique of *Management by values* has been propagated for several decades, which is associated with Ken Blanchard and Michael O'Connor.[1] In sparing their point of view and array of accurate observations, we are after all expressing the conviction that it is not possible to manage solely by values. Such management would be excessively labile and could in addition resemble "management by appeal". Hence, we acknowledge the notion of management that respects and promote values as being the most appropriate, which has been expressed in the sub-title of this report. We are convinced that management should serve the realization of socially and morally proper aims in order to be efficient and effective, while also respecting the law and good practices, basing on values and supporting, promoting and developing them. Nevertheless, in order for them to be efficient and effective, it cannot be restricted to displaying and relying on values. It must avail of the achievements of contemporary management, both soft and hard techniques and tools, while also being universal and harmonized. Values are important, very much so in fact, but are not sufficient in themselves. Aims are also essential, as well as their optimization and harmonization; whereas management by aims is still useful as the most commonly applied technique in the world. Strategies, tactics and operationalization are essential. Systemic management is usually useful, particularly in larger organizations. Integrated management may be better than any specialized management, including management by values. Thus, while respecting values and striving towards their strengthening, we do not perceive management by values as a panaceum for management, nor are we proponents for its absolutization. Nevertheless, in our opinion there is no either/or relation here: either management by values or management without values. We advocate the integration of values in the philosophy of management and attach a high level of importance to values. One of the most significant aims of the research was to establish how it really is in practice, not just (only) in terms of declarations.

The main aim of this research was to recognise the significance of various groups of values in the management of organizations. We had expected that it would be varied in terms of the different types of organization, which generally turned out to be confirmed: differences occurred in the sphere between joint-stock companies, other trading companies and organizations that are not enterprises although they were not very large in general. Likewise, we were also interested in the significance and utilization of values in terms of the formation of the culture of an organization and in the personnel policy, by taking account of values during the course of recruiting and selecting staff,

---

[1] K. Blanchard, M. O'Connor, *Managing by Values*, Berret – Koehler Publishers, San Francisco 1997.

professional development, motivating and rewarding, as well as evaluations and promotions.

The research aims and questions were partly different in the survey research and case studies. These have been more broadly presented in sections one and two of this report. The main thesis and complementary theses have also been presented here.

The authors would like to thank all the people who contributed to making this research possible, thus a particular word of gratitude to His Magnificence, the Rector of the Warsaw School of Economics Prof. Tomasz Szapiro PhD and the Dean of the College of Science on Entrepreneurship Associate Professor Roman Sobiecki, while also all the respondents and participants of the survey research, managing staff and internal experts from enterprises who wanted to respond in a positive manner to the offer of cooperation and who contributed so much. We would like to particularly express our gratitude to the following people:

- Mrs. Agnieszka Jarecka M.A., Head of HR Services and Mrs. Dominika Nawrocka M.A., Talent Acquisition Manager Cracow of Capgemini Poland;
- Mr. Adam Bunsch PhD in Engineering – director, as well as Mrs. Joanna Duliban M.A. from Qumak S.A. company;
- the owners of the firm Five O'Clock: Mr. Bartosz Siess and Mrs. Magdalena Brzezicka and Mr. Mark Brzezicki, and also Mrs. Izabela Kaczyńska M.A., HR Manager of Delphi Automotive Polska.

We would also like to thank the reviewers – Prof. Krzysztof Marecki PhD from the College of Economics and Social Studies of the Warsaw School of Economics.

SECTION ONE

MANAGEMENT OF VALUE AND BY VALUE. SURVEY RESEARCH

1. GENERAL INFORMATION ABOUT RESEARCH SURVEY

1.1. Research aims

The aims of the research carried out in the years 2013–2014 were the following:

- establishing the significance of various groups of values in management and priorities in this field;
- specifying the impact of values on management in organizations of various types;
- establishing, which values gain in terms of importance and which ones lose importance;
- establishing the significance of the chosen economic values (long-term and medium-term profit, competitiveness, innovativeness and effectiveness);
- establishing the significance of the chosen non-economic values(sustainable growth, corporate responsibility, dignity-based values, trust, balancing professional work and other) dimensions of life (personal and family dimensions, spiritual dimensions, participation in culture, social and political life, etc.), broad perception of (not only in an economic dimension) quality, justice and honesty;
- establishing and analysing common values in the analysed organizations;
- recognising the values respected in the personnel policy (in terms of decisions relating to recruitment and redundancies, promotions and demotions, evaluation of work and employees, remuneration, intangible rewards);
- establishing to what extent and in what way values may be availed of in terms of professional management while taking account of the specifics of entities of various legislative and organizational forms.

1.2. Research thesis

The **main thesis** adopted is as follows: **Management that respects the acknowledged values, not only economic ones, increases the level of credibility and effectiveness of an organization, matches the contemporary needs and expectations of the management staff and employees, favours the integration of people in an organization and facilitates the running of personnel policies.**

Detailed thesis:

1. **Values are always taken into account in management and have a driving force, even if this is not done in a very conscious manner. Understanding this fact may have positive impact on the attitude of the management staff and employees in terms of values.**

   A similar notion may be expressed in the following words: Management devoid of values is impossible and does not exist in practice even when the management staff renounce management that respects values. Hence, it is not the case of whether values are respected as certain values are always respected,[2] but rather which values are acknowledged as being important and what their hierarchy is, while also which values in reality (and not only in postulates or desires) constitute the motivation to undertake action on their bases.

2. **It is not possible to manage professionally and efficiently only by means of values. Thus, it is necessary to search for compilatory and integrated techniques where values have a certain, but usually restricted role to fulfil or apply management that respects and promotes values instead of MBV.**

   Hypothesis 2 assumes that although values are necessary in management and are utilized, restricting it to management by values (MBV) exclusively would not be a good idea as this would make management too soft and "underspecified" and would hinder its operationalization (perhaps even render it impossible). Hence, it would be quite necessary to adopt compilatory techniques as MBV is one of two or more techniques of management, e.g. alongside management by aims, management by results, offensive management, or even others that are appropriate to the needs of an organization or to promote <u>management by respecting values</u> (not only economic ones) instead of MBV. In hypothesis 2, the conviction is expressed that values should enrich management and not strip it bare of all the "hard" elements, substan-

---

[2] Profit, profitability of the economic activity is also a value. Thus, if an entrepreneur or another in a managerial position claim that the sole aim of his activities is that of profit, this also matches a defined value, although it is surely excessively one-sided.

tiveness and measurability. There would also not be the deliberate creation and spreading of the illusion that maintaining specific values is sufficient for an efficient and effective management.

3. With relation to the *tyranny of values* of Nicolai Hartmann, we express the conviction that **there is no absolutization, nor excessive promotion of any singular value or homogenous groups of values.**
4. **Economic values play a dominant role in large corporations, particularly in joint-stock companies. In smaller entities, which are not listed, greater balancing of the economic and non-economic values takes place.**
5. **Operationalization of management with the use of values is difficult and this whole process is generally weak in advanced enterprises.**

1.3. Respondents, survey

The target group of the herein research was the representatives of entities from the private sector and the public sector, particularly the managers of the higher, medium and lower levels of management, while also specialists from different organizations. The selection of respondents was deliberate. With reference to the representatives of the managerial staff, the respondents were people employed in trading companies that reacted positively to the proposition of participating in the research, while also students of extramural studies and post-graduate studies from the following colleges: Warsaw School of Economics (College of Science on Entrepreneurship), Jagiellonian University (Faculty of Management and Social Communication), Wyższa Szkoła Finansów i Zarządzania w Warszawie (Faculties of Management, Political Science, Psychology) and Szkoła Główna Gospodarstwa Wiejskiego (Faculty of Economics and Applied IT and Mathematics). The total number of correctly completed survey forms amounted to 512.

We did not undertake representative research as in terms of the time allowed within the framework of the resources at our disposal it was not possible.

The survey utilized in the research has been attached at the end of the herein work. The questions in the survey were constructed in such a way as to first and foremost reflect the qualitative dimension of the research. In the first section of the survey, there were general questions relating to the relevance and significance of the various groups of values in an organization, as well as changes in the significance of values. The subsequent sections contained questions organized according to the groups of values as follows: ranging from economic values to non-economic values and corporate values.

The questions in the final section related to respecting values in the personnel policy of an organization. The specifications were stated at the end of the survey. All the questions in the survey were of a detailed nature and referred to a specific issue.

The majority of the questions were of the nature of the level of importance. The responses to these questions were organized with regard to the growing intensity of the features which the questions related to. The descriptive nature of the responses enabled the precise construction of questions and comprehension of the intentions of the author of the questions. All the questions relating to the level of importance contained the possible response of "other" with the possibility of entering one's own response, while some of the questions also contained the possibility of supplementing the response (a certain number of responses of a partially open nature). Respondents were given the task of choosing one or several responses depending on the question at hand, although as results indicated, the majority of people marked in one answer mainly due to the fact that the manner of description in terms of the responses had the task of completing the space of the possible answers (the responses were to supplement, while simultaneously be separable, but not to overlap in terms of significance). Two questions were of the nature of a symmetric scale in the form of a matrix, defining the intensity of the significance of specific values in an organization and the intensity of the significance of the various aspects of effectiveness in an organization. Two questions were of a descriptive nature (open).

The responses to the survey questions were analysed from a qualitative viewpoint and also from a statistical viewpoint in part, which facilitated the construction of the questions in terms of the level of importance and description. As the scale of the questions on the level of importance was merely serial and descriptive, statistical analysis was rendered impossible, thus the authors restricted themselves to the presentation of the structure of responses by taking account of the groups according to specifications. In the case of questions with responses with numerical scales, the statistical analysis carried out involved a verification of whether the distribution of responses was of a normal nature, as well as the calculation of the basic statistical parameters, while subsequently a comparison of the distribution between the groups of respondents.

All the data included in the tables and diagrams is derived from the self-analysis described here.

The research survey in its first version contained 59 questions and 14 pages of content. Following the collection of opinions, while also within the framework of testing, it was limited to 35 questions and 6 pages of content. This naturally gave rise to some detriment in terms of the depth of the research and thoroughness of the concept, but it was necessary however in order for respondents to feel the desire to complete it as the first version was excessively time-consuming and discouraging in terms of cooperation.

The addresses were also changed. Initially, the target group of the research was the top-management of joint-stock companies listed on the Warsaw Stock Exchange. Due to the insufficient number of those willing to participate in the research, we decided to complement the number of respondents by encompassing working students of second degree studies and post-graduate studies in the afore-mentioned national universities in the research (in managerial and specialized positions). This change made the research more interesting as we consequently not only analysed joint-stock companies in which an excessive amount of research has already been executed and which constitute a mere fraction of a percentage point of the total number of enterprises in Poland, but, also other enterprises that are not joint-stock companies and entities from the public sector. Thanks to this fact, we gained the possibility of becoming familiar with the differences between management respecting and promoting values between joint-stock companies, other enterprises and entities from the public sector. A sample of 512 respondents was adopted, while not statistically representative, it is sufficiently large to observe a multitude of qualitative dependencies.

1.4. IT support of research

Within the framework of the project, software was prepared that was dedicated to running research in an electronic form. With this aim in mind, a domain and a virtual server were purchased on which the software program was initiated, providing the possibility of completing the survey via the Internet. The aforesaid program was based on the PHP Technologies with the aid of MySQL database.

During the course of designing the solution, a key requirement was to preserve the confidentiality of data. Among other aspects, a unique code for the survey was generated for each of the analysed firms facilitating work only within the framework of the installations of the survey designated for the firm at hand.

With the aim of rendering the survey accessible, a link to the survey, together with a code were prepared, which were subsequently sent via electronic mail in the form of *hyperlink* to the e-mail address provided by a particular firm. Access codes to the survey and emails were generated

Likewise, during the course of designing the system, an array of conveniences for the users was taken into account. In the case of each question, the page number was possible to set on which the question was to be presented.

While configurating the questions, the assumption was adopted so that such a number of questions would appear on a page which was opened that would not cause the necessity of tiresome scrolling on the browser. Furthermore, during the course of completing the survey, it was possible to go to any given page by entering its number. Additionally, navigational buttons were placed on each page that facilitated moving to the first/previous/next/last page. A button was placed on the final page that enabled closing the given section of the survey following completion.

Assuming that in a given session of completing the survey the user can not complete the entire survey, a function was added to the program thanks to which after logging into the system again the page where the user had finished the previous session was reopened. Responses to the questions were entered simultaneously without the necessity of manual entry via buttons, as well as without the danger of losing data in random cases.

The IT system was equipped with an interface for the administrator (orderer of the preparation of the survey), facilitating the presentation of the basic statistics of completing the survey with the progress of the completion of the particular survey, as well as a summary of the entire progress.

2. CHARACTERISTICS OF RESEARCH SAMPLE

A total of 512 respondents participated in the survey. A set of tables describing the research sample has been illustrated below in Tables 1–4.

Table 1. Functions fulfilled by the respondents in organizations

No.	Group of positions / functions	No. of indications	% of indications
1.	Managerial	144	28.1
2.	Specialized	368	71.9
	Total	**512**	**100.0**

Source: own research.

In terms of the managerial positions, the following among others, were indicated:

- Directors-relating to Strategy, Relations with Investors, as well as Mergers and Takeovers, HR. Other positions than HR.
- Chairman of the Board (mainly in smaller companies); member of the Board.
- Manager: plant, department, division, branch, office, section, project, process.

Table 2. Market section (according to GUS), in which the organizations of the respondents achieve the greatest revenues

No.	Market sector (according to GUS – Central Statistical Office of Poland)	No. of indications	% of indications
1.	Industry	52	10.1
2.	Trade; repairs of car vehicles	117	22.8
3.	Construction	17	3.3
4.	Transportation and warehouse management	26	5.1
5.	Professional, scientific and technical activities	44	8.6
6.	Financial and insurance activities	78	15.2
7.	Accommodation and catering	27	5.3
8.	Information and communication	57	11.2

9.	Servicing the real estate market	9	1.8
10.	Other (mainly relates to the public sector – self-governing bodies, institutes of culture, health care, etc.)	85	16.6
	Total	**512**	**100.0**

Source: own research.

Table 3. Number of people employed in organizations where the respondents work

No.	Number of those employed	Results of responses (items)	Indications (%)
1.	up to 250 employees	319	62.3
2.	251–500 employees	56	11
3.	over 500 employees	137	**26.7**
	Total	**512**	**100.0**

Source: own research.

As may be seen, small and medium-sized entities are dominant (as in the economy as a whole), whereas a certain over-representation of large entities in comparison with the structure of the economy as a whole.

Table 4. Legislative-organizational forms of entities where the respondents work

No.	Legislative-organizational forms	Number	%
1.	Joint-stock companies	134	26.2
2.	Other enterprises that are not joint-stock companies	329	64.2
3.	Public sector units	49	9.6
	Total	**512**	**100.0**

Source: own research.

The data from Table 4 indicates the over-representation of joint-stock companies in the research.

3. PERCEPTION OF VARIOUS VALUE GROUPS IN MANAGEMENT

There is a significant number of values that both complement each other and compete with each other. Due to the great variety, there is the need for their grouping, which may be executed in various ways. However, it is difficult, or actually impossible to group values in such a manner as for the divisions to be adequate and separable as a multitude of values indicate relations with different groups, while moreover certain values are of an aggregated nature, synthetic so to speak, whereas others are more elementary. There are various sets of values and the ties between them which are frequently of the nature of conjunction – composite values have some common values, while others are separate.

In various eras, periods and regions of the world different values have been preferred; alongside the common and timeless ones, certain values emerged or increased in terms of importance, while others lost their level of significance. Our research relates to the values that are significant in terms of contemporary management in Poland. These values are approximate to those that are acclaimed in the EU, of which we have been formally part of since 10 years ago, although our historical and cultural ties with Europe have an incomparably longer history.

In management that respects values, the significance that is attributed to them is relevant. Without the familiarity of this significance and explicitness of the notions, it would be difficult to analyse these values and deal with the issue in general. Hence, the project of the catalogue of values for use in management was prepared (T. Oleksyn 2012; slightly modified version dating from 2014 is presented in the third section of this report), encompassing 30 chosen values, set out in **four groups of values** as follows:
 – economic;
 – ethical and cultural;
 – competence and development;
 – social and civic.

This type of catalogues are scarce in terms of their preparation in the world; in the majority of cases they relate to the values respected by employees or in business. A catalogue of values for use in management or economics is even more difficult to find.

3.1. Perception of economic values against the background of other value groups

Economic values constitute a rather large group. They encompass the following, among others: value of an enterprise, effectiveness, profitability, viability, competitiveness, innovativeness and exchange rates. This is associated with economics and management, while the theoretical bases for them have provided us with so many excellent economists and people of management that listing the greatest of them exceeds the intentions and possibilities of this report. Of the contemporary representatives of these disciplines that deal with the various aspects of values these are definitely the following (in alphabetical order): K. Blanchard, S. Byrne, S.O. Dolan, P.F. Drucker, R. Kaplan, S. Lachowski, M. O'Connor, M. Porter, R.A. Rappaport, D. Young and J. Welch.

We expected the revelation of the high level of importance of economic values in the research as contemporary societies in our cultural zone pay great attention to them, while enterprises are organizations for whom the economic results are frequently the most important gauge of success. Thus, it was interesting to confront such expectations of the researchers which also resulted from the theory of economics and subject-related literature with the actual research results.

The significance of the economic values and values from other groups have been displayed below in Tables 5–12.

Table 5. Importance of economic values against the background of others according to respondents

No.	Economic values	Number of responses	% of responses
1.	Economic values are the most significant for us, alongside respecting the law	167	32.6
2.	Economic values are of key significance to us; respecting the law, ethical norms and good practices are also of key significance to us	289	56.4
3.	Non-economic and non-ethical and cultural values, civic values associated with development, the ecology are acknowledged by us to be as important as the economic values as no value group is treated as a priority	52	10.2
4.	Other responses (*)	4	0.8
	Total	**512**	**100.0**

(*) Entrepreneurship is also enumerated here, although it may be deemed to be a socio-economic value (it refers to all notes marked by asterisks).

Source: own research.

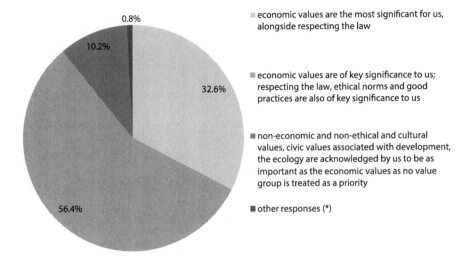

Chart 1. Economic values

Source: own research.

Economic values (and adherence to the law) are perceived as the most important among all the groups of values by <u>only</u> one third of the respondents. Most people accepted variant 2, where there is an additional indication of the significance of ethics and good practices in running a business. Other non-economic and cultural values, as well as civic values associated with competences and development, although perceived to be relevant are not however so important in the opinion of nearly 90% of respondents as the economic, legislative and ethical ones as may be interpreted from the data illustrated in position 3. This indirectly points to the concept of *sustainable development*, where it is assumed that economic development should be carried out with respect for the natural environment and the good of the future generations, while preserving the balance of the axis of professional life–family life–other important dimensions in the life of a person do not find support in terms of the majority of respondents.

In Table 6 it is shown how the responses are formulated depending on the type of enterprise.

Table 6. Importance of particular value groups depending on the type of organization

No.	Significance of value group	Joint-stock companies (*)		Other enterprises		Public sector	
		number	%	number	%	number	%
1.	The most important are economic values, alongside respecting the law	48	35.8	107	32.5	12	24.5
2.	The most important are economic values, alongside respecting the law, ethical norms and good practices	77	57.5	187	56.8	25	51
3.	Non-economic-ethical values, as well as cultural, civic values associated with development, the ecology are acknowledged by us to be equally important as economic values as none of the value groups is treated as a priority	8	6	34	10.3	10	20.4
4.	Other responses	1	0.7	1	0.3	2	4.1
	Total	**134**	**100.0**	**329**	**100.0**	**49**	**100.0**

Source: own research.

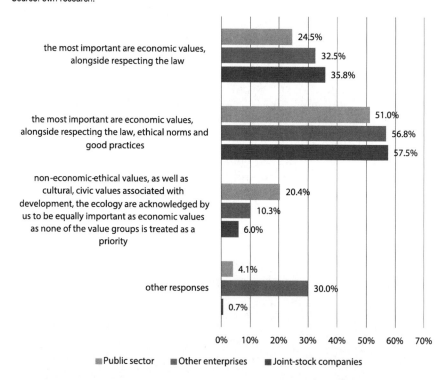

Chart 2. Importance of particular value groups depending on the type of organization

Source: own research.

In accordance with our expectations, the importance of the economic values is at its highest in the joint-stock companies and at a slightly lower level (by 3 percentage points) in other types of enterprises. It is clearly lower however in organizations from the public sector in terms of government and self-governing administration, education, health care, etc. As many as every third respondent in the sector of enterprises acknowledged economic values as being of key importance (as well as adherence to the law), whereas only one fourth in the public sector were of the same view.

The majority of respondents consisted of working students who had frequently encountered such values as effectiveness, efficiency, competitiveness, profitability, etc. at college level and business departments (economic). With relation to this, they acknowledged the superiority of economic values relatively more frequently than the majority of employees of the public sector. Naturally speaking, this is also influenced by significant specifics of the entities from the private sector on the one hand, while from the public sector on the other hand.

3.2. Perception of ethical and cultural values

In subject-related literature and academic teaching, attention has been widely placed on the significance of ethical and cultural values since at least the 1980s. This is associated with among other aspects, the works of such theorists and researchers as (in alphabetical order) K. Blanchard, M. O'Connor, T. Donaldson, E. Fromm, R.R. Gesteland, E. Hall, Ch. Hampden-Turner, A. Havard, G.A. Hofstede, M. Kets de Vries, C. Kluckhorn, A.L. Kroeber, G. Morgan, D. Riesman, L.V. Ryan, E.H. Schein, A. Trompenaars, while also M. Czerska, W. Gasparski, J. Klimek, L. Korporowicz, M. Kostera, B. Pogonowska, M. Rybak, Cz. Sikorski, J. Szczupaczyński, G. Szulczewski, M. Śliwa in Poland.

Ethical and cultural values are numerous in quantity. They are in part convergent in terms of each other and it would be difficult to separate some ethical and cultural values. Hence, they have been perceived in terms of one group of values. This includes the following, among others, responsibility, honesty, justice, involvement, affability, credibility, reliability, trust, respect, cooperation, solidarity, skill of reaching compromise, tolerance, magnanimity, empathy, understanding, civil courage, moderation and loyalty. The results of the research with reference to these groups of values are set out in Tables 7 and 8.

Table 7. Perception of ethical and cultural values in the total organizations analysed

No.	Ethical and cultural values	Number of responses	% of responses
1.	Perceived as important for the realization of the missions, aims and image of a firm and culture promoted; while also sufficiently displayed in the management system of a firm	220	43.0
2.	Important for the realization of the mission, aims and image of a firm and culture promoted, however not fully appreciated and insufficiently displayed in the management system of a firm	204	39.8
3.	Treated in general terms as secondary in the set of economic values	81	15.8
4.	Other responses	7	1.4
	Total	**512**	**100.0**

Source: own research.

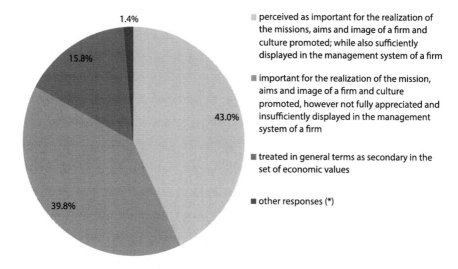

Chart 3. Perception of ethical and cultural values in the total number of organizations analysed

Source: own research.

The majority of respondents acknowledge ethical and cultural values as significant as the total of responses in lines 1 and 2 amounted to 82.8%. These values are deemed to be less important by 16% of respondents.

Table 8. Ethical and cultural values in joint-stock companies, other trading companies and in the public sector according to respondents

No.	Ethical and cultural values	Joint-stock companies		Other enterprises		Public sector	
		num-ber	%	num-ber	%	num-ber	%
1.	Important for the realization of the missions, aims and image of a firm and culture promoted, while also sufficiently displayed in the management system of a firm	50	37.3	145	44.1	25	51
2.	Important for the realization of the missions, aims and image of a firm and culture promoted, however are not fully appreciated and are insufficiently displayed in management system of a firm	58	43.2	131	39.8	15	30.6
3.	Treated in general terms as secondary in the set of economic values	23	17.2	50	15.2	8	16.3
4.	Other responses	3	2.3	3	0.9	1	2.1
	Total	**134**	**100.0**	**329**	**100.0**	**49**	**100.0**

Source: own research.

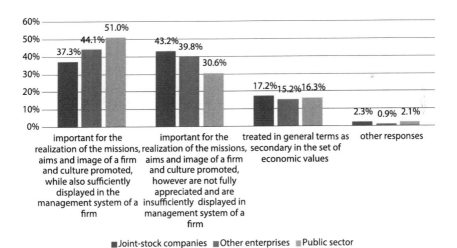

Chart 4. Ethical and cultural values in joint-stock companies and other trading companies, as well as in the public sector according to respondents

Source: own research.

As may be observed, ethical and cultural values are not only deemed to be significant, but also appreciated and sufficiently displayed in the system of managing organizations, particularly in the public sector, although 51% of such responses is not such a distinctive result. Joint-stock companies achieve the lowest result in this case, namely 37.3%.

Of the "other responses", attention was paid to the differences between the declarations ("propaganda") and reality, by using such words as "facade", "fear of partners relating to ethical management", "third plan" treatment of ethical and cultural values. Nevertheless, such critical opinions were rare.

3.3. Perception of competence and developmental values

Values associated with competences and development are also numerous. They may be treated together as professional development or socio-professional development which is strictly associated with the broad perception of competences. We assume that the <u>working competences</u>[3] encompass the following:
- abilities and predispositions;
- internal motivations;
- education and knowledge;
- experience and practical skills;
- personality features, attitudes and behaviour that are important in professional work and in fulfilling the specific organizational roles;
- ability and tendency towards professional development;
- ethical and moral competences; morale of the team / organization;
- state of health and psycho-physical form.

In the case of people managing competences, they encompass hard and soft[4] elements which are useful in professional management, which are particularly associated with leadership. Values in the aforesaid groups are not identical to competences, although they are closely connected. For instance, education and knowledge are both competences, as well as values that are acclaimed in contemporary societies.

The perception of competence and developmental values on the part of respondents is illustrated in Tables 9 and 10.

---

[3] Working competences is a wider notion than the competences of employees / worker competences as they also encompass the management team and those working on their own account that do not have the status of being hired.

[4] Hard competences are the skills and knowledge necessary to carry out a specified job; soft competences are the so-called psycho-social skills as they are associated with the psyche and social skills. They are not born skills, but are acquired during the course of education and experience.

Table 9. Perception of competence and developmental values[5] in the organizations analysed

No.	Competence and developmental values	Number of responses	% of responses
1.	Deemed to be critical for the existence, competitiveness and development of the firm and sufficiently displayed	178	34.8
2.	Significant, although not always displayed in the policies of the firm	266	51.9
3.	General, but rather secondary	63	12.3
4.	Other responses	5	1.0
	Total	**512**	**100.0**

Source: own research.

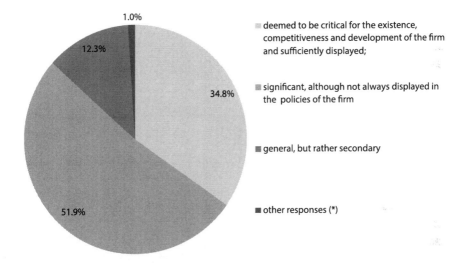

deemed to be critical for the existence, competitiveness and development of the firm and sufficiently displayed;

significant, although not always displayed in the policies of the firm

general, but rather secondary

other responses (*)

Chart 5. Perception of the competence and developmental values[6] in the organizations analysed

Source: own research.

The conviction was most frequently expressed (in half of the cases) that competence and developmental values are important, although not sufficiently displayed in the policies of an organization. Every third respondent felt

---

[5] Competence and developmental values are in particular: education and knowledge, experience and skills, leadership, creativity, activity, communicativeness, attitudes and behaviour, health and psycho-physical form, professionalism, ability to achieve aims and realization of tasks, professional development.

[6] Competence and developmental values are in particular: education and knowledge, experience and skills, leadership, creativity, activity, communicativeness, attitudes and behaviour, health and psycho-physical form, professionalism, ability to achieve aims and realization of tasks, professional development.

that they are not only deemed to be important, but also strongly expressed in the system of management, strategies and policies of an organization.

Table 10. Competence and developmental values according to respondents; aggregated data

No.	Competence and developmental values	Joint-stock companies		Other enterprises		Public sector	
		num-ber	%	num-ber	%	num-ber	%
1.	Critical for the existence, competitive-ness and development of a firm and treated as such	42	31.3	121	36.8	15	30.6
2.	Significant, although not always suffi-ciently displayed in the policies of a firm	69	51.5	172	52.3	26	53.1
3.	Generally speaking, rather secondary, although primary in some areas of activities	21	15.7	34	10.3	7	14.3
4.	Other responses	2	1.5	2	0.6	1	2
	Total	134	100.0	329	100.0	49	100.0

Source: own research.

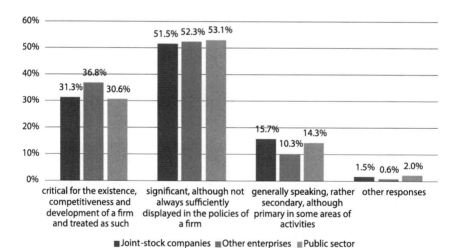

Chart 6. Competence and developmental values according to respondents; aggregated data

Source: own research.

It may come as some surprise that it is relatively rare to perceive the significance of the competence and developmental values in the public sector.

Of the (few) "other responses", it was possible to find the claim that promotions are decided more by seniority and not competences, as well as the treatment of competences as "decisively secondary", or "of little significance to the firm".

3.4. Perception of social and civic values

Social and civic values also play a certain role in the management of organizations, both due to the fact that it is also necessary to refer to them, as well as the fact that the people associated with the organization avow to them. Ignoring or violating them, even unconsciously, may be the source of conflicts and weaken the ability to manage. Social and civic values are in particular civic involvement, action towards the common good (in the name of the good of the state and local communities, restriction of unemployment, environmental protection, development of culture, protection of health and life, sport and recreation, charity, etc.), social cohesion, adherence to the law, patriotism and others from this group.

We expected that these values may not be perceived as particularly important in the management of an organization and in the formation of its culture, however they shall not be completely marginalized. Marginalization would not be beneficial from the viewpoint of the realization of the notion of a civic society and the realization of the concept of sustainability. The results have been indicated in Tables 11–12.

Table 11. Social and civic values[7] of the total organizations analysed

No.	Social and civic values	Number of responses	% of responses
1.	Equally important as economic values	115	22.4
2.	Significant, but less important than economic ones	166	32.4
3.	Perceived rather as secondary, taking on significance in an organization rather sporadically	222	43.4
4.	Other responses	9	1.8
	Total	512	100.0

Source: own research.

---

[7] These are as follows: civic involvement, activity for the common good (on behalf of restricting unemployment, environmental protection, development of culture, protection of health and life, sport and recreation, charity, etc.), social cohesion, adherence to the law, patriotism, as well as others from this group.

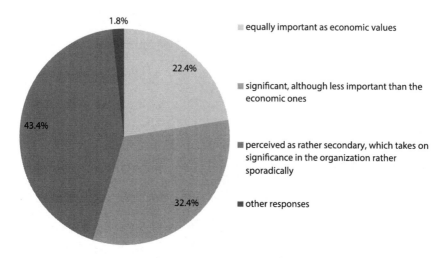

Chart 7. Social and civic values[8] in the total organizations analysed

Source: own research.

Social and civic values were most frequently perceived as "secondary" in organizations (among respondents), taking on significance only sporadically with 43.4% of such responses. Of the sporadic "other responses", the marginality of these values strengthened in the life of an organization, using such words as "insignificant", "rather insignificant".

Table 12. Social and civic values in the cross-section of the particular types of organizations according to respondents

No.	Social and civic values	Joint-stock companies		Other enterprises		Public sector	
		number	%	number	%	number	%
1.	Equally important as economic values	29	21.6	69	21.0	17	34.7
2.	Significant, but less important than economic ones	40	29.8	110	33.4	16	32.6
3.	Perceived rather as secondary, taking on significance in an organization rather sporadically	63	47.1	145	44.1	14	28.6
4.	Other responses	2	1.5	5	1.5	2	4.1
	Total	134	100.0	329	100.0	49	100.0

Source: own research.

---

[8] These are as follows: civic involvement, activity for the common good (on behalf of restricting unemployment, environmental protection, development of culture, protection of health and life, sport and recreation, charity, etc.), social cohesion, adherence to the law, patriotism, as well as others from this group.

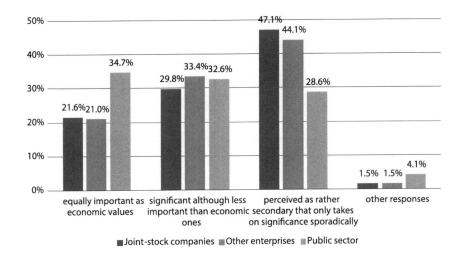

Chart 8. Social and civic values in the cross-section of the particular types of organization according to respondents

Source: own research.

The greater significance of social and civic values is clearly visible from the viewpoint of the representatives of the public sector rather than in the private sector, which should be of no surprise, although it could certainly have been expected that the differences would be even more profound than what was revealed by the research.

4. IMPACT OF VALUES ON MANAGEMENT IN THE OPINIONS OF RESPONDENTS

In this section, an attempt has been made to establish the qualitative impact of values, as indicated in chapter I in terms of management and the differentiation of the assessment of respondents with relation to the 4 types of groups. The impact of values on 10 distinct areas was analysed: the integration of people with an organization, the motivational system, overcoming crises and difficulties, discipline in an organization (including work discipline), the culture of an organization, the effectiveness of the operations of an organization, the satisfaction of employees, restricting pathology, the expectations of employees and the image of an organization. The results have been indicated in Tables 13–17.

Table 13. Impact of values on management in the opinions of respondents, aggregated data

No.	Types of impact	Very weak		Weak		Average		Rather strong		Strong	
		I.	%	I.	%	I.	%	I.	%	I.	%
1.	Integrate people in organizations	10	1.9	44	8.6	119	23.3	221	43.1	118	23.1
2.	Constitute a real element of the motivational system	12	2.3	46	9	141	27.6	232	45.3	81	15.8
3	Facilitate overcoming crises and difficulties	7	1.4	44	8.6	148	28.9	331	43.2	92	17.9
4.	Increase discipline	7	1.4	58	11.3	173	33.8	198	38.7	76	14.8
5.	Have a favourable impact on the culture of an organization	13	2.5	44	8.6	152	29.7	185	36.1	118	23.1
6.	Serve the higher level of effectiveness of an organization	7	1.4	29	5.7	109	21.3	228	44.5	139	27.1
7.	Favour greater satisfaction among employees	14	2.8	48	9.3	118	23.1	211	41.2	121	23.6
8.	Have a restrictive impact on pathology	24	4.7	102	19.9	167	32.6	152	29.7	67	13.1
9.	Cause people to expect their presence and respect	14	2.7	49	9.6	168	32.8	205	40.1	76	14.8
10.	Have an impact on the external image of the firm	7	1.4	29	5.7	68	13.3	203	39.6	205	40

Source: own research.

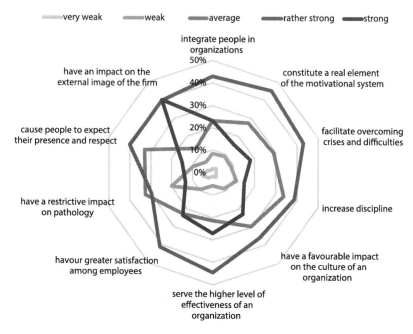

Chart 9. Impact of values on management in joint-stock companies

Source: own research.

It is surely surprising (and uplifting), but respondents most frequently indicate the strong or rather strong impact of values on the system of management in an organization. This particularly relates to the impact of values on the following:

- external image of an organization (as many as 79.6% of respondents feel that it is strong, or rather strong);
- motivating employees (72.9% indicate a strong impact or rather strong impact);
- strengthening the organizational and work disciplines (72.5% of respondents assess this as strong);
- overcoming crises (72.1% of such indications);
- growth in the effectiveness of the operations of an organization (71.6% of people are of the opinion that it is strong, or rather strong);
- integrating people in an organization (66.3% of people indicate as above).

There are certain differences, albeit not very significant, between the impact of the values on the management of an organization, depending on the legislative and organizational form and area of activities. The impact of values on management in joint-stock companies is slightly weaker than in the remaining enterprises and in organizations from the public sector.

Table 14. Impact of values on management in joint-stock companies

No.	Impact of values	Very weak		Weak		Average		Rather strong		Strong	
		I.	%	I.	%	I.	%	I.	%	I.	%
1.	Integrate people in organizations	2	1.5	11	8.2	33	24.6	61	45.6	27	20.1
2.	Constitute a real element of the motivational system	4	3	13	9.7	32	23.9	69	51.5	16	11.9
3	Facilitate overcoming crises and difficulties	1	0.7	10	7.5	37	27.6	66	49.2	20	15
4.	Increase discipline	3	2.2	17	12.7	43	32.1	46	34.3	25	18.7
5.	Have a favourable impact on the culture of an organization	4	3	9	6.7	35	26.1	49	36.6	37	27.6
6.	Serve the higher level of effectiveness of an organization	3	2.3	6	4.6	29	21.6	60	44.7	36	26.8
7.	Favour greater satisfaction among employees	3	2.2	13	9.7	36	26.9	56	41.8	26	19.4
8.	Have a restrictive impact on pathology	7	5.2	22	16.4	47	35.1	40	29.9	18	13.4
9.	Cause people to expect their presence and respect	5	3.7	14	10.4	38	28.4	57	42.6	20	14.9
10.	Have an impact on the external image of the firm	1	0.7	7	5.2	16	11.9	53	39.6	57	42.6

Source: own research.

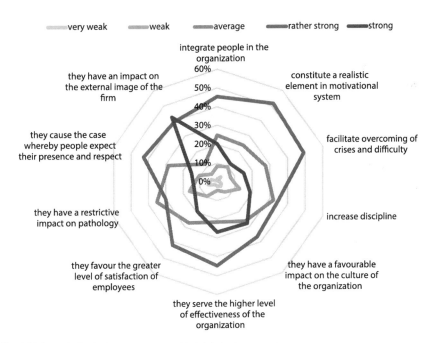

Chart 10. Impact of values on management in joint-stock companies

Source: own research.

Table 15. Impact of values on management in the remaining enterprises

No.	Impact of values	Very weak		Rather weak		Average		Rather strong		Strong	
		I.	%	I.	%	I.	%	I.	%	I.	%
1.	Integrate people in organizations	7	2.1	29	8.8	72	21.9	141	42.9	81	24.3
2.	Constitute a real element of the motivational system	6	1.8	29	8.8	98	29.8	140	42.6	56	17.0
3	Facilitate overcoming crises and difficulties	5	1.5	34	10.3	93	28.3	136	41.3	61	18.5
4.	Increase discipline	2	0.6	34	10.3	114	34.7	136	41.3	43	13.1
5.	Have a favourable impact on the culture of an organization	8	2.4	29	8.8	103	31.3	118	35.9	71	21.6
6.	Serve the higher level of effectiveness of an organization	3	0.9	19	5.8	69	21.0	146	44.4	92	28.0
7.	Favour greater satisfaction among employees	9	2.7	31	9.4	69	21.0	133	40.4	87	26.4
8.	Have a restrictive impact on pathology	16	4.9	70	21.3	104	31.6	95	28.9	44	13.4
9.	Cause people to expect their presence and respect	7	2.1	32	9.7	115	35.0	128	38.9	47	14.3
10.	Have an impact on the external image of the firm	5	1.5	20	6.1	40	12.2	133	40.4	131	39.8

(not joint-stock companies) I = number of indications
Source: own research.

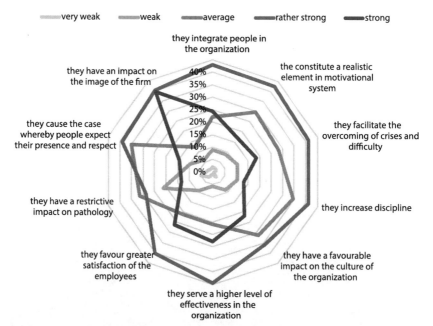

Chart 11. Impact of values on management in the remaining enterprises

(not joint-stock companies) I = number of indications
Source: own research.

Table 16. Impact of values on management in the public sector according to respondents

No.	Impact of values	Very weak		Rather weak		Average		Rather strong		Strong	
		I.	%	I.	%	I.	%	I.	%	I.	%
1.	Integrate people in organizations	1	2.0	4	8.2	14	28.6	19	38.8	11	22.4
2.	Constitute a real element of the motivational system	2	4.1	4	8.2	11	22.4	23	46.9	9	18.4
3	Facilitate overcoming crises and difficulties	1	2.0	0	0	18	36.7	19	38.8	11	22.4
4.	Increase discipline	2	4.1	7	14.3	16	32.7	16	32.7	8	16.3
5.	Have a favourable impact on the culture of an organization	1	2.0	6	12.2	14	28.6	18	36.7	10	20.4
6.	Serve the higher level of effectiveness of an organization	1	2.0	4	8.2	11	22.4	22	44.9	11	22.4
7.	Favour greater satisfaction among employees	2	4.1	4	8.2	13	26.5	22	44.9	8	16.3
8.	Have a restrictive impact on pathology	1	2.0	10	20.4	16	32.7	17	34.7	5	10.2
9.	Cause people to expect their presence and respect	2	4.1	3	6.1	15	30.6	20	40.8	9	18.4
10.	Have an impact on the external image of the firm	1	2.0	2	4.1	12	24.5	17	34.7	17	34.7

Source: own research.

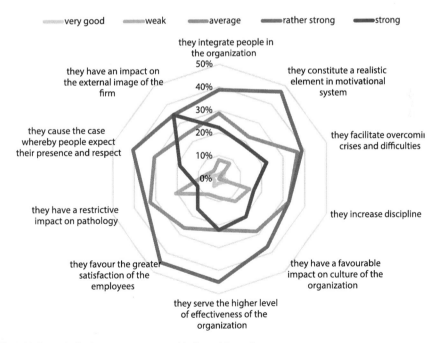

Chart 12. Impact of values on management in the public sector

Source: own research.

Analysis was carried out on the differences of the distribution of the specified distribution of the intensity of the features in the groups designated by the specifications: depending on the legislative and organizational form, scale of employment, sector of the market in which the organization operates and the function fulfilled by the respondent at hand in an organization. In the statistical analysis, the following tests were applied:

Shapiro-Wilk Test[9] – a test defining the type of variable distribution (normal or abnormal).

Table 17. Descriptive statistics of the impact of values on management in the opinions of respondents

	Medium	Median	Dominant	Standard deviation	Skewness	Kurtosis	Shapiro-Wilk Statistics	Significance
Integrate people in organizations	3.76	4.0	4	.977	−.687	.275	.872	.00
Constitute a real element of the motivational system	3.63	4.0	4	.947	−.634	.381	.876	.00
Facilitate overcoming crises and difficulties	3.67	4.0	4	.927	−.512	.198	.880	.00
Increase discipline	3.54	4.0	4	.938	−.324	−.097	.892	.00
Have a favourable impact on the culture of an organization	3.68	4.0	4	1.013	−.519	−.027	.886	.00
Serve the higher level of effectiveness of an organization	3.90	4.0	4	.925	−.790	.696	.854	.00
Favour greater satisfaction among employees	3.73	4.0	4	1.023	−.691	.137	.875	.00
Have a restrictive impact on pathology	3.26	3.0	3	1.074	−.162	−.569	.915	.00
Cause people to expect their presence and respect	3.54	4.0	4	.962	−.488	.176	.889	.00
Have an impact on the external image of the firm	4.10	4.0	5	.950	−1.128	1.190	.808	.00

Source: own research.

ANOVA Kruskal-Wallis Test[10] – analysis of the variables of a distribution that diverges from the normal and multi-faceted variants was carried out by the ANOVA Rang Kruskal-Wallis test. This test verifies whether differences exist between the groups for comparison. The aim of specification and definition of which groups specifically differ from each other was carried out by the so-called post-hoc analysis (test after test), in the case of ANOVA Kruskal-Wallis – a multi-comparable test.

---

[9] Further information in: S.S. Shapiro, M.B. Wilk, H.J. Chen H.J., *A Comparative Study of Various Tests of Normality*. "Journal of the American Statistical Association" 1968, 63, http://www.jstor.org/stable/pdfplus/2285889.pdf [18.06.2012].

[10] Further information in: W.H. Kruskal, W.A. Wallis, *Use of Ranks in One-criterion Variance Analysis*. "Journal of the American Statistical Association", December 1952, 47 (260), pp. 583–621, http://www.jstor.org/stable/pdfplus/2280779.pdf [18.06.2012].

Mann-Whitney U Test[11] – a test comparing the quantitative variables (numbers) between two groups serves to compare numbers relating to the distribution not approximate to the normal distribution.

According to respondents, the values have on average a relatively large impact on the analysed issues (on average above 3.54 with the dominant = 4, and deviations from the range < 0.927; 1.023 >). A lower impact was noted only with relation to the restriction of pathology, albeit still high (medium = 3.26, dominant = 3, standard deviations = 1.074).

Table 18. Histogram of variable distribution

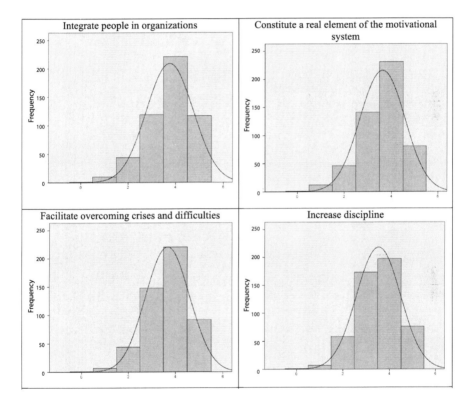

[11] Further information in: H.B. Mann, D.R. Whitney, *On a Test of Whether One of Two Random Variables Is Stochastically Larger than the Other*, "Annals of Mathematical Statistics" 1947, 18, pp. 50–60, http://www.jstor.org/stable/pdfplus/2236101.pdf [18.06.2012].

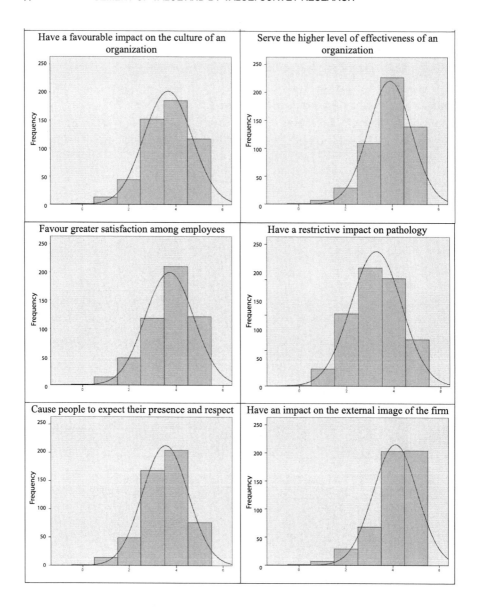

Source: own research.

On the histograms in Table 18, the precise distribution of the responses provided for the issues associated with the impact of values on the sphere of operations in organizations has been presented. In all of the diagrams, it is possible to observe the left-leaning variable skewness of varying intensity, which was confirmed by a test (−1.128; −0.324), whose results are indicated in Table 12.

The distribution of all the variables are to a small extent approximate to the normal distribution, which was statistically confirmed by the Shapiro–Wilk test in that the variables significantly differ from the normal distribution (significance < 0.05). In such a case, the utilization of non-parametric statistical tests is suggested.

5. IN SEARCH OF DEPENDENCY

5.1. Values in an organization and the legislative-organizational form

With the aim of verifying whether organizations of varying legislative forms differ from each other with regard to the assessment of the significance of values in the management of an organization analysis was carried out with the aid of the Kruskal-Wallis test (record nature of the dependent variables). In Table 19, the descriptive statistics of the analysis carried out have been presented.

Table 19. Values in an organization and its legislative-organizational form

Variable	Grouping variable			Statistics of the Kruskal-Wallis test		
	Legislative form	N	Average impor-tance	Chi-square	df	Asymp-totic signifi-cance
Integrate people in organizations	Joint-stock companies	134	249.0	.869	2	.648
	Other enterprises that are not joint-stock companies	329	260.80			
	Entities from public sector	49	248.15			
	Total	**512**				
Constitute a real element of the mo-tivational system	Joint-stock companies	134	251.53	.480	2	.787
	Other enterprises that are not joint-stock companies	329	256.89			
	Entities from public sector	49	267.49			
	Total	**512**				
Facilitate over-coming crises and difficulties	Joint-stock companies	134	257.49	.708	2	.702
	Other enterprises that are not joint-stock companies	329	253.83			
	Entities from public sector	49	271.69			
	Total	**512**				

Increase discipline	Joint-stock companies	134	256.01	.59	2	.775
	Other enterprises that are not joint-stock companies	329	258.66			
	Entities from public sector	49	243.36			
	Total	**512**				
Have a favourable impact on the culture of an organization	Joint-stock companies	133	271.62	2.260	2	.323
	Other enterprises that are not joint-stock companies	329	251.17			
	Entities from public sector	49	246.02			
	Total	**511**				
Serve the higher level of effectiveness of an organization	Joint-stock companies	134	254.55	1.019	2	.601
	Other enterprises that are not joint-stock companies	329	259.93			
	Entities from public sector	49	238.82			
	Total	**512**				
Favour greater satisfaction among employees	Joint-stock companies	133	243.05	3.048	2	.218
	Other enterprises that are not joint-stock companies	329	263.99			
	Entities from public sector	49	237.5			
	Total	**511**				
Have a restrictive impact on pathology	Joint-stock companies	134	258.71	.162	2	.922
	Other enterprises that are not joint-stock companies	329	254.74			
	Entities from public sector	49	262.26			
	Total	**512**				
Cause people to expect their presence and respect	Joint-stock companies	134	257.23	.711	2	.701
	Other enterprises that are not joint-stock companies	329	253.90			
	Entities from public sector	49	271.94			
	Total	**512**				
Have an impact on the external image of the firm	Joint-stock companies	134	263.21	1.771	2	.413
	Other enterprises that are not joint-stock companies	329	257.30			
	Entities from public sector	49	232.79			
	Total	**512**				

Source: own research.

On the basis of the importance in the Kruskal-Wallis test, whose values for all variables are formulated at above 0.05, <u>there are grounds for stating the statistically significant differences</u> between organizations of various legislative forms with regard to the importance of different values in the management of an organization.

5.2. Values in an organization and the size of the entity according to employment figures

With the aim of verifying whether the organizations of various magnitude in accordance with the number of workers employed differ from each other in terms of the assessment of the importance of values in the management of an organization, analysis was carried out with the aid of the Kruskal-Wallis test, whose results have been indicated in Table 20.

Table 20. Values in an organization and the size of the entity according to level of employment

Variable	Grouping variable			Statistics of Kruskal-Wallis test		
	Number employed	N	Average importance	Chi-square	df	Asymptotic significance
Integrate people in organizations	up to 250 employees	319	260.10	5.171	2	.075
	251–500 employees	56	284.38			
	over 500 employees	137	236.72			
	Total	512				
Constitute a real element of the motivational system	up to 250 employees	319	258.43	3.50	2	.174
	251–500 employees	56	281.89			
	over 500 employees	137	241.62			
	Total	512				
Facilitate overcoming crises and difficulties	up to 250 employees	319	255.18	5.087	2	.079
	251–500 employees	56	293.86			
	over 500 employees	137	244.30			
	Total	512				
Increase discipline	up to 250 employees	319	257.73	4.787	2	.091
	251–500 employees	56	288.80			
	over 500 employees	137	240.43			
	Total	512				
Have a favourable impact on the culture of an organization	up to 250 employees	319	249.96	1.671	2	.434
	251–500 employees	56	271.46			
	over 500 employees	136	263.80			
	Total	511				
Serve the higher level of effectiveness of an organization	up to 250 employees	319	255.43	1.496	2	.473
	251–500 employees	56	277.09			
	over 500 employees	137	250.58			
	Total	512				

Favour greater satisfaction among employees	up to 250 employees	319	256.40	2.441	2	.295
	251–500 employees	56	279.96			
	over 500 employees	136	245.19			
	Total	511				
Have a restrictive impact on pathology	up to 250 employees	319	252.69	4.027	2	.134
	251–500 employees	56	292.5			
	over 500 employees	137	250.65			
	Total	512				
Cause people to expect their presence and respect	up to 250 employees	319	258.05	.180	2	.914
	251–500 employees	56	249.57			
	over 500 employees	137	255.73			
	Total	512				
Have an impact on the external image of the firm	up to 250 employees	319	248.67	3.044	2	.218
	251–500 employees	56	278.34			
	over 500 employees	137	265.80			
	Total	512				

Source: own research.

On the basis of the importance in the Kruskal-Wallis test, there is no basis to state the statistically significant differences between organizations of varying numbers of people employed with regard to the importance of the different values in the management of an organization.

5.3. Values in an organization and the market sector

With the aim of verifying whether the responses of respondents from firms operating in various sectors of the market differ from each other with regard to the assessment of the importance of values in the management of an organization, analysis was carried out with the aid of the Kruskal-Wallis test, whose results have been presented in Table 21.

Table 21. Values in an organization and the market sector

Variable	Grouping variable			Statistics of Kruskal-Wallis test		
	Market section (according to GUS)	N	Average impor- tance	Chi- square	df	Asymp- totic signifi- cance
Integrate people in organizations	industry	52	257.38	14.193	9	.116
	trade; repair of car vehicles	117	250.40			
	construction	17	205.35			
	transportation and warehouse management	26	304.54			
	professional, scientific and technical activities	44	267.15			
	financial and insurance activities	78	257.48			
	accommodation and catering	27	272.37			
	information and communication	57	217.73			
	serving the real estate market	9	341.22			
	other (mainly relating to the public sector – self-governing unit, institutes of culture, health care, etc.)	85	265.48			
	Total	**512**				
Constitute a real element of the motiva- tional system	industry	52	263.57	10.276	9	.329
	trade; repair of car vehicles	117	251.49			
	construction	17	263.47			
	transportation and warehouse management	26	254.15			
	professional, scientific and technical activities	44	237.19			
	financial and insurance activities	78	264.88			
	accommodation and catering	27	305.87			
	information and communication	57	262.82			
	serving the real estate market	9	333.61			
	other (mainly relating to the public sector – self-governing unit, institutes of culture, health care, etc.)	85	232.61			
	Total	**512**				

Facilitate over-coming crises and difficulties	industry	52	249.29	8.807	9	.455
	trade; repair of car vehicles	117	242.37			
	construction	17	217.0			
	transportation and warehouse management	26	281.27			
	professional, scientific and technical activities	44	265.47			
	financial and insurance activities	78	271.88			
	accommodation and catering	27	275.54			
	information and communication	57	261.59			
	serving the real estate market	9	335.83			
	other (mainly relating to the public sector – self-governing unit, institutes of culture, health care, etc.)	85	244.06			
	Total	512				
Increase discipline	industry	52	279.60	8.855	9	.451
	trade; repair of car vehicles	117	245.48			
	construction	17	244.56			
	transportation and warehouse management	26	265.54			
	professional, scientific and technical activities	44	259.14			
	financial and insurance activities	78	269.15			
	accommodation and catering	27	295.54			
	information and communication	57	253.68			
	serving the real estate market	9	293.83			
	other (mainly relating to the public sector – self-governing unit, institutes of culture, health care, etc.)	85	229.72			
	Total	512				
Have a favour-able impact on the culture of an organi-zation	industry	51	231.28	11.800	9	.225
	trade; repair of car vehicles	117	245.18			
	construction	17	189.12			
	transportation and warehouse management	26	264.5			
	professional, scientific and technical activities	44	245.72			
	financial and insurance activities	78	281.78			
	accommodation and catering	27	283.31			
	information and communication	57	266.62			
	serving the real estate market	9	312.94			
	other (mainly relating to the public sector – self-governing unit, institutes of culture, health care, etc.)	85	256.35			
	Total	511				

Serve the higher level of effectiveness of an organi-zation	industry	52	256.40	8.039	9	.530
	trade; repair of car vehicles	117	263.0			
	construction	17	224.88			
	transportation and warehouse management	26	224.12			
	professional, scientific and technical activities	44	270.5			
	financial and insurance activities	78	280.81			
	accommodation and catering	27	254.44			
	information and communication	57	259.58			
	serving the real estate market	9	263.33			
	other (mainly relating to the public sector – self-governing unit, institutes of culture, health care, etc.)	85	232.15			
	Total	**512**				
Favour greater satisfaction among employees	industry	51	258.77	2.416	9	.983
	trade; repair of car vehicles	117	249.17			
	construction	17	256.18			
	transportation and warehouse management	26	260.42			
	professional, scientific and technical activities	44	251.47			
	financial and insurance activities	78	260.5			
	accommodation and catering	27	278.65			
	information and communication	57	267.52			
	serving the real estate market	9	276.94			
	other (mainly relating to the public sector – self-governing unit, institutes of culture, health care, etc.)	85	243.44			
	Total	**511**				
Have a restric-tive impact on pathology	industry	52	227.64	9.273	9	.412
	trade; repair of car vehicles	117	268.83			
	construction	17	266.24			
	transportation and warehouse management	26	277.77			
	professional, scientific and technical activities	44	233.55			
	financial and insurance activities	78	260.56			
	accommodation and catering	27	275.31			
	information and communication	57	229.94			
	serving the real estate market	9	320.94			
	other (mainly relating to the public sector – self-governing unit, institutes of culture, health care, etc.)	85	261.89			
	Total	**512**				

Cause people to expect their presence and respect	industry	52	237.51	9.734	9	.372
	trade; repair of car vehicles	117	267.53			
	construction	17	203.24			
	transportation and warehouse management	26	236.77			
	professional, scientific and technical activities	44	258.85			
	financial and insurance activities	78	261.24			
	accommodation and catering	27	276.61			
	information and communication	57	238.82			
	serving the real estate market	9	343.33			
	other (mainly relating to the public sector – self-governing unit, institutes of culture, health care, etc.)	85	260.34			
	Total	**512**				
Have an impact on the external image of the firm	industry	52	269.06	11.399	9	249
	trade; repair of car vehicles	117	261.31			
	construction	17	186.53			
	transportation and warehouse management	26	277.46			
	professional, scientific and technical activities	44	227.95			
	financial and insurance activities	78	271.75			
	accommodation and catering	27	257.28			
	information and communication	57	269.98			
	serving the real estate market	9	297.44			
	other (mainly relating to the public sector –self-governing unit, institutes of culture, health care, etc.)	85	236.94			
	Total	**512**				

Source: own research.

On the basis of the importance in the Kruskal-Wallis test, whose values for all variables are formulated above 0.05, there is no basis to state the statistically significant differences between organizations from various sectors of the market with regard to the importance of various values in the management of an organization.

5.4. Values in an organization and the function of the respondent in an organization

With the aim of verifying whether the functions fulfilled in an organization differ in terms of the importance of values in the management of an organization, analysis was carried out with the aid of the Mann-Whitney U test. The results of the analysis executed have been presented in Table 22.

Table 22. Values in an organization and the function of the respondent in an organization

Variable	Grouping variable				Mann-Whit-ney U test	z	Asymptotic significance(bilateral)
	Function executed	N	Average importance	Sum of importance			
Integrate people in organizations	managerial	144	**276.42**	39805.0	23627.0	−2.015	**.044**
	specialized	368	248.70	91523.0			
	Total	512					
Constitute a real element of the motivational system	managerial	144	251.92	36277.0	25837.0	−.466	.641
	specialized	368	258.29	95051.0			
	Total	512					
Facilitate overcoming crises and difficulties	managerial	144	272.89	39295.5	24136.5	−1.662	.097
	specialized	368	250.09	92032.5			
	Total	512					
Increase discipline	managerial	144	234.90	33825.5	23385.5	−2.179	**.029**
	specialized	368	**264.95**	97502.5			
	Total	512					
Have a favourable impact on the culture of an organization	managerial	143	**283.20**	40498.0	22422.0	−2.716	**.07**
	specialized	368	245.43	90318.0			
	Total	511					
Serve the higher level of effectiveness of an organization	managerial	144	259.41	37355.0	26077.0	−.296	.767
	specialized	368	255.36	93973.0			
	Total	512					
Favour greater satisfaction among employees	managerial	143	272.98	39036.0	23884.0	−1.704	.088
	specialized	368	249.40	91780.0			
	Total	511					
Have a restrictive impact on pathology	managerial	144	256.89	36992.0	26440.0	−.039	.969
	specialized	368	256.35	94336.0			
	Total	512					

Cause people to expect their presence and respect	managerial	144	272.85	39291.0			
	specialized	368	250.10	92037.0	24141.0	−1.652	.099
	Total	512					
Have an impact on the external image of the firm	managerial	144	266.32	38350.0			
	specialized	368	252.66	92978.0	25082.0	−1.06	.314
	Total	512					

Source: own research.

On the basis of the analysis of the importance in the Mann-Whitney U test accepted at the level of 0.05, it is possible to state the <u>existence of the statistical dependency between the function fulfilled in an organization and the assessment of the importance of values in the management of an organization</u>.

Fulfilling the managerial functions in an organization has a significant impact on the more frequent perception of values as the factor of integrating people in an organization, rather than by specialists (medium importance for a manager = **276.42** *vs* medium importance for specialists = 248,70). Likewise, managers are also noticing the beneficial impact of values on the culture of an organization (medium importance for a manager = **283.20** *vs* medium importance for specialists = 245.43). In turn, specialists more frequently identify the value of the factor increasing the discipline (medium importance for specialists = **264.95** *vs* medium importance for a manager = 234.90).

6. VALUES WHOSE SIGNIFICANCE HAS CHANGED THE MOST

Not only is the level of importance significant, but the change in the importance of the particular values over time also. Certain values rise in terms of importance, while others lose importance. Respondents were asked to on the one hand, indicate the values whose importance grew the most over the past three years at least, while on the other hand, those that decreased the most over the same period. The three-year time period defined arbitrarily was to encompass the period in which certain values remain unchanged, while others may change. Over a longer time period, it is possible to expect that the importance of all the values changes to a greater or lesser extent, whereas over a shorter time period, it is possible to expect that the significance of no value would manage to change. Each respondent could indicate up to three values. The results have been displayed in Tables 23 and 24.

6.1. Values whose significance has grown over the past three years

Table 23. Suggested growth in significance of values in the organizations analysed by the respondents (10 values of the greatest number of indications)

No.	Values whose significance has grown in the views of respondents	Number of indications
1.	Effectiveness, profitability	94
2.	Creativity	65
3.	Knowledge, education	61
4.	Professional development	53
5.	Competitiveness	52
6.	Integration, involvement	48, 47
7.	Motivation	36
8.	Innovativeness	30
9.	Responsibility, cooperation	27
10.	Professionalism	25

Source: own research.

Most frequently, the <u>growth in the significance of the effectiveness / profitability was indicated</u>, which is possible to attach to the particularly high ranking in importance of the economic values in society, as well as the profile of education of the respondents (economics, management). Likewise, the following were given a high rating: creativity, knowledge, professional development and competitiveness. What is surprising is the ranking of competitiveness in 8th position and honesty in 15th position.

6.2. Values whose significance has dropped over the past three years

Table 24. Values whose significance has dropped over the past three years

No.	Indicated values whose significance has dropped	Quantitative indications
1.	Trust	40
2.	Respect	30
3.	Solidarism / solidarity	27
4.	Loyalty Understanding	26
5.	Justice	24
6.	Health care and life	22
7.	Goodwill	19
8.	Flexibility	18
9.	Empathy	17
10.	Discipline Patriotism	15

Source: own research.

Self-analysis has confirmed what has also been indicated by other researchers, namely the fall in significance of such values as trust, respect, social solidarity, solidarity, moreover loyalty, understanding, justice, protection of health and life, amiability, flexibility, empathy, discipline and patriotism. The most drastic aspect is however the noted fall in trust.

7. IMPORTANCE OF ECONOMIC VALUES

Table 1 reveals that the economic values are acknowledged to be the most significant in an organization, alongside adherence to the law and ethics in the case of every third respondent on average. There was no restriction to mere questions relating to the total groups of economic and non-economic values as indicated in chapter I, but also focus on the establishment of the level of importance of the values chosen within the framework of their particular groups.

In Tables 25–38, the level of importance of the chosen economic values according to the opinions of respondents has been illustrated. Likewise, such economic values as profit (long-term and short-term), competitiveness, innovativeness, effectiveness, while also fair remuneration that may be ranked between economic values and social values have been evaluated. Social values are perceived in a manner that is in accordance with the entry of art. 4 European Social Card, signed and partially ratified by Poland.

7.1. Importance of profit over long periods of time

Table 25. Importance of profit over long periods of time (at least 3 years) according to the opinions of those under analysis

No.	Importance of profit over long periods of time	Number of responses	% of responses
1.	The most important of all economic values	290	56.6
2.	Some of the most important values in a firm are ranked among the group	133	25.9
3.	High; however some others are ranked higher	62	12.2
4.	Other responses	27	5.3
	Total	512	100

Source: own research.

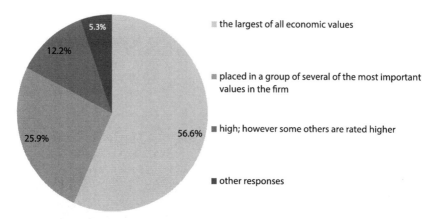

Chart 13. Importance of profit over long periods of time (at least 3 years) according to the opinions of those under analysis

Source: own research.

Profit over long periods of time is thus acknowledged to be the most significant economic value by nearly 57% of respondents. A further 26% sees this in a group of the most significant on equal terms as effectiveness, competitiveness and innovativeness. Some of the respondents had difficulty with responding to this question, or profit was not significant to them (in the public sector), which was reflected in the relatively high indicator of "other responses".

In Table 26, the differences in the perception of profit as economic values depending on the legislative and organizational form of entities have been highlighted. In accordance with the assumptions, the highest ranking of importance is that of long-term profit in joint-stock companies, whereas the lowest is in the public sector, while simultaneously it is worth remembering that the majority of the latter notion of profit does not exist.

Table 26. Importance of profit over long periods of time (at least 3 years) according to those under analysis in joint-stock companies, other trading companies and the public sector

No.	Importance of long-term profit is as follows:	Joint-stock companies		Other enterprises		Public sector	
		number	%	number	%	number	%
1.	The greatest of all values	82	61.2	186	56.5	21	42.9
2.	Some of the most important values in a firm are ranked among the group	35	26.1	87	26.4	11	22.4
3.	High; however some other economic values are ranked higher	14	10.5	39	11.9	9	18.4
4.	Other responses	3	2.2	17	5.2	8	16.3
	Total	134	100	329	100	49	100

Source: own research.

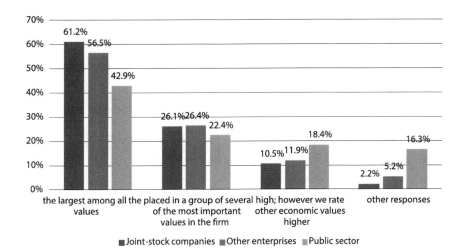

Chart 14. Importance of profit over long periods of time

Source: own research.

7.2. Importance of short-term profit

Responses to questions relating to the perception of the role of short-term profit by respondents have been indicated in Tables 27–28.

Table 27. Importance of short-term profit according to the opinions of those under analysis; aggregated data

No.	Importance of short-term profit is as follows:	Number of responses	% of responses
1.	The highest	243	47.5
2.	Several of the most important economic values in the company are ranked in the group (most frequently, alongside effectiveness, long-term profit, the mission of the organization, competitiveness, innovativeness, quality and customer satisfaction are also enumerated)	146	28.5
3.	High, although lower than some others (long-term profit, mission, customer satisfaction, quality)	87	17
4.	Other responses–profit does not occur or is less signifi-cant (mainly the public sector); it is to be sufficient to exist; in several cases the inappropriate relation between the organization and profit (among others, "driving up costs", in order to avoid paying tax)	36	7
	Total	**512**	**100**

Source: own research.

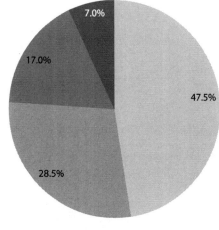

the highest

placed in a group of several of the most important economic values in the company (most frequently listed alongside effectiveness, long-term profit, mission of the organization, competitiveness, innovativeness, quality, customer satisfaction)

high, although lower than some others (long-term profit, mission, customer satisfaction, quality)

other response – profit does not occur or is less significant than (mainly public sector); it is to be sufficient in order to exist, in several cases inappropriate relation of organization to profit (among other things, "driving up costs", in order to avoid paying tax)

Chart 15. Importance of short-term profit

Source: own research.

Short-term profit is perceived as relatively less significant (by approximately 10 percentage points), than the long-term profit, although what is interesting and surprising is the fact that it is relatively less significant for joint-stock companies than the remaining enterprises. This has been illustrated in Table 28.

Table 28. Importance of short-term profit according to the opinions of those under analysis in joint-stock companies, other enterprises and in the public sector

No.	Importance of short-term profit is as follows:	Joint-stock companies		Other enterprises		Public sector	
		number	%	number	%	number	%
1.	The greatest of all values	60	44.8	168	51.1	15	30.6
2.	Several of the most important values in the firm are ranked in the group (indicated in Table 17)	45	33.6	85	25.8	16	32.7
3.	High; although others are ranked higher, particularly those indicated in position 3 of Table 17	23	17.1	57	17.3	7	14.3
4.	Other responses	6	4.5	19	5.8	11	22.4
	Total	134	100	329	100	49	100

Source: own research.

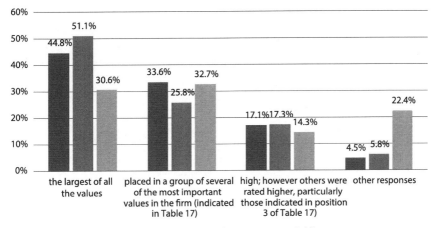

Chart 16. Importance of short-term profit

Source: own research.

The free descriptions referring to joint-stock companies reveal that the ranking of importance of short-term profit is not the most significant. The "long-term development of a firm" and "market share" count for more. The ranking of importance of short-term profit was defined as "of medium importance". Likewise, the data indicates that the cash flow "is more significant" and "payments of dividends".

7.3. Perception of competitiveness of an enterprise

In subject-related literature and academic teaching, economics and management place a strong emphasis (sometimes too strong) on competitiveness, by perceiving it to be "the be or not to be" for enterprises. This is certainly the case with an array of situations, although it does not relate to monopolies and oligopolies. A multitude of weak and non-competitive entities also function on the market (more frequently vegetating than functioning) that exist thanks to low costs and the modest expectations of their owners and employees. The opinions of respondents associated with the competitiveness of firms are presented in Tables 29–30.

Table 29. Perception of the competitiveness of an enterprise – aggregated data

No.	Competitiveness is perceived as the following value:	Number of responses	% of responses
1.	Key, decisive to a fundamental extent in terms of survival and development, strongly advocated by managerial staff	198	38.7
2.	Significant, however we are not only oriented towards competing, but also cooperating (also with market competitors)	259	50.5
3.	Less significant; due to its position (natural monopoly, oligopoly, etc.) there is no need to compete strongly	44	8.6
4.	Other responses	11	2.2
	Total	**512**	**100.0**

Source: own research.

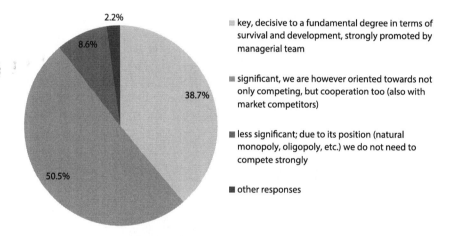

Chart 17. Perception of the competitiveness of an enterprise – aggregated data

Source: own research.

As may be observed, respondents most frequently choose variant 2 by indicating the fact that their enterprises are oriented towards both competing, as well as cooperating, with their market rivals also. Such a conviction was expressed by 50.5% of respondents. What gives food for thought is the fact that enterprises that are not joint-stock companies were more frequently oriented towards cooperation with other entities than joint-stock companies. In accordance with the assumptions, the least oriented towards competition and the most oriented towards cooperation and competition were entities from the public sector. This has been illustrated in Table 30.

Table 30. Perception of competitiveness according to the opinions of those under analysis in joint-stock companies, other enterprises and in the public sector

No.	Competitiveness is as follows:	Joint-stock companies		Other enterprises		Public sector	
		number	%	number	%	number	%
1.	Key, decisive to a fundamental extent in terms of survival and development; strongly supported	58	43.3	133	40.4	7	14.3
2.	Significant, however we are not only oriented towards competing, but also cooperating (also with market competitors)	65	48.5	164	49.8	30	61.2
3.	Less significant; due to its position (natural monopoly, oligopoly, etc.) there is no need to compete strongly	9	6.7	25	7.6	10	20.4
4.	Slightly important	2	1.5	7	2.1	2	4.1
	Total	134	100.0	329	100.0	49	100.0

Source: own research.

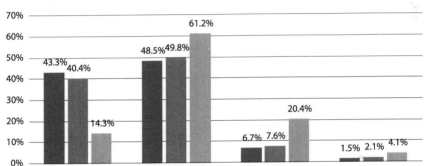

Chart 18. Perception of competitiveness according to the opinions of those under analysis in joint-stock companies, other enterprises and in the public sector

Source: own research.

8. PERCEPTION OF INNOVATIVENESS

Innovativeness[12] is a value which has been debated in detail for many years, indicating both its significance in the creation of new demand and development of markets, as well as its ties with an economy based on knowledge and Polish backwardness (our country is to be found at the end of the EU ranking in terms of innovativeness[13]). On the other hand however, it is worth being aware of the fact that in a multitude of cases, these attributes are not innovations, but traditional (classical) solutions and technologies; while in monopolies and oligopolies innovativeness does not have to be in first place. Such opinions are convergent with the later views of P.F. Drucker, who claimed that not everyone must be innovative: it is necessary not to set innovative goals before people, those responsible for maintenance, utilization and the optimization of the existing processes. He also drew attention to the fact that innovative activities that take firms away from their current activities rarely become a success.[14]

A certain impact on the registered changes (not actual changes) in the sphere of the level of innovativeness is also exerted by ownership changes in the structure of the economy. In large foreign and international corporations present in Poland, very frequently the designing, construction and technologies are solely created by the parent organizations abroad, while the Polish employees deal exclusively with the general execution (production, sales, etc.). A further factor is the insufficient number of educated engineers and surplus of humanists, with the former being in general more innovative.

Information about how respondents perceive innovativeness in their enterprises is presented in Tables 31–32.

---

[12] Innovation is a process involving the transformation of the existing possibilities into new notions and implementing them into practical application.

[13] Innovation Union Scoreboard 2014, European Commission, http://ec.europa.eu/enterprise/policies/innovation/files/ius/ius-2014_en.pdf [15.01.2015].

[14] P.F. Drucker, *Myśli przewodnie Druckera*, przeł. A. Doroba, MT Biznes, Warszawa 2002, pp. 215–216.

Table 31. Perception of innovativeness of a firm

No.	Innovativeness is perceived as the following:	Number of responses	% of responses
1.	Value of key significance, strongly supported to a sufficient level	146	28.5
2.	Value of key significance, although frequently supported in an insufficient manner	222	43.3
3.	Significant value, nevertheless in the reality of our organization not of key significance	95	18.6
4.	Value of little importance in our case	39	7.6
5.	Other responses	10	2
	Total	**512**	**100**

Source: own research.

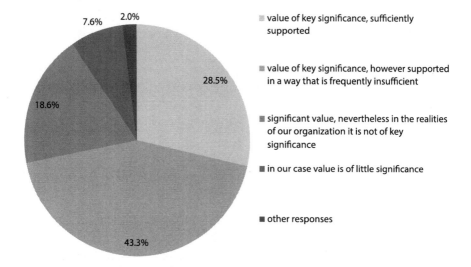

Chart 19. Perception of innovativeness of a firm

Source: own research.

Table 30 reveals that 72% of respondents acknowledge innovativeness to be a value of key significance (the total responses in variants 1 and 2), although more frequently insufficiently supported rather than strongly supported. Nevertheless, almost 30% of the respondents deemed that in their organizations, competitiveness is not a value of key significance.

In joint-stock companies the pressure on innovativeness is greater than in other types of enterprises (Table 31).

Table 31. Perception of innovativeness according to the opinions of those analysed in joint-stock companies, other enterprises and the public sector

No.	Innovativeness is the following:	Joint-stock companies		Other enterprises		Public sector	
		number	%	number	%	number	%
1.	Value of key significance, strongly supported in our firm	44	32.9	81	27.1	13	26.5
2.	Value of key significance, although frequently supported in an insufficient manner in our firm	62	46.3	141	42.9	19	38.8
3.	Significant value, nevertheless in the reality of our organization not of key significance	20	14.9	68	20.7	7	14.2
4.	Value of little importance in our case	7	5.2	23	7.0	9	18.4
5.	Other responses (lack of innovative products and technologies)	1	0.7	8	2.4	1	2.1
	Total	134	100.0	329	100.0	49	100.0

Source: own research.

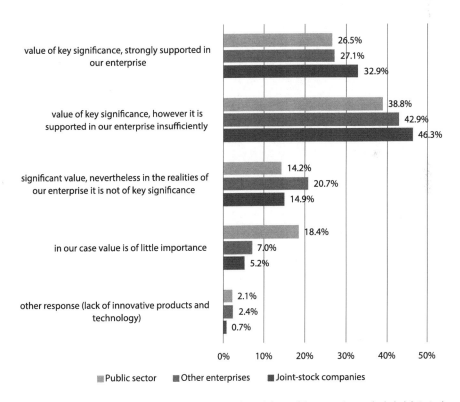

Chart 20. Perception of innovativeness according to the opinions of those under analysis in joint-stock companies, other enterprises and the public sector

Source: own research.

9. PERCEPTION OF EFFECTIVENESS

Economic effectiveness is widely perceived as the relation between the results (effects) and the costs of their acquisition. In contemporary times, it is perceived as the most significant economic value. Effectiveness and being effective is also commonly expected of enterprises, as well as undertakings, people and their work.

One of the aims of the survey research was to establish how important effectiveness is as the criteria of evaluating an organization, its particular areas, organizational units and employees. The results are presented in Tables 32-35.

Table 32. Perception of effectiveness (understood as the relation between results and costs)

No.	Feature or aspect of effectiveness	1		2		3		4		5	
		I.	%	I.	%	I.	%	I.	%	I.	%
1.	Effectiveness as criteria for the evaluation of an enterprise	6	1.2	16	3.1	81	15.9	204	39.9	204	39.9
2.	Effectiveness as criteria for the evaluation of the particular areas / organizational units	5	1	20	3.9	122	23.9	222	43.4	142	27.8
3.	Effectiveness as criteria for the evaluation of the managerial staff	10	2	23	4.5	117	22.9	207	40.5	154	30.1
4.	Effectiveness as criteria for the evaluation of the employees in areas where it is measurable/ easily countable	4	0.8	21	4.2	100	19.6	209	40.8	177	34.6
5.	Effectiveness as criteria for the evaluation of the employees in areas where it is slightly measurable / difficult to count	23	4.5	104	20.4	201	39.3	123	24.1	60	11.7
6.	Effectiveness (work, activity) as competence of the managerial staff	8	1.6	28	5.5	126	24.6	208	40.7	141	27.6
7.	Effectiveness (work, activity) as competence of the employees	5	1	26	3.4	91	19.6	188	45.3	201	30.7
8.	Increasing effectiveness in areas where it is deemed to be excessively low	5	1	26	5.1	91	17.8	188	36.8	201	39.3
9.	Increasing effectiveness in areas where it is already high	29	5.7	92	18	205	40.1	141	27.6	44	8.6

Legend: 1 – significance entirely subordinate; 2 – of little importance; 3 – of moderate importance; 4 – important; 5 – very important.

Source: own research.

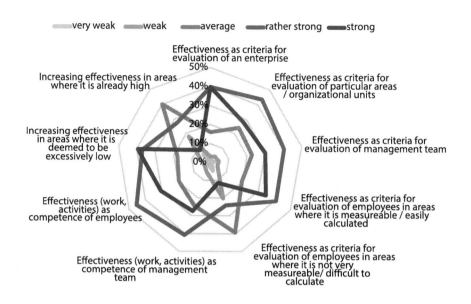

Chart 21. Perception of effectiveness (understood as the relation between results and costs)

Source: own research.

Effectiveness is a value that is in general highly rated among the respondents. It is essential to remember that the respondents are managers and working students of the faculties of management, economics and IT, for whom such a conviction is learned. The large number of indications of the pursuit of increasing effectiveness in these enterprises too may be surprising, as it is already very high. This would seem to confirm the contemporary trend towards maximization and minimization, while abandoning optimization. Over time, this may lead to a lack of moderation, over-exploitation of resources and great problems for such organizations in the future. Pressure in this direction is more frequent among enterprises that are not joint-stock companies than in the case of joint-stock companies themselves. A completely different situation exists in the public sector. Such trends among others, are illustrated in the Tables 33–35.

Table 33. Perception of effectiveness in joint-stock companies

No.	Feature or aspect of effectiveness	1		2		3		4		5	
		I.	%	I.	%	I.	%	I.	%	I.	%
1.	Effectiveness as criteria for the evaluation of an enterprise	2	1.5	2	1.5	26	19.4	51	38.1	52	38.8
2.	Effectiveness as criteria for the evaluation of the particular areas / organizational units	0	0	5	3.7	28	20.9	55	41.1	45	33.6

3.	Effectiveness as criteria for the evaluation of the managerial staff	1	0.7	5	3.7	21	15.8	61	45.5	45	33.6
4.	Effectiveness as criteria for the evaluation of the employees in areas where it is measurable / easily countable	1	0.7	6	4.5	26	19.5	50	37.3	50	37.3
5.	Effectiveness as criteria for the evaluation of the employees in areas where it is slightly measurable / difficult to count	2	1.4	26	19.4	53	39.6	30	22.4	22	16.5
6.	Effectiveness (work, activity) as competence of the managerial staff	2	1.5	7	5.2	28	20.9	57	42.5	39	29.2
7.	Effectiveness (work, activity) as competence of the employees	1	0.7	5	3.8	26	19.4	58	43.3	43	32.1
8.	Increasing effectiveness in areas where it is deemed to be excessively low	0	0	15	4.5	15	11.2	50	37.3	62	46.3
9.	Increasing effectiveness in areas where it is already high	10	7.4	21	15.7	55	41.1	30	22.4	17	12.7

Legend: 1 – significance entirely subordinate; 2 – of little importance; 3 – of moderate importance; 4 – important; 5 – very important.

Source: own research.

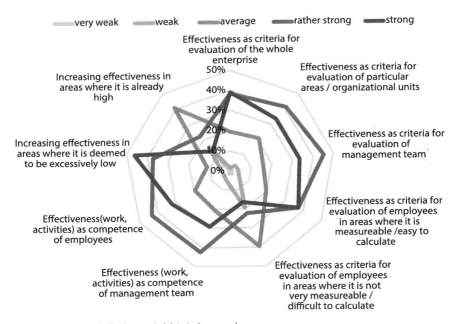

Chart 22. Perception of effectiveness in joint-stock companies

Source: own research.

Table 34. Perception of effectiveness in the remaining enterprises (not joint-stock companies)

No.	Feature or aspect of effectiveness	1		2		3		4		5	
		l.	%	l.	%	l.	%	l.	%	l.	%
1.	Effectiveness as criteria for the evaluation of an enterprise	3	0.9	12	3.6	51	15.5	130	39.5	133	40.4
2.	Effectiveness as criteria for the evaluation of the particular areas / organizational units	4	1.2	14	4.3	79	24.0	147	44.7	85	25.8
3.	Effectiveness as criteria for the evaluation of the managerial staff	7	2.1	15	4.6	83	25.2	129	39.2	95	28.9
4.	Effectiveness as criteria for the evaluation of the employees in areas where it is measurable / easily countable	3	0.9	14	4.3	57	17.3	141	42.9	114	34.7
5.	Effectiveness as criteria for the evaluation of the employees in areas where it is slightly measurable / difficult to count	19	5.8	66	20.1	125	38.0	82	24.9	37	11.2
6.	Effectiveness (work, activity) as competence of the managerial staff	6	1.8	19	5.8	83	25.2	131	39.8	90	27.4
7.	Effectiveness (work, activity) as competence of the employees	4	1.2	10	3.0	65	19.8	152	46.2	98	29.8
8.	Increasing effectiveness in areas where it is deemed to be excessively low	4	1.2	18	5.5	66	20.1	118	35.9	123	37.4
9.	Increasing effectiveness in areas where it is already high	17	5.2	64	19.5	120	36.5	102	31.0	26	39.8

Source: own research.

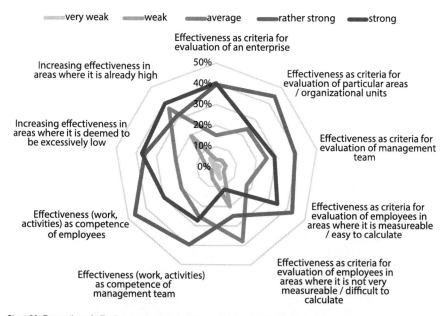

Chart 23. Perception of effectiveness in the remaining enterprises (not joint-stock companies)

Source: own research.

Table 35. Perception of effectiveness in the public sector

No.	Feature or aspect of effectiveness	1		2		3		4		5	
		I.	%	I.	%	I.	%	I.	%	I.	%
1.	Effectiveness as criteria for the evaluation of a firm	1	2.0	2	4.1	4	8.2	23	46.9	19	38.8
2.	Effectiveness as criteria for the evaluation of the particular areas / organizational units	1	2.0	1	2.0	15	30.6	20	40.8	12	24.5
3.	Effectiveness as criteria for the evaluation of the managerial staff	2	4.1	3	6.1	13	26.5	17	34.7	14	28.6
4.	Effectiveness as criteria for the evaluation of the employees in areas where it is measurable / easily countable	0	0	1	2.0	17	34.7	18	36.7	13	26.5
5.	Effectiveness as criteria for the evaluation of the employees in areas where it is slightly measurable / difficult to count	2	4.1	12	24.5	23	46.9	11	22.4	1	2.0
6.	Effectiveness (work, activity) as competence of the managerial staff	0	0	2	4.1	15	30.6	20	40.8	12	24.5
7.	Effectiveness (work, activity) as competence of the employees	0	0	2	4.1	9	18.4	22	44.9	16	32.7
8.	Increasing effectiveness in areas where it is deemed to be excessively low	1	2.0	2	4.1	10	20.4	20	40.8	16	32.7
9.	Increasing effectiveness in areas where it is already high	2	4.1	7	14.3	30	61.2	9	18.4	1	2.0

Source: own research.

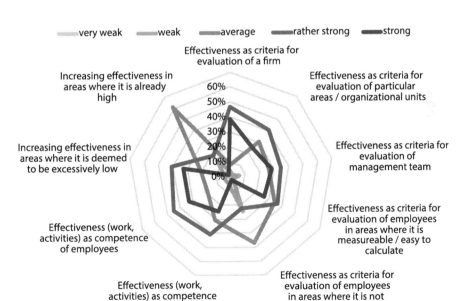

Chart 24. Perception of effectiveness in the public sector

Source: own research.

For the purpose of analysing the dependency of effectiveness as one of the values in an organization depending on the legislative and organizational form, scale of employment, market sector in which the organization operates, as well as the function fulfilled by the respondent in the organization at hand, a thorough statistical analysis was carried out in which the same statistical tests were utilized as in the case of the analysis of the intensified impact of values on management.

Table 36. Descriptive statistics of the impact of value on management in the opinions of respondents

	Medium	Median	Dominant	Standard deviation	Skewness	Kurtosis	Shapiro-Wilk Statistics	Significance
Effectiveness as criteria for the evaluation of a firm	4.13	4.00	4	.913	−1.179	1.901	.805	.000
Effectiveness as criteria for the evaluation of the particular areas / organizational units	3.91	4.00	4	.903	−.792	1.100	.850	.000
Effectiveness as criteria for the evaluation of the managerial staff	3.91	4.00	4	.969	−.888	.987	.850	.000
Effectiveness as criteria for the evaluation of the employees in areas where it is measurable / easily countable	4.03	4.00	4	.915	−.932	1.183	.833	.000
Effectiveness as criteria for the evaluation of the employees in areas where it is slightly measurable / difficult to count	3.17	3.00	3	1.049	−.048	−.338	.914	.000
Effectiveness (work, activity) as competence of the managerial staff	3.86	4.00	4	.962	−.772	.728	.861	.000
Effectiveness (work, activity) as competence of the employees	4.00	4.00	4	.886	−.963	1.620	.832	.000
Increasing effectiveness in areas where it is deemed to be excessively low	4.07	4.00	5	.959	−1.016	1.042	.823	.000
Increasing effectiveness in areas where it is already high	3.14	3.00	3	1.020	−.207	−.164	.912	.000

Source: own research.

According to the respondents, effectiveness has on average a relatively large impact on the analysed issues (medium over 3.86, dominant 4, with deviations ranging from < 0.886; 0.969 >). The lower significance of effectiveness appears in the context of the criteria of the assessment of employees in areas where it is not very measureable or difficult to enumerate (medium = 3.17, dominant = 3, standard deviations = 1.049), as well as the increase of effectiveness in areas where it is already high (medium = 3.14, dominant = 3, standard deviations = 1.02).

In the histograms illustrated in Table 37, a precise distribution of the responses provided on the issue of effectiveness in the sphere of operations of organizations has been presented. It is possible to observe in all of the diagrams the left-leaning skewness of varying intensity, which was confirmed by a test (-1.179; -0.048), from which the results have been displayed in Table 37.

Table 37. Histograms of variable distribution

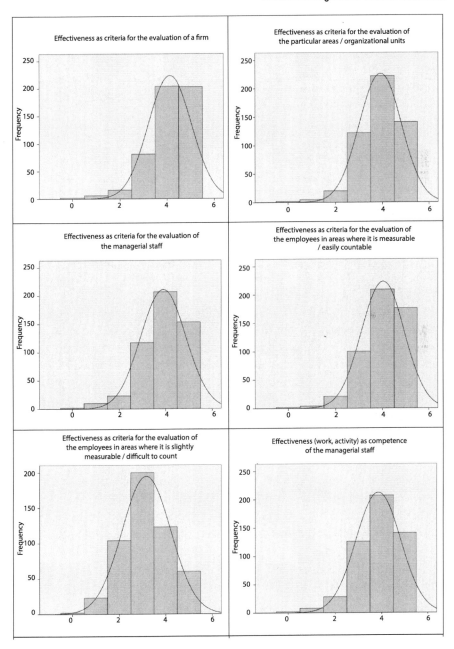

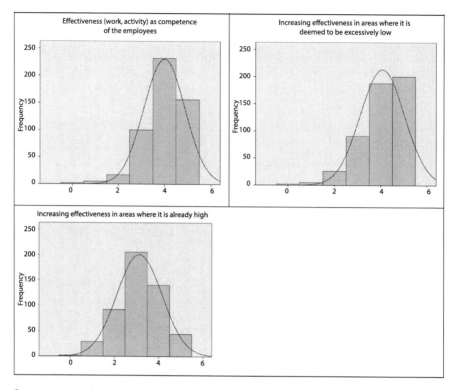

Source: own research.

The distribution of all the variables differ from the normal distribution, which was statistically proven by the Shapiro-Wilk test with the level of importance at < 0.05, while accepting the statistical hypothesis that the distribution is not normal, thus the non-parametric statistical tests shall be reused.

9.1. Perception of effectiveness as a legislative-organizational form

With the aim of verifying whether the organizations of varying legislative forms differ from each other in terms of the various aspects of effectiveness, analysis was executed with the aid of the Kruskal-Wallis test. In Table 38, the descriptive statistics of the analysis performer have been presented.

Table 38. Perception of effectiveness as a legislative-organizational form

Variable	Grouping variable			Statistics of Kruskal-Wallis test		
	Legislative form	N	Average impor-tance	Chi-square	df	Asymp-totic signifi-cance
Effectiveness as criteria for the evaluation of a firm	Joint-stock companies	132	250.10	.311	2	.856
	Other enterprises that are not joint-stock companies	329	256.87			
	Public sector units	49	260.86			
	Total	510				
Effectiveness as criteria for the evaluation of the particular areas / organizational units	Joint-stock companies	132	273.31	3.194	2	.203
	Other enterprises that are not joint-stock companies	329	250.64			
	Public sector units	49	240.12			
	Total	510				
Effectiveness as criteria for the evaluation of the managerial staff	Joint-stock companies	132	277.56	4.735	2	.094
	Other enterprises that are not joint-stock companies	329	249.24			
	Public sector units	49	238.10			
	Total	510				
Effectiveness as criteria for the evaluation of the employees in areas where it is measurable / easily countable	Joint-stock companies	132	259.53	2.976	2	.226
	Other enterprises that are not joint-stock companies	329	258.71			
	Public sector units	49	223.08			
	Total	510				
Effectiveness as criteria for the evaluation of the employees in areas where it is slightly measurable / difficult to count	Joint-stock companies	132	273.17	4.774	2	.092
	Other enterprises that are not joint-stock companies	329	253.27			
	Public sector units	49	222.90			
	Total	510				
Effectiveness (work, activity) as competence of the managerial staff	Joint-stock companies	132	265.22	.919	2	.632
	Other enterprises that are not joint-stock companies	329	252.76			
	Public sector units	49	247.70			
	Total	510				
Effectiveness (work, activity) as competence of the employees	Joint-stock companies	132	257.24	.188	2	.910
	Other enterprises that are not joint-stock companies	329	253.80			
	Public sector units	49	262.19			
	Total	510				

Increasing effectiveness in areas where it is deemed to be excessively low	Joint-stock companies	132	**281.30**			
	Other enterprises that are not joint-stock companies	329	247.62	6.343	2	**.042**
	Public sector units	49	238.94			
	Total	**510**				
Increasing effectiveness in areas where it is already high	Joint-stock companies	132	256.50			
	Other enterprises that are not joint-stock companies	329	258.70	1.629	2	.443
	Public sector units	49	231.34			
	Total	**510**				

Source: own research.

On the basis of the level of importance in the Kruskal-Wallis test, whose value in terms of all the variables bar one are formulated above 0.05, **there is no basis to claim the statistically significant differences** between organizations of varying legislative forms with regard to the assessment of the different aspects of effectiveness.

Only the "response increasing effectiveness in areas where it is deemed to be excessively low" indicates the dependency with relation to the legislative form of an organization. In joint-stock companies, greater significance is attached to the role of effectiveness in terms of increasing the rather ineffective areas (medium ranking of importance = **281.30**), than in the remaining enterprises (medium ranking of importance = 247.62), while the least importance in this area occurs in the entities of the public sector (medium ranking of importance = 238.94).

9.2. Perception of effectiveness and the size of the entity according to the levels of employment

With the aim of verifying whether organizations of varying scale according to the numbers of people employed differ from each other with regard to the assessment of different aspects of effectiveness, analysis was run with the aid of the Kruskal-Wallis test, whose results are illustrated in Table 39.

Table 39. Perception of effectiveness and the size of the entity according to the level of employment

Variable	Grouping variable			Statistics of Kruskal-Wallis test		
	Legislative form	N	Average impor-tance	Chi-square	df	Asymp-totic signifi-cance
Effectiveness as criteria for the evaluation of a firm	up to 250 employees	319	247.47	3.575	2	.167
	251–500 employees	56	256.37			
	over 500 employees	135	274.13			
	Total	510				
Effectiveness as criteria for the evaluation of the particular areas / organizational units	up to 250 employees	319	233.61	22.639	2	.000
	251–500 employees	56	274.04			
	over 500 employees	135	**299.54**			
	Total	510				
Effectiveness as criteria for the evaluation of the managerial staff	up to 250 employees	319	242.71	7.304	2	.026
	251–500 employees	56	271.36			
	over 500 employees	135	**279.15**			
	Total	510				
Effectiveness as criteria for the evaluation of the employees in areas where it is measurable / easily countable	up to 250 employees	319	242.50	8.284	2	.016
	251–500 employees	56	**290.90**			
	over 500 employees	135	271.53			
	Total	510				
Effectiveness as criteria for the evaluation of the employees in areas where it is slightly measurable / difficult to count	up to 250 employees	319	239.21	11.380	2	.003
	251–500 employees	56	**284.35**			
	over 500 employees	135	282.03			
	Total	510				
Effectiveness (work, activity) as competence of the managerial staff	up to 250 employees	319	254.32	.171	2	.918
	251–500 employees	56	262.69			
	over 500 employees	135	255.30			
	Total	510				
Effectiveness (work, activity) as competence of the employees	up to 250 employees	319	256.70	1.242	2	.537
	251–500 employees	56	236.74			
	over 500 employees	135	260.44			
	Total	510				
Increasing effectiveness in areas where it is deemed to be excessively low	up to 250 employees	319	244.45	6.241	2	.044
	251–500 employees	56	259.83			
	over 500 employees	135	**279.81**			
	Total	510				

Increasing effectiveness in areas where it is already high	up to 250 employees	319	252.09	1.013	2	.603
	251–500 employees	56	249.95			
	over 500 employees	135	265.87			
	Total	510				

Source: own research.

Analysis of the Kruskal-Wallis test with the level of importance at < 0.05 reveals that the statistically significant difference between organizations of varying numbers of people employed due to the perception of several aspects of effectiveness: "as the criteria of evaluating the particular areas or organizational units", "as the criteria of evaluating the management team", "as the criteria of evaluating the employees in areas where it is measureable or easy to enumerate", "as the criteria of evaluating the employees in areas where it is not measureable or difficult to enumerate „and "serves to increase the effectiveness in areas where it is deemed to be excessively low". In the case of utilizing effectiveness for the assessment of areas or organizational units, as well as assessment of the management team, while also to increase the effectiveness in areas of low effectiveness, the greatest level of significance is placed on this by the large organizations, namely those with over 500 employees (respective medium ranking of importance = 299.54; 279.15; 279.81). Organizations employing between 251 and 500 workers in the same areas place less significance on this (respective medium ranking of importance = 274.04; 271.36; 259.83), but attach greater importance to "effectiveness as the criteria of evaluating employees in areas where it is measurable or easy to enumerate", while also in "areas where it is not very measurable or difficult to enumerate" (respective medium ranking of importance = 290.90; 284.35). Relatively speaking, the least importance of effectiveness in an organization is placed by enterprises employing less than 250 workers.

9.3. Perception of effectiveness and the market sector

With the aim of verifying whether organizations of various sectors of the economy differ from each other with regard to the different aspects of effectiveness, analysis was run with the aid of the Kruskal-Wallis test, of which the results are illustrated in Table 40.

Table 40. Perception of effectiveness and the market sector

Variable	Grouping variable			Statistics of the Kruskal-Wallis test		
	Market section (according to GUS)	N	Average impor-tance	Chi-square	df	Asymp-totic signifi-cance
Effectiveness as criteria for the evaluation of a firm	industry	52	244.71	6.879	9	.650
	trade; repair of car vehicles	117	280.46			
	construction	17	243.03			
	transportation and warehouse management	26	264.33			
	professional, scientific and technical activities	44	251.53			
	financial and insurance activities	78	260.51			
	accommodation and catering	27	219.72			
	information and communication	57	252.79			
	serving the real estate market	9	238.28			
	other (mainly relating to the public sector – self-governing units, institutes of culture, health care, etc.)	85	246.02			
	Total	512				
Effectiveness as criteria for the evaluation of the particular areas / organizational units	industry	52	237.20	13.467	9	.143
	trade; repair of car vehicles	117	257.71			
	construction	17	197.76			
	transportation and warehouse management	26	273.56			
	professional, scientific and technical activities	44	242.18			
	financial and insurance activities	78	289.58			
	accommodation and catering	27	211.30			
	information and communication	57	269.61			
	serving the real estate market	9	216.50			
	other (mainly relating to the public sector – self-governing units, institutes of culture, health care, etc.)	85	260.03			
	Total	512				

| Variable | Grouping variable | | | Statistics of the Kruskal-Wallis test | | |
	Market section (according to GUS)	N	Average impor-tance	Chi-square	df	Asymp-totic signifi-cance
Effectiveness as criteria for the evaluation of the managerial staff	industry	52	243.70	9.891	9	.359
	trade; repair of car vehicles	117	261.85			
	construction	17	230.91			
	transportation and warehouse management	26	234.54			
	professional, scientific and technical activities	44	258.30			
	financial and insurance activities	78	292.00			
	accommodation and catering	27	234.74			
	information and communication	57	267.78			
	serving the real estate market	9	254.22			
	other (mainly relating to the public sector – self-governing units, institutes of culture, health care, etc.)	85	234.88			
	Total	**512**				
Effectiveness as criteria for the evaluation of the employees in areas where it is measurable / easily countable	industry	52	233.63	14.372	9	.110
	trade; repair of car vehicles	117	258.71			
	construction	17	163.50			
	transportation and warehouse management	26	271.67			
	professional, scientific and technical activities	44	259.00			
	financial and insurance activities	78	266.51			
	accommodation and catering	27	215.31			
	information and communication	57	274.06			
	serving the real estate market	9	244.67			
	other (mainly relating to the public sector – self-governing units, institutes of culture, health care, etc.)	85	273.49			
	Total	**512**				

Variable	Grouping variable			Statistics of the Kruskal-Wallis test		
	Market section (according to GUS)	N	Average impor- tance	Chi- square	df	Asymp- totic signifi- cance
Effectiveness as criteria for the evaluation of the employees in areas where it is slightly measurable / difficult to count	industry	52	249.97	7.823	9	.552
	trade; repair of car vehicles	117	260.14			
	construction	17	211.76			
	transportation and warehouse management	26	231.06			
	professional, scientific and technical activities	44	238.83			
	financial and insurance activities	78	280.72			
	accommodation and catering	27	287.78			
	information and communication	57	253.04			
	serving the real estate market	9	214.72			
	other (mainly relating to the public sector – self-governing units, institutes of culture, health care, etc.)	85	255.95			
	Total	512				
Effectiveness (work, activity) as competence of the managerial staff	industry	52	268.32	4.573	9	.870
	trade; repair of car vehicles	117	261.32			
	construction	17	261.59			
	transportation and warehouse management	26	250.02			
	professional, scientific and technical activities	44	238.08			
	financial and insurance activities	78	234.16			
	accommodation and catering	27	272.87			
	information and communication	57	267.75			
	serving the real estate market	9	289.83			
	other (mainly relating to the public sector – self-governing units, institutes of culture, health care, etc.)	85	257.36			
	Total	512				

| Variable | Grouping variable | | | Statistics of the Kruskal-Wallis test | | |
	Market section (according to GUS)	N	Average impor-tance	Chi-square	df	Asymp-totic signifi-cance
Effectiveness (work, activity) as competence of the employees	industry	52	231.81	11.903	9	.219
	trade; repair of car vehicles	117	250.29			
	construction	17	181.76			
	transportation and warehouse management	26	263.77			
	professional, scientific and technical activities	44	263.17			
	financial and insurance activities	78	278.88			
	accommodation and catering	27	271.85			
	information and communication	57	282.06			
	serving the real estate market	9	231.39			
	other (mainly relating to the public sector – self-governing units, institutes of culture, health care, etc.)	85	249.53			
	Total	**512**				
Increasing effectiveness in areas where it is deemed to be excessively low	industry	52	258.90	8.529	9	.482
	trade; repair of car vehicles	117	259.95			
	construction	17	176.26			
	transportation and warehouse management	26	276.71			
	professional, scientific and technical activities	44	242.78			
	financial and insurance activities	78	273.94			
	accommodation and catering	27	252.17			
	information and communication	57	248.82			
	serving the real estate market	9	230.17			
	other (mainly relating to the public sector – self-governing units, institutes of culture, health care, etc.)	85	260.56			
	Total	**512**				

Variable	Grouping variable			Statistics of the Kruskal-Wallis test		
	Market section (according to GUS)	N	Average impor-tance	Chi-square	df	Asymp-totic signifi-cance
Increasing effectiveness in areas where it is already high	industry	52	259.80	8.895	9	.447
	trade; repair of car vehicles	117	270.54			
	construction	17	258.76			
	transportation and warehouse management	26	251.56			
	professional, scientific and technical activities	44	246.85			
	financial and insurance activities	78	255.78			
	accommodation and catering	27	288.65			
	information and communication	57	213.54			
	serving the real estate market	9	222.39			
	other (mainly relating to the public sector – self-governing units, institutes of culture, health care, etc.)	85	264.07			
	Total	512				

Source: own research.

On the basis of the level of importance in the Kruskal-Wallis test, there is no basis to state the statistically significant differences between organizations of various sectors of the economy with relation to the evaluation of the various aspects of effectiveness.

9.4. Perception of effectiveness and the function of the respondent in an organization

With the aim of verifying whether the functions fulfilled in organizations differ from the assessment of the various aspects of effectiveness, analysis was run with the aid of the Mann-Whitney U test, of which the results are illustrated in Table 41.

Table 41. Perception of effectiveness and the function of the respondent in an organization

Variable	Function executed	N	Average importance	Sum of importance	Mann-Whitney U test	Z	Asymptotic significance (bilateral)
			Grouping variable				
Effectiveness as criteria for the evaluation of a firm	managerial	144	268.61	38680.0			
	specialized	368	251.76	92648.0	24752.0	−1.242	.214
	Total	512					
Effectiveness as criteria for the evaluation of the particular areas / organizational units	managerial	144	253.01	36434.0			
	specialized	368	257.86	94894.0	25994.0	−.355	.723
	Total	512					
Effectiveness as criteria for the evaluation of the managerial staff	managerial	144	267.93	38581.5			
	specialized	368	252.03	92746.5	24850.5	−1.155	.248
	Total	512					
Effectiveness as criteria for the evaluation of the employees in areas where it is measurable / easily countable	managerial	144	257.83	37127.5			
	specialized	368	255.98	94200.5	26304.5	−.135	.892
	Total	512					
Effectiveness as criteria for the evaluation of the employees in areas where it is slightly measurable / difficult to count	managerial	144	241.72	34808.0			
	specialized	368	262.28	96520.0	24368.0	−1.477	.140
	Total	512					
Effectiveness (work, activity) as competence of the managerial staff	managerial	144	268.26	38630.0			
	specialized	368	251.90	92698.0	24802.0	−1.188	.235
	Total	512					
Effectiveness (work, activity) as competence of the employees	managerial	144	270.14	38900.0			
	specialized	368	251.16	92428.0	24532.0	−1.398	.162
	Total	512					
Increasing effectiveness in areas where it is deemed to be excessively low	managerial	144	238.15	34293.5			
	specialized	368	263.68	97034.5	23853.5	−1.866	.062
	Total	512					
Increasing effectiveness in areas where it is already high	managerial	144	268.25	38627.5			
	specialized	368	251.90	92700.5	24804.5	−1.179	.238
	Total	512					

Source: own research.

On the basis of the analysis of the level of importance in the Mann-Whitney U test accepted at the level of 0.05, it is possible to state that <u>there is no basis to claim the significant differences between the function fulfilled in an organization and the assessment of the various aspects of effectiveness</u>.

10. FAIR REMUNERATION

Fair remuneration[15] for work executed is placed at the point of contact of economic, cultural and social values. This is associated with the accepted philosophy of management in the EU, as well as the values and socio-political system promoted in the EU. Unfortunately, Poland admittedly ratified art. 4 of the European Social Card relating to fair remuneration, but did not sign the most important points, namely points 1 and 3. Likewise, this concept in a formal and legislative sense does not need to be realized. Art. 13 of the Polish Labour Code with reference to fair remuneration is so general that it does not make anything binding with the exception of respect for the minimum level of remuneration, which in turn most certainly cannot be identified in Poland with fair remuneration.

Table 42. Fair remuneration[16] in the organizations analysed

No.	Criteria of fair remuneration	Number of indications	% of responses
1.	Are currently respected with relation to all those employed in the firm	107	20.9
2.	Are respected with relation to the majority of professional and qualified groups and we are heading towards their complete realization in the upcoming years (with relation to the total number employed)	110	21.5
3.	Are respected with relation to the key managers and specialists; in the case of the remaining ones, this value is not realized, however we have this in our plans for the future	144	28.1
4.	Are respected with relation to the key managers and specialists; in the case of the remaining people, this value is not realized and we do not have this in our plans	124	24.2
5.	Other responses	27	5.3
	Total	**512**	**100**

Source: own research.

---

[15] This remuneration guarantees a decent standard of living. In the opinion of experts, fair remuneration should be formulated at the level of 60% of the average salary in a given country. Compare: art. 4. European Social Card, dated 1961.

[16] Its essence is defined in the art. 4. European Social Card. Out of the five criterions stipulated there, two of them are the most significant: fair remuneration should be sufficient to maintain an employee and his family at a level that is acknowledged to be dignified in a given local community (which in practice signifies various levels in various countries and regions); remuneration in a given organization should be similar for similar types of work and their effects, regardless of sex, age, nationality, race, outlook, political convictions.

On a national scale, the postulate of fair remuneration in general is not executed, although there is a multitude of organizations that treat and execute the notion of fair remuneration seriously. The results of research on this issue have been set out in Tables 42–43.

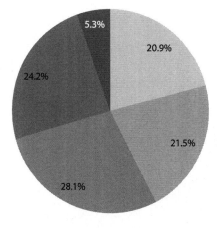

■ are already respected at present with relation to all those employed in the firm

■ are respected with relation to the majority of professional and qualification groups and we are aiming to achieve full realization of this in the coming years (with regard to the total number of employed)

■ are respected with relation to key managers and specialists; in the case of the others this value is not realized, although it is in our plans for the future

■ are respected with relation to key managers and specialists; in the case of the others this value is not realized and we do not have this in our plans

Chart 24. Fair remuneration in the organizations analysed

Source: own research.

Responses to the question relating to the ranking of importance of fair remuneration and the approach to this issue were distributed rather equally: a similar number of people acknowledged that fair remuneration is already applied in their organizations with relation to all employees (21%), as well as informing that a significant move towards its realization had occurred and is not ceasing to pursue its full implementation. Almost all of the others stated that the obligation by means of the code in terms of the realization of the principles of fair remuneration (Labour Code, art. 13) is executed with reference to positions of key significance, such as managers and specialists. With regard to the remaining employees, this is a matter for the future (28%), or do not think about whether employees outside of the areas of key significance should earn a fair salary at all (24%).

The public sector is rather closer to the realization of the principles of fair remuneration than the private sector, which initially arouses surprise. The stereotype form of thinking is associated with the conviction about worse salaries in the public sector than in the private sector, which generally speaking is not correct, particularly with relation to the lower positions.

Table 43. Fair remuneration according to the opinions of respondents with a division into joint-stock companies, the remaining enterprises and public sector units

No.	Fair remuneration	Joint-stock companies		Remaining enterprises		Public sector	
		number	%	number	%	number	%
1.	Is currently realized with relation to all those employed	28	20.9	68	20.7	11	22.4
2.	Is realized with relation to the majority of professional and qualified groups and we are heading towards its expansion in terms of the remaining employees also	30	22.4	69	21.0	11	22.4
3.	Is realized with relation to the key managers and specialists; in the case of the remaining ones, this value is not realized although we have this in our plans for the future	31	23.1	102	31.0	11	22.4
4.	Is realized with relation to the key managers and specialists; in the case of the remaining ones, this value is not realized and we do not have this in our plans for the foreseeable future	34	25.4	77	23.4	13	26.6
5.	Other responses	11	8.2	13	4.0	3	6.2
	Total	134	100.0	329	100.0	49	100.0

Source: own research.

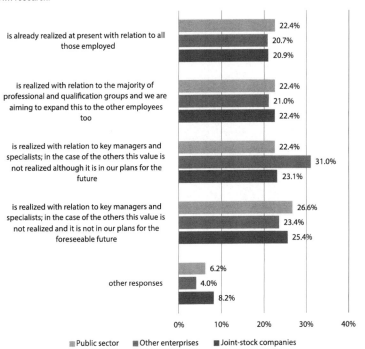

Chart 25. Fair remuneration according to the opinions of respondents with a division into joint-stock companies, the remaining enterprises and public sector units

Source: own research.

In terms of "other responses" there was the following information:
- "Remuneration depends on contacts with the Board. Older employees are overlooked".
- "Fair remuneration is offered to the newly employed; people with many years of work experience are paid too low"; may be confirmed by the opinions that despite the nominal unemployment, there are difficulties with finding the appropriate new employees with competence and it is necessary to pay them more than the people already employed.
- "Remuneration is proportional to the type and effects of work".
- "Fair remuneration is an abstract notion here".
- "The levels of remuneration are defined centrally (public administration)".

11. IMPORTANCE OF THE CHOSEN NON-ECONOMIC VALUES

The ranking of importance of such values as the following is analysed here:
- sustainability;
- social responsibility of enterprises (CSR);
- the so-called dignity values;
- balancing professional work, personal and family life, as well as civic involvement;
- quality (broad perception encompassing products and processes, as well as work; this of course did not refer tithe assessment of the quality of products, etc., but also the significance provided by quality as a value);
- justice;
- honesty.

These were not all the values stipulated in the catalogue of values as there are no such technical possibilities (analysis taking account of all the values from the catalogue would be too troublesome for the respondents). It is worth noting that the catalogue of values was not prepared exclusively from the viewpoint of this research and we hope that the scope of the applications of the catalogue shall be wider. The results have been displayed in Table 44.

11.1. Sustainable development

The concept of sustainability is more known in Poland by the term "sustainable development" or "long-lasting growth". This explanation is not entirely accurate as this development is achieved in leaps and bounds, rather than evenly. Nevertheless, if sustainability is to be understood as the appropriate relations between the product, technological and economic development on the one hand, while the social development on the other hand, thirdly protection of the natural environment, as well as fourthly, attention to the future generations, as such a perception of a term does not arouse reservations.

The concept of sustainable growth is quickly gaining acceptance in a multitude of developed countries. As can be seen from the data below provided in Tables 44–45, it is well-received by the respondents from the organizations analysed.

Table 44. Value of sustainable development in the organizations analysed

No.	Sustainable development (sustainability) is as follows:	Indications	% of indications
1.	Precious value which we treat seriously and are currently executing	155	30.2
2.	Precious value which we are currently executing only to a limited scope	322	62.9
3.	Controversial value; I do not think that the concept of sustainable development was appropriate in the case of our organization	23	4.5
4.	Other responses	12	2.4
	Total	**512**	**100.0**

Source: own research.

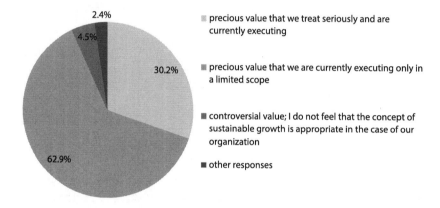

Chart 26. Value of sustainable development (sustainability) in the organizations analysed

Source: own research.

The responses of the respondents are of an optimistic tone; which reveal that the concept of sustainable growth (together with their value) enjoys decidedly strong support, although twice more people claim that it is realized in a restricted sphere than those expressing the opinion that it is already fully implemented. The indicators of the support are the highest in joint-stock companies, although the differences of the assessments between them and the remaining organizations are not large as indicated in Table 45.

Table 45. Value of sustainable development in the opinions of respondents with a division into joint-stock companies, the remaining enterprises and the public sector

No.	Sustainable development is as follows:	Joint-stock companies		Other enterprises		Public sector	
		number	%	number	%	number	%
1.	Precious value which we treat seriously and are currently executing	43	32.1	97	29.5	15	30.6
2.	Precious value which we are currently executing only to a limited scope	85	63.4	207	62.9	30	61.2
3.	Controversial value; I do not think that the concept of sustainable development was appropriate in the case of our organization	5	3.7	15	4.6	3	6.1
4.	Other responses	1	0.8	10	3.0	1	2.1
	Total	134	100.0	329	100.0	49	100.0

Source: own research.

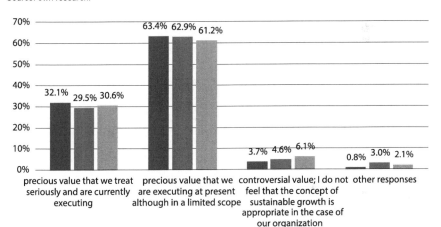

Chart 27. Value of sustainable development in the opinions of respondents with a division into joint-stock companies, the remaining enterprises and the public sector

Source: own research.

11.2. Social responsibility of enterprises

The corporate social responsibility (CSR) signifies such a concept of the operations of enterprises where they do not restrict themselves to the formal and legislative correctness, but are geared towards the interests of all stakeholders (not only owners / shareholders), by protecting the natural environment and indicate care for the fate of future generations. The beginnings of CSR may be sourced back to the end of 19th century and the beginning of 20th century in the so-called area of entrepreneurs in the USA (to be precise, in the phase of its civilization). In contemporary times, it is present and realized in all the developed countries, although there are rather frequently opinions that CSR is a cynical game that is full of hypocrisy.

In our research, we wanted to become familiar with the opinions of the respondents in terms of issues with regard to CSR and the actual intentions, by among other questions, whether enterprises undergo an objectified ethical audit (according to the principles accepted in EBEN). The responses have been presented in Tables 46–47.

Table 46. Social responsibility of enterprises in the opinions of those analysed

No.	Corporate social responsibility	Number of responses	% of responses
1.	It is treated in our firm in a universal and responsible way; we are subjected to regular external audits and we acquire good results	173	33.7
2.	It is treated in our firm in a universal and responsible way; however up to now we have not been subjected to regular external audits	172	33.6
3.	We are not distinguishable either in a positive or negative sense in this sphere in terms of groups similar to our organization	150	29.3
4.	I feel that we are adhering to CSR well, however we should work intensively on some particular issues	3	0.6
5.	Other responses	14	2.8
	Total	**512**	**100.0**

Source: own research.

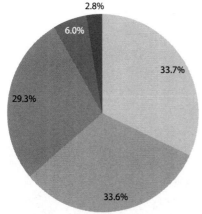

2.8%
6.0%
33.7%
29.3%
33.6%

■ is treated in a universal and responsible way; we are subject to regular external audits and we acquire good results

■ is treated in a universal and responsible way; up to now we have not been subject to regular external audits

■ we do not distinguish ourselves either favourably or unfavourably in this sphere in terms of the entities similar to our organization

■ I feel that we are adhering to CSR well in general terms, although we should work more intensively on certain issues

■ other responses

Chart 28. Corporate social responsibility in the opinions of those analysed

Source: own research.

Table 47. CSR in joint-stock companies, the remaining enterprises and in the public sector according to respondents

No.	Corporate social responsibility	Joint-stock companies		Trading companies		Public sector	
		number	%	number	%	number	%
1.	It is treated in our firm in a universal and responsible way; we are subjected to regular external audits and we acquire good results	47	35.1	111	33.7	15	30.6
2.	It is treated in our firm in a universal and responsible way; however up to now we have not been subjected to regular external audits	45	33.6	106	32.2	21	42.9
3.	We are not distinguishable either in a positive or negative sense in this sphere in terms of groups similar to our organization	40	29.8	101	30.7	9	18.3
4.	I feel that we are adhering to CSR well, however we should work intensively on some particular issues	0	0	2	0.6	1	2.1
5.	Other responses	2	1.5	9	2.7	3	6.1
	Total	134	100.0	329	100.0	49	100.0

Source: own research.

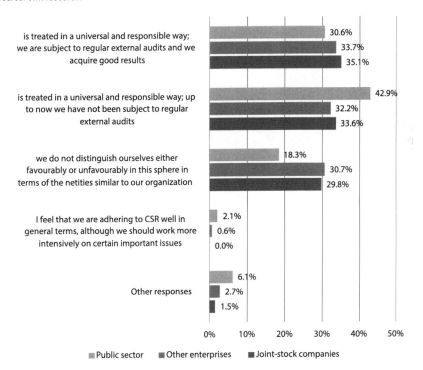

Chart 29. CSR in joint-stock companies, the remaining enterprises and in the public sector according to respondents

Source: own research.

Other responses:
- "It is something unnecessary as it does not bring in profits".
- "Audits are not run".
- "CSR does not function in our company".
- "CSR functions in a very restricted sphere".

A small number of responses drew attention to the case whereby CSR does not occur at all or is mainly utilized for promotional purposes/PR.

11.3. Values associated with dignity

Values associated with dignity are, in the opinions of some psychologists (e.g. Prof. Mark Kosewski) of fundamental importance in terms of management and the creation of organizational culture. These in particular include respect, respect for human dignity, amiability, respect for freedom and privacy. Responses to questions relating to dignity-based values are illustrated in Tables 48–49.

Table 48. Values associated with dignity in organizations in the opinions of respondents

No.	Values associated with dignity are as follows:	Number of responses	% of responses
1.	The real pillar in shaping the relations with people both within the framework of the firm, as well as outside of it (in shaping the relations with clients, trading partners, local communities, etc.)	249	48.6
2.	This is a more intentional pillar than the real one in terms of shaping the relations with people both in terms of the company, as well as in terms of relations with clients, trading partners, local communities, etc.	164	32
3.	Values treated rather as secondary, although in a way that does not violate good practices	83	16.2
4.	Other responses	16	3.2
	Total	512	100

Source: own research.

Other responses:
- "Very bad in relations with superiors".
- "Frequent".
- "Lack of respect in internal relations and outside the firm".
- "Employers have no idea about dignity".
- "Some Polish managers swear more often than a drunk outside a shop".
- "People are often treated as of secondary importance".
- "Lack of values inside the firm, feigning them on the outside".

However, it is necessary to add that this type of very critical opinions are few and far between (3%).

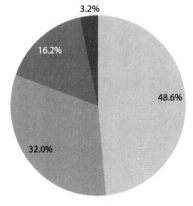

realistic pillar in shaping relations with people both within the framework of the firm, as well as outside of it (in shaping relations with clients, trading partners, local communities, etc.)

pillar more intentional than realistic in shaping relations with people within the framework of the company, as well as outside of it – in relations with clients, trading partners, local communities, etc.

values treated as rather secondary, although in a way that does not violate good practices

other responses

Chart 30. Values associated with dignity in organizations in the opinions of respondents

Source: own research.

Table 49. Values associated with dignity in joint-stock companies, the remaining enterprises and the public sector

No.	Values associated with dignity are as follows:	Joint-stock companies		Other enterprises		Public sector	
		number	%	number	%	number	%
1.	The real pillar in shaping the relations with people both within the framework of the firm, as well as outside of it (in shaping the relations with clients, trading partners, local communities etc.).	61	45.5	158	48	30	61.2
2.	This is a more intentional pillar than the real one in terms of shaping the relations with people both in terms of the company, as well as in terms of relations with clients, trading partners, local communities, etc.	51	38.1	104	31.6	9	18
3.	Values treated rather as secondary, although in a way that does not violate good practices.	20	14.9	53	16.1	10	20.4
4.	Other responses	2	1.5	14	4.3	0	0
	Total	134	100.0	329	100.0	49	100.0

Source: own research.

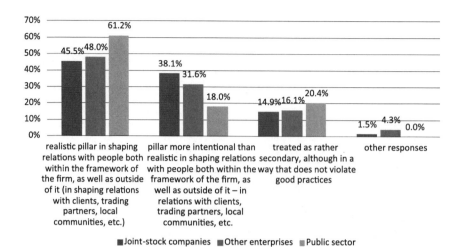

Chart 31. Values associated with dignity in joint-stock companies, the remaining enterprises and the public sector

Source: own research.

In the public sector, there are no such critical comments with relation to the lack of respect for dignity-based values as in the private sector.

11.4. Trust

Trust is a significant value that is essential to the normal functioning of the society and development of business. Kenneth Arrow, laureate of the Noble Prize, wrote 30 years ago that almost every commercial transaction includes an element of trust. Its lacking signifies economic backwardness.[17]

In research by CBOS dating from 2012, 23% of Polish people expressed the conviction that "Generally speaking, the majority of people can be trusted". In the same research, a mere 2% "had absolute trust in strangers", while 32% "rather trusted" them. Trust in large enterprises was expressed by 35% of Polish people and this is a similar level to the level of trust in newspapers (34%) and towards the government (39%), whereas slightly lower in terms of the officials of public administration and to the courts of law (both 45%). Trust shown towards trade unions is much lower than towards large enterprises and amounts to 29%, whereas only 20% towards political parties. The indica-

---

[17] See: http://www.findict.pl/frontpageheadline/zaufanie-w-biznesie [15.02.2015].

tors of trust among Polish people rise together with the levels of education, which are higher in large cities than in smaller towns.[18]

Against the background of this data, our results may be acknowledged to be moderately optimistic, although it is necessary to make allowances for questions that are asked differently, while also the environment of educated people and professionally associated with enterprises (they would not talk about strangers). These results are presented in Tables 50–51.

Table 50. Trust as value in organizations according to the opinions of those surveyed

No.	Trust in our firm is a value which:	Number of responses	% of responses
1.	Is well exposed both in terms of internal relations (we are able to display this and we do so), as well as external relations (we also enjoy a great level of trust among our clients and other external partners)	290	56.6
2.	Requires strengthening mainly in terms of relations with clients and other external partners	213	41.6
3.	Other responses	9	1.8
	Total	**512**	**100.0**

Source: own research.

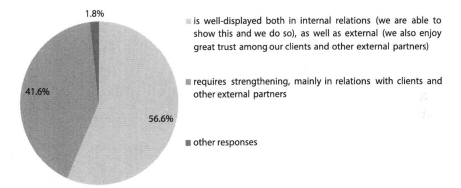

Chart 32. Trust as value in organizations according to the opinions of those surveyed

Source: own research.

Other responses (combined total of only 9, but all were very critical):
- "Reduced drastically".
- "Complete abstraction, you cannot trust anyone".
- "Lack of internal firm".

---

[18] CBOS, *Komunikat z badań «Zaufanie społeczne»*, BS/33/2012, March, Warszawa, 2012.

It is necessary to remember the data from tables, 13 of which reveal that trust is indicated in first place among the values that over the past 2–3 years have been falling in terms of significance.

Table 51. Value of trust in joint-stock companies, the remaining enterprises and in the public sector

No.	Trust in our firm is a value which:	Joint-stock companies		Other enterprises		Public sector	
		number	%	number	%	number	%
1.	Is well exposed both in terms of internal relations (we are able to display this and we do so), as well as external relations (we also enjoy a great level of trust among our clients and other external partners)	82	61.2	178	54.1	30	61.2
2.	Requires strengthening	50	37.3	146	44.4	17	34.7
3.	Other responses	2	1.5	5	1.5	2	4.1
	Total	134	100	329	100.0	49	100.0

Source: own research.

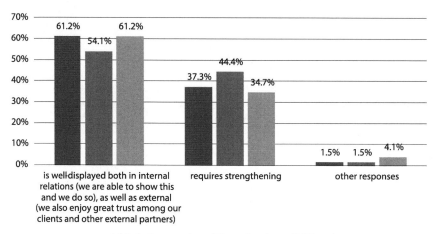

Chart 33. Value of trust in joint-stock companies, the remaining enterprises and in the public sector

Source: own research.

Attention is drawn to the fact that a percentage of respondents acknowledge that their organizations enjoy a great level of trust among clients and other external partners in the case of joint-stock companies that are clearly higher than the remaining enterprises and are to be found at an identical level as the entities of the public sector (61.2%).

11.5. Balancing professional work and other spheres of life

Many employers expect a huge level of involvement and total devotion of the managers and employees on behalf of their organizations, by means of very intensive and strenuous work in a dimension that exceeds all norms. A multitude of people are also excessively absorbed by their professional work to the detriment of other dimensions of life: finding time and devoting sufficient attention to the family, rest and recreation, civic involvement and on behalf of local communities, spiritual development, culture, hobbies, etc. Revealing and documenting a new (and unfortunately mass) phenomenon of death from overwork, termed *karoshi*[19] in Japan, SCD[20] in USA, in terms of heart attacks and strokes, lead to the case, or at least should lead to the case whereby both employers and employees should accordingly strive towards a more complete balance of professional work and other spheres of life. This is done in a conscious and effective manner in a multitude of organizations in various countries; one of the first to describe his activities in this sphere and widely recommend it to the world was the corporation of Hewlett Packard.

The research was to indicate in what way the approach to this issue is in Polish organizations, as well as what specific activities are undertaken. The results are illustrated in Tables 52–53.

As can be seen, the response of variant 2 is most frequently indicated, where an organization is not run in any direction relating to a uniform policy, while the balancing that is referred to remains at the discretion of the direct superiors and employees, as well as their agreements. In precisely one fourth of cases, an employer takes on an active approach and aims to enable the balancing of professional work and other spheres of life for employees. Likewise, there is a similar percentage of indicators (22%) in terms of the lack of interest among employers with regard to the issue raised here.

---

[19] This was officially acknowledged to be a different cause of death at the beginning of the 1990s, following a battle that lasted many years between the widows and the government of Japan, as well as the opinions of independent experts and the accepted national programs of counteracting the problem. It is the second most common cause of death in Japan among those aged between 40–50.

[20] Sudden Cardiac Death. This is the first cause of death among those aged between 40–50 in the USA; these are not heart attacks. Approximately 550,000 people die from this cause in the USA annually, mainly men of the type of «hot reactors» (in: R.S. Eliot, Director of the American Institute of Stress Medicine, *From Stress to Strength*, Wydawnictwo Amber, Warszawa 1997, p. 11).

Table 52. Balancing professional work and other dimensions of life in the opinions of respondents

No.	Variants of responses	Number of indications	% of indications
1.	The employer has an active influence and moves successfully in the direction of the aforesaid sustainability in particular by means of the following: not imposing exorbitant requirements with relation to the quantity and pace of work, openness with regard to the wishes of employees in terms of making the dimension and time of work flexible (in as much as possible), restricting work in terms of overtime and other actions	128	25.0
2.	The employer requires the adherence to law and good practices, however apart from this he/she does not interfere in the aforesaid issues by acknowledging that they are at the discretion of the employees and their direct superiors	258	50.4
3.	We require a high level of effectiveness, great level of involvement in professional work and sacrifices for the good of the company. The afore-mentioned balance is of no interest to us	115	22.4
4.	Other responses	11	2.2
	Total	**512**	**100.0**

Source: own research.

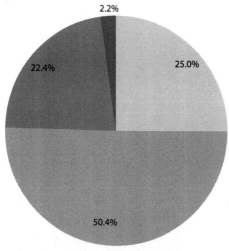

employer has an active and effective impact in terms of the aforesaid sustainability, particularly by means of: no imposition of exorbitant requirements relating to the amount and pace of work, openness with regard to the wishes of employees regarding fle

employer requires adherence to the law and good practices, however apart from this he does not interfere in the aforesaid issues as a rule, acknowledging that they are at the discretion of employees and their direct superiors

we require a high level of effectiveness, great involvement in professional work and devotion for the good of the company. The aforesaid balancing is of no interest to me

Chart 34. Balancing professional work and other dimensions of life in the opinions of respondents

Source: own research.

Other (open) opinions:
- "Balance of work–life in general is of no interest to our employer."
- "He is inconsistent and insincere – he forces us to do overtime and simultaneously praises family life."
- "The boss cares more about the personal life of parents with children than a single employee."
- "The Management Board is floundering and the requirements are a pretext to conflicts with the employees."

Table 53. Balancing professional work and other dimensions of life in joint-stock companies, other enterprises and public sector units

No.	Balance of professional life, personal life / family and social and civic involvement	Joint-stock companies		Other enterprises		Public sector	
		number	%	number	%	number	%
1.	The employer has an active influence and moves successfully in the direction of the aforesaid sustainability in particular by means of the following: not imposing exorbitant requirements with relation to the quantity and pace of work, openness with regard to the wishes of employees in terms of making the dimension and time of work flexible (in as much as possible), restricting work in terms of overtime and other actions	32	23.9	79	24	17	34.7
2.	The Management of the Company requires the adherence to the law and good practices of the company require the adherence to the law and good practices, however apart from this he/she does not interfere in the aforesaid issues by acknowledging that they are at the discretion of the employees and their direct superiors	73	54.5	160	48.6	25	51.1
3.	We require a high level of effectiveness, great level of involvement in professional work and sacrifices for the good of the company. The afore-mentioned balance is of no interest to us	26	19.4	83	25.2	6	12.2
4.	Other responses	3	2.2	7	2.1	1	2
	Total	134	100.0	329	100.0	49	100.0

Source: own research.

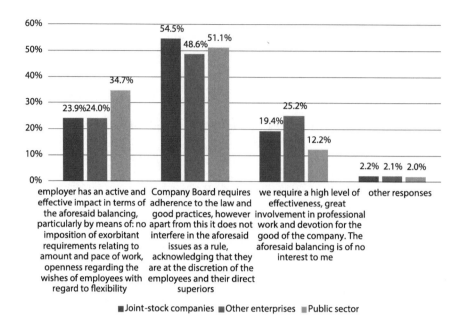

Chart 35. Balancing professional work and other dimensions of life in joint-stock companies, other enterprises and public sector units

Source: own research.

As can be seen, relatively speaking the greatest balance of the axis of "professional work – other dimensions of life" occur in the entities of the public sector. In joint-stock companies, this dilemma is most frequently at the discretion of the particular managers.

11.6. Quality as a value

The quality of products was of great and even key significance in the second half of the 20th century. Indeed, this is still the case in theory. However, in recent times the conviction has spread in business circles that "excessively high" quality and lifespan of products is not in the interests of producers and service providers as this restricts the demand and revenue for enterprises. A multitude of producers at the stage of designing plan a specific sphere of wear and tear of equipment (i.e. by utilizing one chosen element of weak quality). Likewise, consumers / users are more and more frequently expressing the conviction that the previous generations of products were more long-lasting and could be used significantly longer and that the designers, technologists and producers are deliberately shortening their lifecycle to be able to produce and sell more. The interests of clients are not taken into account, nor are the shrinking natural resources or protection of the natural environment. Specific trademarks of specific products are listed (an ever-increasing number), while various forms of technical evidence are provided.

One of the aims of this research was to become familiar with the opinions of respondents on the issue of the contemporary meaning of quality as such, but not as a tool in the pursuit of other aims, e.g. economic ones; in as much as this is a worthwhile value in reality, and not in literature and declarations. These opinions have been illustrated in Tables 54–55.

Table 54. Quality as a value in the opinions of respondents

No.	Variants of responses	Number of indications	% of indications
1.	Quality, including the durability of goods and services, has remained an immeasurably important value and its significance is not decreasing, but rather growing	258	50.4
2.	Quality remains very important, however the relation between durability / lifespan / period of usage or utilization of products undergo change; the latter are deliberately restricted timewise and this has not much in common with the good of the client or protection of the natural environment	161	31.4
3.	Quality is losing out to price; in spite of political correctness but in accordance with the truth, it is necessary to say that due to the main barriers to demand, the expectations of clients that require never-ending promotions and price reductions, we have a multitude of various tacky markets in Poland and likewise, a multitude of various tacky products	80	15.6
4.	Other responses	13	2.6
	Total	512	100.0

Source: own research.

The responses were distributed equally in approximate terms between those who feel that quality is still of priority importance and whose importance is still growing and those who are more sceptical and also perceive negative phenoma in this sphere (expressed in some variants of responses).

The representatives of the public sector (apart from the material sphere) should in principle abstain from giving opinions. Those who responded surely reacted as clients- consumers and not as representatives of their organizations.

In choosing another response, they informed that the accepted variants of responses do not take account of the specifics of the operations of their organizations, which is confirmed by the afore-mentioned thesis.

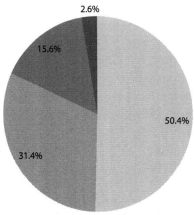

quality, including the durability of goods and services remains an extricably important value and its significance is not falling, but rather growing

quality remains very important, however the relation of durability / lifespan / time of use or utilization of products is undergoing change; the latter are deliberately limited timewise and this has little to do with the good of the client or protection

quality is losing out to price; in spite of political correctness but in agreement with the truth, it is necessary to say that mainly with regard to the barriers of demand and expectations of clients demanding constant promotions and price reductions

other responses

Chart 36. Quality as value in the opinions of respondents

Source: own research.

Table 55. Quality as a value in the opinions of respondents in joint-stock companies, other enterprises and public sector units

No.	Quality	Joint-stock companies		Other enterprises		Public sector	
		number	%	number	%	number	%
1.	Quality, including the durability of goods and services, has remained an immeasurably important value and its significance is not decreasing, but rather growing	78	58.2	162	49.2	18	36.7
2.	Quality remains very important, however the relation between durability / lifespan / period of usage or utilization of products undergo change; the latter are deliberately restricted timewise and this has not much in common with the good of the client or protection of the natural environment	32	23.9	107	32.5	22	44.9
3.	Quality is losing out to price; in spite of political correctness but in accordance with the truth, it is necessary to say that due to the main barriers to demand and the expectations of clients that require never-ending promotions and price reductions, we have a multitude of various tacky markets in Poland and likewise, a multitude of various tacky products	22	16.4	54	16.4	4	8.2
4.	Other responses	2	1.5	6	1.8	5	10.2
	Total	134	100	329	100	49	100

Source: own research.

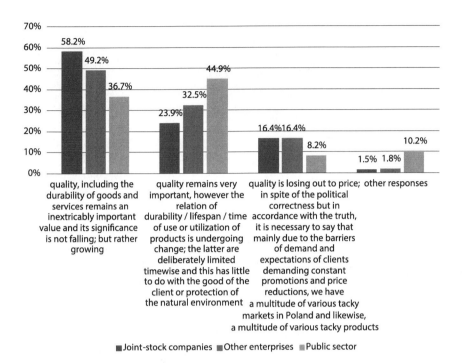

■ Joint-stock companies ■ Other enterprises ■ Public sector

Chart 37. Quality as a value in the opinions of respondents in joint-stock companies, other enterprises and public sector units

Source: own research.

11.7. Justice as a value

Justice, widely perceived as "honest, proper conduct" was acknowledged by Plato as the most important of virtues. The need for justice has constantly accompanied people down through the ages, while simultaneously a multitude of wickedness has been committed on behalf of this value. It is additionally a notion that is very subjective and potentially conflicting. How do respondents perceive justice in their organizations? The results have been presented in Tables 56–57.

The results are perceived to be optimistic as they certify to the fact that in the majority of organizations (almost two thirds) the approach towards justice is profound and active; the management team do not exclusively rely on the educated perception of justice from a customary and cultural point of view, but also consider what is fair and what is not and why in their organizations, while also developing the associated communication.

Table 56. Justice in the management of an organization in the opinions of respondents

No.	Variants of responses	Number of responses	% of responses
1.	The management staff try to be fair in taking decisions and expect the same from others by basing on the socially and culturally educated perception of justice	163	31.8
2.	There are attempts to be fair in terms of managerial decisions and action by basing on the socially and culturally educated perception of justice, but also consideration of what is just and what is not in the firm, while also communicating with others with relation to these issues	31	61.9
3.	Other responses	32	6.3
	Total	**512**	**100.0**

Source: own research.

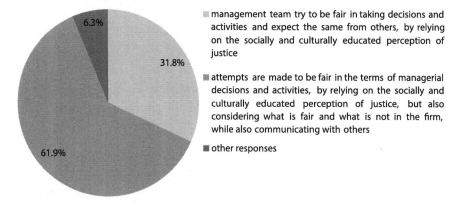

management team try to be fair in taking decisions and activities and expect the same from others, by relying on the socially and culturally educated perception of justice

attempts are made to be fair in the terms of managerial decisions and activities, by relying on the socially and culturally educated perception of justice, but also considering what is fair and what is not in the firm, while also communicating with others

other responses

Chart 38. Justice in the management of an organization in the opinions of respondents

Source: own research.

Other opinions (critical); constitute a total of 6% of the general opinions:
- Organization is solely geared towards profit, while justice is less significant/not significant at all.
- Justice is reserved for the Board/shareholders/; subject to arbitrary decisions.
- It is a theoretical notion. The person who is higher in the hierarchy is always right.
- Justice is frequently violated. Employees who do not have results at work are favourized.
- Widespread lack of objectivity.
- Good relations are above justice.
- Justice is not important in my firm.
- There is no justice.

- Lack of fair assessment of employees, their competences and results of work.
- Lack of justice, particularly with relation to the employees at lower levels.

Table 57. Justice in the management of an organization in the opinions of respondents from joint-stock companies, other enterprises and the public sector

No.	Variants of responses	Joint-stock companies		Other enterprises		Public sector	
		number	%	number	%	number	%
1.	The management staff try to be fair in taking decisions and expect the same from others by basing on the socially and culturally educated perception of justice	44	32.8	97	29.5	22	44.9
2.	There are attempts to be fair in terms of managerial decisions and action by basing on the socially and culturally educated perception of justice, but also consideration of what is just and what is not in the firm, while also communicating with others with relation to these issues	85	63.5	209	63.5	23	46.9
3.	Other responses	5	3.7	23	7.0	4	8.2
	Total	134	100	329	100	49	100

Source: own research.

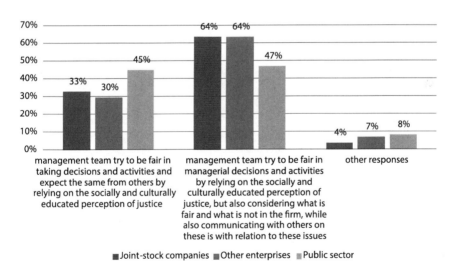

Chart 39. Justice in the management of an organization in the opinions of respondents from joint-stock companies, other enterprises and the public sector

Source: own research.

11.8. Honesty as a value

Honesty in business, mutual ties of employers and employees, intentions, etc., would seem to be a value that is commonly acknowledged to be important and expected. How do respondents perceive honesty in their organizations? Responses to these questions are included in Tables 58–59.

Table 58. Honesty in an organization in the opinions of respondents

No.	Variants of responses	Number of responses	% of responses
1.	Our organization is honest both in terms of internal relations, as well as external relations. This facilitates the restriction of the number and frequency of inspections	139	27.1
2.	The majority of people are honest, although not everyone is. Hence, the principle of limited trust is applied. In places acknowledged to be critical, inspection and monitoring are applied	283	55.3
3.	We feel that there is too much dishonesty and that it constitutes a serious problem; we apply inspections and monitoring on a widespread level	68	13.3
4.	Other responses	22	4.3
	Total	512	100

Source: own research.

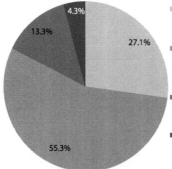

Chart 40. Honesty in an organization in the opinions of respondents

Source: own research.

The assessment of moderately positive is predominant (response of variant 2) – 55% of indicators. The assessment of very positive is twice more frequent than the opinion that dishonesty is excessive (27% and 13% respectively).

Of the remaining opinions (open and generally critical) which totalled 4%, the following were noted:

- we operate according to the simplified principle that "what is not forbidden is honest";
- employees are admittedly trusted, but inspections and audits are very frequent;
- not everyone is treated equally;
- firm places trust in chosen people, most frequently the management team;
- there is a lot of dishonesty and many issues are swept under the carpet.

Table 59. Honesty in an organization in the opinions of respondents in joint-stock companies, other enterprises and in the public sector

No.	Variants of responses	Joint-stock companies		Other enterprises		Public sector	
		number	%	number	%	number	%
1.	Our organization is honest both in terms of internal relations, as well as external relations. This facilitates the restriction of the number and frequency of inspections	33	24.6	97	29.5	9	18.4
2.	The majority of people are honest, although not everyone is. Hence, the principle of limited trust is applied. In places acknowledged to be critical, inspection and monitoring are applied	71	53.0	182	55.3	30	61.2
3.	We feel that there is too much dishonesty and that it constitutes a serious problem; we apply inspections and monitoring on a widespread level	25	18.7	40	12.2	3	6.1
4.	Other responses	5	3.7	10	3.0	7	14.3
	Total	134	100.0	329	100.0	49	100.0

Source: own research.

The conviction that dishonesty is excessive is relatively speaking the most frequently alluded to view by the respondents from the joint-stock companies (19%). The view that "admittedly the majority is honest, but it is necessary to apply the principle of limited trust, whereas in neuralgic cases inspections and monitoring should be applied", is most frequently expressed in the public sector (61%).

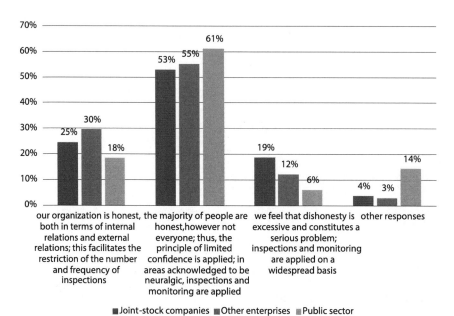

Chart 41. Honesty in an organization in the opinions of respondents in joint-stock companies, other enterprises and in the public sector

Source: own research.

12. COMMON VALUES FOR PEOPLE IN AN ORGANIZATION (CORPORATE)

Common values for people in an organization are a set of the values that the people associated with the given organization adopt, accept and want to execute together. Rather frequently, the values that are significant for the given organization are created by its founders who express in them their own hierarchy of values, as well as ideals and dreams, while also the desire to instigate in the organization and the world around it their own particle of good. They subsequently try to select such top-managers whose ideals are shared and create the impression of individuals capable and determined to realize them, together with the people selected by them.

Such a perception of common values is more frequently termed *corporate values* even in organizations that are not corporations, or more seldom *core values*. If the process of selection of "adjusting to" and accepting common values in an organization is run skilfully, thus on a sufficiently wide scale, the common values may be an additional element that connects people that are associated with the given organization constituting one of the factors of motivational impact and a significant element of culture. Likewise, they may also facilitate management and make it both easier and more effective. The significant factors and conditions of success are as follows:

- sincerity of intentions;
- authenticity (values should be in accordance with the internal need and profound convictions of the people; shared, but not imposed);
- partnership of the managerial staff and employees;
- avoiding ideologization, temptation to utilize (overuse) the values for the purposes of image (PR) and manipulation of people;
- determination and consistency in their adherence, managing them, associating with a wide perception of personnel policy (recruitment and employment reduction, selection of people, evaluation, development, while also leadership, motivation and promotion).

The notion and values constitute the first element of the widely perceived mission of the organization at hand, "something for the spirit". Of course, not all organizations formulate their missions in a broader manner (if at all), while not all work on educating and adhering to the common values. These may be encountered much earlier in large corporations (hence the term "corporate values"), than in small and medium-sized enterprises. Nevertheless, in the latter case some system of values functions, although it is seldom discussed, agreed on, registered or utilized in a methodical way in management. Without values in general it would be impossible to function. We are guided by them even when we are unaware of this fact.

In our survey research, we asked several questions relating to the common values. We asked whether they were separate and more widely known, how they are termed, which specific values are accepted as being common, whether they were distinguished as one value, acknowledged as the most important and what that value is, how realistic it is (non-declarative), the usefulness of the common values in the management of an organization. The set of questions relating to the common values was one of the most strongly displayed in the research carried out.

12.1. Distinguishing the common values for an organization

The set of questions described was aimed at establishing how often common values are distinguished in organizations and if joint-stock companies indicate any advantage here in terms of the other types of organizations. The results are formulated in Tables 60–61.

Table 60. Responses of the analysed people to the question of whether the values expected of managers and employees have been defined in the organization

No.	In our enterprises the values expected from managers and employees have been defined	Results of responses (item)	Results of responses (%)
1.	Yes	335	65.4
2.	No	177	34.6
	Total	**512**	**100**

Source: own research.

The responses reveal that almost 2/3 of organizations had values distinguished and acknowledged as common for the people as a whole that were associated with that organization (those employed and managing, as well as other people that were not hired employees). This is a high indicator which we had not expected. Nevertheless, we did not ask if the common values had been registered (and in which documents), or functioned as Iliad and Odyssey during the times of Homer and also several centuries later.

Table 61. Responses of the analysed people to the question of whether the values expected of managers and employees have been defined in the organization with a division into joint-stock companies, the remaining enterprises and the public sector units

No.	Were the values expected from the managers and employees common	Joint-stock companies		Other enterprises		Public sector	
		number	%	number	%	number	%
1.	Yes	106	79.1	205	62.3	24	49
2.	No	28	20.9	124	37.7	25	51
	Total	134	100	329	100	49	100

Source: own research.

The responses reveal that there is a prevalence of the joint-stock companies here with almost 80% of the common values distinguished in them (corporate values). The private sector is decidedly ahead of the public sector in this case.

12.2. Used names of common values for people from organization

We expected that the notion of "corporate values" may be most often used in Poland, which has been confirmed by the results of the research. The results have been illustrated in Tables 62 and 63.

Table 62. Used name of values in organizations according to those surveyed

No.	Applied names of "common values in an organization"	Number of indications	% of indications
1.	Corporate values	96	28.7
2.	Common values	109	32.5
3.	Universal values	58	17.3
4.	Company values	58	17.3
5.	Otherwise (our values, the values of the enterprise, the organizational values, the values provided from the name of the organization)	14	4.2
	Total	335	100

Source: own research.

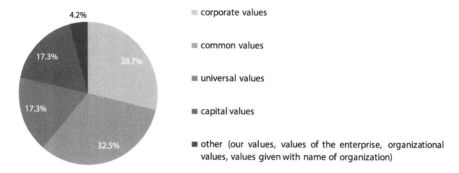

Chart 42. Used names of values in organizations according to those surveyed

Source: own research

Table 63. Used name of "common values" in organizations in joint-stock companies, other enterprises and public sector units

No.	How these values are termed:	Joint-stock companies		Other enterprises		Public sector	
		number	%	number	%	number	%
1.	Corporate values	37	35	45	22	6	25
2.	Common values	53	50	72	35.1	6	25
3.	Universal values	14	13.2	39	19.0	7	29.1
4.	Stock values	0	0	38	18.5	4	16.7
5.	Other (our value, value of the enterprise, organizational value, value provided from name of organization)	2	1.8	11	5.4	1	4.2
	Total	106	100.0	205	100.0	24	100.0

Source: own research.

12.3. Familiarity with common values in an organization

From the viewpoint of management and its effectiveness, it is a very significant issue whether the "common values" are commonly known, rather widely known, but not widespread, or whether familiarity with them is rather miniscule. This naturally has an impact on their real significance and certifies to the approach to this issue on the part of the people responsible for organization. The results of the research on this issue have been presented in Tables 64–65.

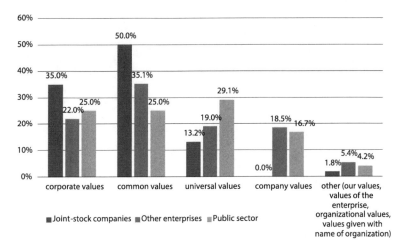

Chart 43. Used term of "common values" in joint-stock companies, other enterprises and public sector units

Source: own research.

Table 64. Familiarity with common values / corporate values according to the opinions of respondents

No.	Familiarity with "common values" is as follows:	Number	%
1.	Widespread	114	34
2.	Relatively high, but not widespread	172	51.4
3.	Not very high	37	11
4.	Slight	9	2.7
5.	Other responses (It is difficult for me to say)	3	0.9
	Total	335	100.0

Source: own research.

Table 65. Familiarity with common values / corporate values in joint-stock companies, other enterprises and public sector units

No.	Familiarity with common values is as follows:	Joint-stock companies		Other enterprises		Public sector	
		number	%	number	%	number	%
1.	Widespread	62	34.1	11	26.2	36	34
2.	Relatively high, but not widespread	89	48.9	26	61.9	57	53.8
3.	Not very high	22	12.1	5	11.9	10	9.4
4.	Slight, very limited	9	4.9	0	0	0	0
5.	Other responses	0	0	0	0	3	2.8
	Total	182	100	42	100	106	100

Source: own research.

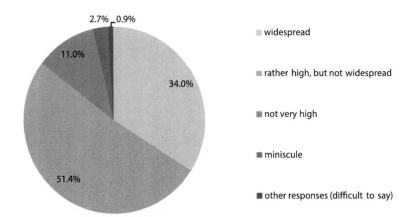

Chart 44. Familiarity with common values / corporate values according to the opinions of respondents

Source: own research.

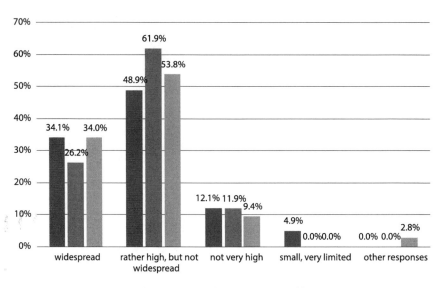

Chart 45. Used term of "common values" in joint-stock companies, other enterprises and public sector units

Source: own research.

12.4. Values most frequently accepted as common

What is of particular interest is the fact that from the viewpoint of the subject matter undertaken, the response to the question of which specific values were acknowledged in the particular organizations as common / organizational / corporate. The appropriate data has been illustrated in Tables 66–67.

Table 66. Most frequently accepted common values in joint-stock companies
(array of decreasing responses, indicating the given value)

No.	Accepted common values / corporate values
1.	Effectiveness, profit
2.	Quality, broad perception (products, processes, work, relations, etc.)
3.	Responsibility (also for the environment)
4.	Professionalism
5.	Teamwork
6.	Honesty
7.	Trust
8.	Loyalty
9.	Creativity, innovativeness
10.	Business orientation

Source: own research.

Table 67. Most frequently indicated common values in other enterprises
(not joint-stock companies) – decreasing sequence

No.	Accepted common values / corporate values
1.	Effectiveness, profit
2.	Professionalism
3.	Quality, broad perception
4.	Responsibility
5.	Cooperation, teamwork
6.	Creativity, innovativeness
7.	Business orientation
8.	Honesty
9.	Trust
10.	Loyalty

Source: own research.

The low position of creativity and innovativeness, as well as business orientation is surprising. With regard to the business orientation, perhaps it had not been entered into the business values as it is acknowledged to be so obvious in joint-stock companies that it was not necessary to enter them on "the flag". However, in terms of creativity and innovativeness, perhaps their rarity is one of the reasons why we are to be found "at the tail-end of Europe". It is difficult to have high levels of creativity and innovativeness of employees when these values are not promoted or required.

Comparing the common values of joint-stock companies and the remaining enterprises indicates that in as much as the afore-mentioned values are the same (although they differ in terms of order), the further positions of honesty, trust and loyalty are in the remaining enterprises even more seldom acknowledged to be organizational values than in the joint-stock companies. Nevertheless, in the remaining enterprises, innovativeness and creativity are noted at a higher level than in the joint-stock companies. Could it be that the strong orientation (excessively strong?) towards finance and dividends in the joint-stock companies has led to the case whereby real issues are losing importance in the world? Such a conclusion would not be sufficiently justified on the basis of the results presented here, but certain unease remains.

In the majority of cases, the number of common values adopted into one organization ranged between 3 and 7. Admittedly, the surveys did not contain such a question, although such numbers most frequently arise from the markings and personal entries made by the particular respondents.

Table 68. Ten most frequently accepted common values in public sector units

No.	Accepted common values / organizational values
1.	Quality, broad perception (products, processes, work, relations, etc.)
2.	Orientation towards results
3.	Effectiveness (work)
4.	Professionalism
5.	Responsibility (broad perception)
6.	Creativity, innovativeness
7.	Trust
8.	Cooperation, teamwork
9.	Loyalty
10.	Honesty

Source: own research.

In terms of the common values, such ones as "environmental protection" or "sustainable growth" appear only sporadically. This may be acknowledged to be a weakness of the survey (such variants of responses had not been presented and were only possible to enter in the position of "other", which was rarely executed). However, environmental protection and sustainable growth are more frequently perceived in enterprises as aims and tasks than as corporate values that are to connect people.

The low position of cooperation and teamwork is surprising (only in eighth position). Trust, honesty and loyalty close the list, as in the case of the sector of enterprises.

Table 69. Response to the question of whether the most important common value / corporate value in the organization is specified – aggregated data

No.	Variants of responses	Number	%
1.	Yes (most frequently: effectiveness, professionalism, quality)	161	31.4
2.	We do not distinguish one most important value	174	34.0
3.	Difficult to say	177	34.6
	Total	512	100.0

Source: own research.

The question was awkward for a significant portion of those analysed, as such an issue is rarely touched on in organizations. Thus, it is no wonder that a significant proportion of responses were termed as "difficult to say". In cases whereby the respondents felt competent to provide a clear response, they more frequently indicated the lack of one specific value to term as the most important. This question may be significant in the context of the deliberations, among other aspects, whether profit or effectiveness are deemed to be the most important value.

12.5. Evaluation of the practical usefulness of common values

It is possible to establish the common values. Nevertheless, the question of what practical use comes out of this is significant. The responses of the respondents to such a question posed have been illustrated in Tables 70–71. The positive ones are prevalent; they may be acknowledged as generally encouraging for working with the common values.

Table 70. Evaluation of the practical usefulness of the registered corporate values by those surveyed – aggregated data (for the responses provided)

No.	Variants of responses	Number	%
1.	In essence, they are not useful and do not result in much	50	14.9
2.	They are known and generally accepted; we included them in the system of management (its various sub-systems), with varying degrees of effects	159	47.5
3.	They are known and accepted; we included them in the system of management to a generally good effect	97	28.9
4.	They are known and accepted; we included them in the system of management to a very good effect; we feel that it brings significant effects	29	8.7
	Difficult to say, lack of response	177	x
	Total	**335**	**100**

Source: own research.

As can be seen, a large number of respondents was not able to respond to the question.

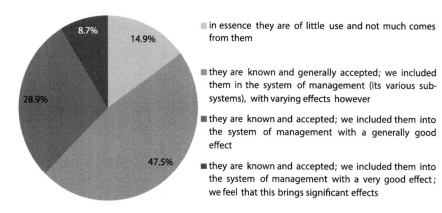

in essence they are of little use and not much comes from them

they are known and generally accepted; we included them in the system of management (its various sub-systems), with varying effects however

they are known and accepted; we included them into the system of management with a generally good effect

they are known and accepted; we included them into the system of management with a very good effect; we feel that this brings significant effects

Chart 46. Usefulness of common values / corporate values according to the opinions of respondents

Source: own research.

Table 71. Evaluation of the practical usefulness of corporate values in the cross-section of a group of entities (data for respondents who did not avoid this evaluation)

No.	Variants of responses	Joint-stock companies		Other enterprises		Public sector	
		number	%	number	%	number	%
1.	In essence, they are not useful and do not result in much	13	12.3	35	17.1	2	8.3
2.	They are known and generally accepted; we included them in the system of management with varying degrees of effects	49	46.2	93	45.4	17	70.8
3.	They are known and accepted; we included them in the system of management to a generally good effect	29	27.4	64	31.2	4	16.7
4.	They are known and accepted; we included them in the system of management to a very good effect; we feel that it brings significant effects	15	14.1	13	6.3	1	4.2
	Total	106	100	205	100	24	100

Source: own research.

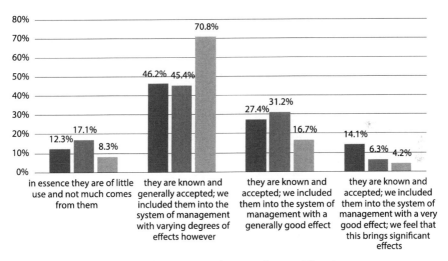

Chart 47. Evaluation of the practical usefulness of the registered corporate values by those surveyed – disaggregated data

Source: own research.

13. RESPECTING VALUES IN THE PERSONNEL POLICIES OF AN ORGANIZATION

One of the most significant and most difficult issues in management by values that is significantly decisive in terms of the sense and effectiveness of such management is the relation of values deemed to be important for the personnel policy and management of human capital. Due to the nature of material, it does not seem that there would be more possibilities of creating close, algorithmic ties in connection with all the values that are acknowledged to be important. Nevertheless, we present the view that such ties should not be restricted to the issue of notions, or designating directions, but it would be necessary to move one by establishing at least sensible principles that are possible to accept and which are binding within the personnel policy and management of human capital.

In the afore said research, we asked the respondents to take account of the values in terms of the following:
– recruitment and selection of staff;
– evaluation of employees;
– promotions;
– remuneration;
– non-material motivation.

13.1. Taking account of values during the recruitment and selection of people

This is a compelling and promising, yet a difficult issue from a substantive viewpoint. On the basis of personal experience and contacts, as well as subject-related literature, we thought that values acknowledged by a candidate for work are rarely analysed profoundly in routine procedures. It is usually the requirements of the work position that are taken into account, which are defined in the profile of the position either in the professiogram or in more modest terms, in the analysis by the specialist of issues of personnel or "head-hunters" with the manager the one to commission such activity in search of an employee. In smaller organizations, the entrepreneur /employer generally runs the interview with the candidate and asks him about professional issues that he feels are significant from the viewpoint of his own expectations. Likewise, he also takes account of the general impression and tries to imagine if the candidate would "fit" into the organization, tasks and with other people. In terms of values, as we thought they are seldom touched on in detail both from the point of view of running direct talks on this issue, as well as the assumption that the candidate would rather say what he feels should be said in order to get the job than what is true.

Sometimes it is possible to encounter propositions of a different approach. Izabela Bartnicka, an independent expert with relation to the recruitment and selection of staff, claims that the model of recruitment has changed, in that the employers are not only viewing the hard competences now, but are increasingly trying to analyse the soft competences of a candidate for work, in terms of the values held by him and their compliance with the values promoted in the firm at hand. She emphasizes that such procedure is more difficult than the traditional one, in which the values are not paid attention to.[21]

The results of research on this issue give room for greater optimism. They reveal that the values are the subject matter of interest for the majority of people who run the recruitment and selection of personnel, although only 23% of them feel that their organization has the appropriate methodics at its disposal.

Table 72. Taking account of values during the recruitment process according to the opinions of respondents – disaggregated data

No.	Taking account of values during the recruitment process and selection of people – evaluation of practices	Number	%
1.	This takes place in the sphere that is dependent on individual knowledge, abilities and inquisitiveness of the particular personnel specialists and managers; we do not have the tools and procedures at our disposal that would facilitate the analysis of candidates for work in the context of values in a credible way and common within the company, which is comparable and routine by nature	208	40.6
2.	As above, however with relation to some professional and qualified positions and groups we have carried out a satisfactory operationalization	153	29.9
3.	We take account of values with relation to the majority of candidates for work and we have a system of methodics that may be deemed to be appropriate	120	23.4
4.	Other responses	31	6.1
	Total	512	100.0

Source: own research.

---

[21] I. Bartnicka, *Pracodawcy muszą walczyć o kandydatów do pracy*, http://biznes.onet.pl/video/pracodawcy-musza-walczyc-o-kandydatow-do-pracy.14910.w.html [15.01.2015].

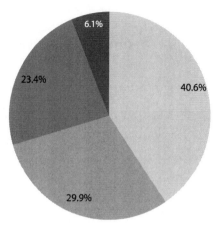

takes place in the sphere of abilities and curiosity, depending on individual knowledge of particular personnel specialists and managers; we do not have tools and procedures at our disposal that would facilitate analysis of candidates for work

as above, although with relation to certain positions and professional and qualification groups we have carried out a satisfactory operationalization

we take account of values with relation to the majority of candidates for work and we have methodics at our disposal that may be acknowledged to be appropriate

other responses

Chart 48. Taking account of values during the recruitment process according to the opinions of respondents – disaggregated data

Source: own research.

Other opinions (6% of the total, very critical and not completely on the subject matter):

- selection of people depends on one person – unfortunately;
- the Board searches for the cheapest people, even at the cost of knowledge, level of involvement or personal culture;
- paying attention to experience and choice according to self-discretion, lack of professionalism in recruitment;
- we constitute a closed environment, there is a small number of people who got work according to competences or values held; only favouritism counts;
- others in a similar tone.

Table 73. Taking account of values during the recruitment process according to the opinions of respondents – disaggregated data

No.	Taking account of values in the recruitment and selection of people	Joint-stock companies		Other enterprises		Public sector	
		number	%	number	%	number	%
1.	This takes place in the sphere that is dependent on individual knowledge, abilities and inquisitiveness of the particular personnel specialists and managers; we do not have the tools and procedures at our disposal that would facilitate the analysis of candidates for work in the context of values in a credible way and common within the company, which is comparable and routine by nature	48	35.8	144	43.8	16	32.7
2.	As above, however with relation to some professional and qualified positions and groups we have carried out a satisfactory operationali-zation and we are able to do this	41	30.6	95	28.9	17	34.7
3.	We take account of values with relation to the majority of candidates for work and we have a system of methodics that may be deemed to be appropriate	38	28.4	74	22.5	8	16.3
4.	Other responses	7	5.2	16	4.9	8	16.3
	Total	**134**	**100.0**	**329**	**100.0**	**49**	**100.0**

Source: own research.

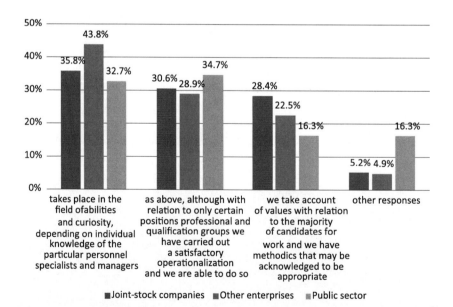

Chart 49. Taking account of values during the recruitment process according to the opinions of respondents – disaggregated data

Source: own research.

13.2. Taking account of values in the assessment of employees

If the values in an organization are perceived to be important, they should also be taken into account in the evaluation of employees, not only the formalized and periodical ones. This may be difficult and troublesome for the assessor. The information on how it looks in practice is included in Tables 74–75.

Table 74. Taking account of values in the assessment of employees according to the opinions of respondents – aggregated data

No.	Variants of responses	Number	%
1.	In the assessment of the employees, in essence we do not take account of the professed and respected values; we are guided by the evaluation of the results of work and qualifications	214	41.8
2.	We take them into account in individual and rather exceptional cases	145	28.3
3.	We take them into account in a routine manner with relation to the chosen professional groups	68	13.3
4.	We take them into account with relation to the majority of professional groups / employees	57	11.1
5.	Other responses	28	5.5
	Total	512	100.0

Source: own research.

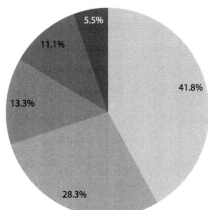

in the evaluation of employees in essence, we do not take the professed and respected values by them into consideration; we are guided by the evaluation of the results of work and qualifications

we take them into account in individual and rather exceptional cases

we take account of them in a routine way with relation to the chosen professional groups

we take account of them with relation to the majority of professional groups / employees

other responses

Chart 50. Taking account of values in the assessment of employees according to the opinions of respondents – aggregated data

Source: own research.

Table 75. Taking account of values in the assessment of employees according to the opinions of respondents – disaggregated data

No.	Variants of responses	Joint-stock companies		Other enterprises		Public sector	
		number	%	number	%	number	%
1.	In the assessment of the employees, in essence we do not take account of the professed and respected values; we are guided by the evaluation of the results of work and qualifications	59	44.1	139	42.2	16	32.7
2.	We take them into account in individual and rather exceptional cases	31	23.1	95	28.9	19	38.8
3.	We take them into account in a routine manner with relation to the chosen professional groups	18	13.4	42	12.8	8	16.3
4.	We take them into account with relation to the majority of professional groups/employees	22	16.4	34	10.3	1	2.0
5.	Other responses	4	3	19	5.8	5	10.2
	Total	134	100.0	329	100.0	49	100.0

Source: own research.

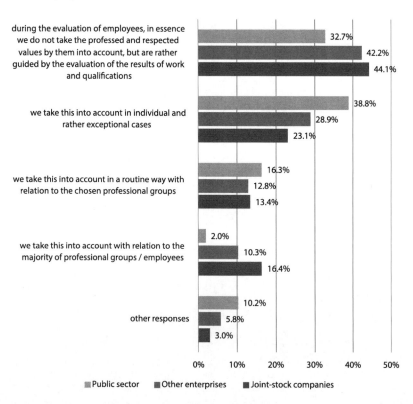

Chart 51. Taking account of values in the assessment of employees

Source: own research.

Free responses (mostly critical):
- there is no evaluation of employees;
- evaluation of employees (is known to them) is not run in a methodological way;
- only effectiveness is assessed;
- values are taken into account during the periodical evaluation, but the criteria arouses doubts;
- during the evaluation personal liking and antipathy are mainly taken into account;
- members of the families of the board members are favourized; values are in the background.

In sum, in the public sector values are taken into consideration in the evaluation of employees more frequently than in the private sector.

13.3. Taking account of values while making decisions relating to promotion

A further question in the survey related to the scope of taking values into account when promoting employees, particularly for managerial positions. The intention of the researcher was to recognise which values are generally taken into account during the course of considering and making decisions relating to promotions and if so, does this refer to certain positions or the majority of cases. We had not assumed the possibilities that values may be taken into consideration in terms of big promotions as being excessively abstract; although if there had been such cases, they could have been registered in the variant of "other responses".

It would have been worth analysing which specific values are deemed to be significant in terms of considering decisions about promotions. We assumed that thorough analysis would take place in case studies as the survey research could not be excessively extended.

The results have been illustrated in Tables 76–77.

Table 76. Taking account of values while making decisions relating to promotion – aggregated data

No.	Taking account of values while making decisions relating to promotion	Number	%
1.	We do not take account of the acknowledged values; we are guided by competences and the hitherto results / successes	178	34.8
2.	We take values into account only with relation to some positions, particularly managerial ones; we do not have any professional instrumentarium	125	24.4
3.	We take values into account only with relation to some positions, particularly managerial ones; we have a professional instrumentarium at our disposal	65	12.7
4.	We take values into account with relation to the majority of positions, however we do not have specialized techniques and tools at our disposal	79	15.5
5.	We take values into account with relation to the majority of positions and we have specialized techniques, tools and procedures at our disposal	33	6.4
6.	Other responses	32	6.2
	Total	**512**	**100.0**

Source: own research.

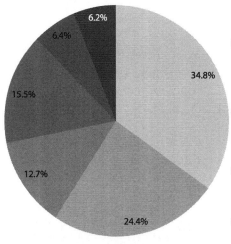

we do not take account of the acknowledged values; we are guided by competences and hitherto results / successes

we take values into account only with relation to certain positions, particularly managerial ones; we do not have any professional instrumentrium at our disposal

we take values into account only with relation to certain positions, particularly managerial ones; we have any professional instrumentrium at our disposal

we take account of the values with relation to the majority of positions, although we have specialized techniques and tools

we take account of the values with relation to the majority of specialized techniques, tools and procedures

Chart 52. Taking account of values while making decisions relating to promotion – aggregated data

Source: own research.

The majority of those analysed indicated variant 1, informing that these values were not taken into consideration during the course of decisions relating to promotions (35% of such responses). Every fourth respondent was of the opinion that values are to some extent taken into account during the course of promotions for <u>only certain </u>positions (mainly managerial), although there is no instrumentarium here; by which we mean the prepared, agreed and widely known principles, criteria, procedures, etc. Almost 13% informed that the values were taken into account for some positions, while some form of instrumentarium is applied, or in other words, the systemic approach, thanks to which being guided by values during the course of taking decisions relating to promotions (expected in the organization and appreciated by candidates) may be based on the appropriate principles, criteria, while also procedures. More thorough analysis of this in the survey research was acknowledged by us as impossible, in the hope of gaining access to this type of information in case study research.

In "other responses", as in the case of the other questions, there was a prevalence of critical comments, not necessarily connected with the content and point of the question. We were also informed of the following:

- There are no promotions in the enterprise (are they very rare?); over twenty of this type of response.
- Acquaintances of the management team or Supervisory Board receive promotion, without paying attention to value (several such responses).
- Values are taken into account during the course of promotions for all positions (several such responses).
- Promotions are mostly decided by pacts and personal liking; competences and values are less significant.

The "other responses" were in general few and far between (approximately 6%).

Table 77. Taking account of values while making decisions relation to promotion – disaggregated data

No.	Variants of responses	Joint-stock companies		Other enterprises		Public sector units	
		number	%	number	%	number	%
1.	We do not take account of the acknowledged values; we are guided by competences and the hitherto results / successes	51	38.1	109	33.1	18	36.7
2.	We take values into account only with relation to some positions, particularly managerial ones; we do not have any professional instrumentarium	28	20.9	85	25.8	12	24.5

3.	We take values into account only with relation to some positions, particularly managerial ones; we have a professional instrumentarium at our disposal	14	10.4	46	14.0	5	10.2
4.	We take values into account with relation to the majority of positions, however we do not have specialized techniques and tools at our disposal	21	15.7	54	16.4	4	8.2
5.	We take values into account with relation to the majority of positions and we have specialized techniques, tools and procedures at our disposal	14	10.4	17	5.2	2	4.1
6.	Other responses	6	4.5	18	5.5	8	16.3
	Total	**134**	**100.0**	**329**	**100.0**	**49**	**100.0**

Source: own research.

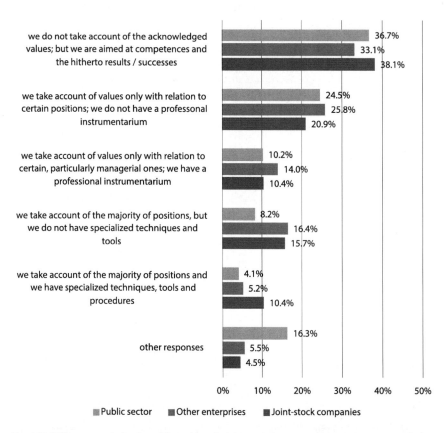

Chart 53. Taking account of value while making decisions relating to promotion – disaggregated data

Source: own research.

13.4. Taking account of values during remuneration process

This is one of the most delicate and difficult issues associated with management that respects (and strengthens) values. If the aim of the organization is to strengthen values, it is necessary to connect them with the system of remuneration. This connection should be in a creative way: by providing additional money for honesty and other "decent" approaches and behaviour that comes under civilized norms, which could be acknowledged as strange and even evoke mockery. On the other hand, the commonly applied jubilee awards are direct rewards for the value that is the many years of loyalty with relation to the employer. The issue of what specific way to connect the system of remuneration with the values that are precious for the organization is worthy of separate analysis. We suppose that this is not resolved in either theory or practice and is still awaiting its discoverers. In the questions put forth here, we did not venture deeper, limiting ourselves to providing the sample ties of premiums and rewards, as well as penalties for critical events (both positive and negative), as well as the ties of values with the formulation of the fundamental wage structure. The content of the questions and answers have been provided in Tables 78–79.

Table 78. Taking account of values during remuneration process – aggregated data

No.	Variants of responses	Number	%
1.	We are not guided by the evaluation of the degree of conformity with the expectations of values in our company during the course of rewarding managers and employees	134	26.2
2.	We are guided by this sporadically, mainly with relation to critical events (very positive-subject to rewards on occasions, or very negative-subject to penalties on occasions)	177	34.6
3.	We take them into account rather frequently, particularly with the use of the system of rewards and penalties, although sometimes increasing the level of the basic remuneration	127	24.8
4.	We apply routine systemic ties, generally relating to managers and employees	53	10.3
5.	Other responses (there are no rewards nor penalties; personal liking and antipathy, but not values)	21	4.1
	Total	512	100.0

Source: own research.

The results are generally positive as only approximately 30% of respondents claimed no ties between remuneration and values (the total number of people choosing variants 1 and 5 in terms of responses with relation to the combined total of respondents). The majority, namely 35% of respondents however claimed that the ties between remuneration and values are sporadic and are restricted to critical events. The routine and systemic ties were referred to by every tenth respondent.

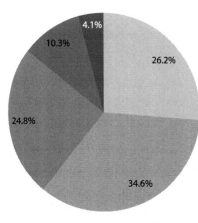

we are not guided by the evaluation of the degree of conformity with values in our company and in rewarding managers and employees

we are guided by this sporadically, mainly with relation to critical events (very positive, sometimes subject to rewarding or very negative, sometimes subject to penalties)

we take this into account rather frequently, particularly with the aid of the system of rewards and penalties while also increasing the level of basic pay

we apply a routine systemic connection by relating to the managers and employees in general

other responses – there are no rewards nor penalties; personal liking and antipathy are taken into account, but not values

Chart 54. Taking account of values during remuneration process – aggregated data

Source: own research.

Table 79. Taking account of values during remuneration process – detailed data

No.	Variants of responses	Joint-stock companies		Other enterprises		Public sector units	
		number	%	number	%	number	%
1.	We are not guided by the evaluation of the degree of conformity with the expectations of values in our company during the course of rewarding managers and employees	34	25.4	89	27.1	11	22.4
2.	We are guided by this sporadically, mainly with relation to critical events (very positive-subject to rewards on occasions, or very negative-subject to penalties on occasions)	42	31.4	119	36.2	16	32.7
3.	We take them into account rather frequently, particularly with the use of the system of rewards and penalties, although sometimes increasing the level of the basic remuneration	40	29.8	74	22.5	13	26.5
4.	We apply routine systemic ties, generally relating to managers and employees	13	9.7	36	10.9	4	8.2
5.	Other responses	5	3.7	11	3.3	5	10.2
	Total	134	100.0	329	100.0	49	100.0

Source: own research.

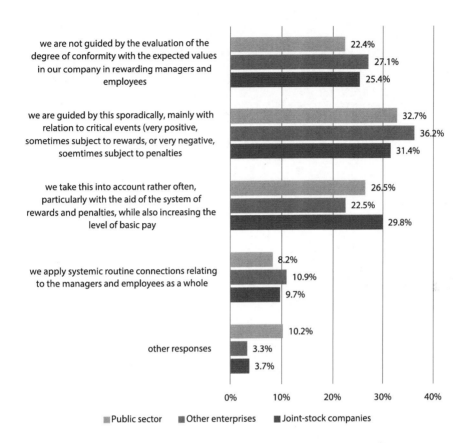

Chart 55. Taking account of values during remuneration process – detailed data

Source: own research.

13.5. Promoting values by means of intangible rewards

It is easier to promote values via intangible rewards than via remuneration. Whether this is effective or not is another matter. Responses to this question relating to ties between the promotion of values and intangible rewards are illustrated in Tables 80–87.

Table 80. Ties between promoting values and non-material rewards – aggregated data

No.	Variants of responses	Number of responses	% of responses
1.	There are no ties	149	29.1
2.	Ties are rather sporadic	235	45.9
3.	Ties are relatively frequent	98	19.1
4.	Ties are routine and systemic	30	5.9
	Total	**512**	**100.0**

Source: own research.

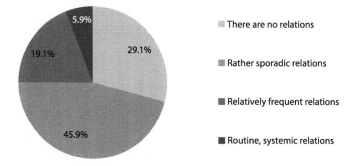

Chart 56. Relations between promoting values and intangible rewards – aggregated data

Source: own research.

Table 81. Relations between promoting values and intangible rewards – aggregated data

No.	Variants of responses	Joint-stock companies		Other enterprises		Public sector units	
		number	%	number	%	number	%
1.	Ties are rather sporadic	38	28.4	99	30.1	12	24.5
2.	Ties are relatively frequent	61	45.5	151	45.9	23	46.9
3.	Ties are routine and systemic	26	19.4	65	19.8	7	14.3
4.	There are no ties	9	6.7	14	4.3	7	14.3
	Total	**134**	**100.0**	**329**	**100.0**	**49**	**100.0**

Source: own research.

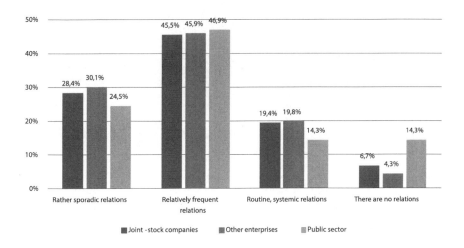

Chart 57. Relations between promoting values and intangible rewards – detailed data

Source: own research.

Table 82. Forms of intangible rewards associated with promoting values

No.	Applied forms of intangible rewards
1.	Praise and words of acknowledgement on public forums
2.	Awarding the title employee of the year, month, etc.
3.	Titles: the incest manager, colleague, employee etc., as well as publicly granting diplomas or associated badges and medals
4.	Honorary titles: excellent inventor, rationalizer, role model for youth, etc.
5.	Additional leave
	Trips as rewards (they have a certain tangible value)
7.	Article in company press, local or national press with a picture
8.	Local, community order of distinction, etc.
9.	Plaques, busts, naming of buildings, rooms, libraries etc. after distinguished / excellent / particularly of merit / heroic people
10.	Proclaiming the services, attitudes, impact etc. of the distinguished person in the community of the given organization (and wider spectrum) with the use of the Internet, Extranet, company and local media, TV, etc.

Source: own research.

14. FINDINGS AND CONCLUSIONS FROM RESEARCH ANALYSIS

1. The results of the survey research would seem to be more optimistic and uplifting than we had expected. It turned out that this issue enjoys great interest and there is currently a favourable social vibe for the spreading of management with greater use of (and promotion of) values. This may be a benefit to both the effectiveness of management, as well as the integration of people in the organization and their motivation, while also cooperation with other stakeholders, the realization of the concept of sustainability, organizational vibe and behaviour and the perception of the organization from the outside.

2. Almost all of the respondents from the private sector acknowledge economic values as at least important. 56% of respondents deem them to be the most important, alongside adherence to the law and ethical norms; whereas in joint-stock companies this percentage is even higher. This is confirmed by the high level of importance of economic values among the total values, which was to be expected.

3. The group of ethical and cultural values is perceived to be significant and sufficiently displayed in their organizations by 43% of respondents. In joint-stock companies, this indicator is clearly lower (37%), while the highest in the entities of the public sector where it amounts to 51%. This is also a high indicator, although it may certify to the fact that in joint-stock companies the orientation towards profit in some cases pushes non-economic values into the background. Such a conviction also strengthens the analysis of the differences in the perception of the groups of values as follows: competence and developmental, as well as civic and social in joint-stock companies and other entities.

4. Competence and developmental values are acknowledged to be important by 87% of respondents, of whom 35% state that they are sufficiently displayed, while 52% state that they are insufficiently so. 12% think that in their organizations they are of rather secondary importance (in the opinions of 16% of respondents working there). A large proportion of respondents are convinced that these values require strengthening in their organizations.

5. Social and civic values are deemed to be secondary by 43% of respondents (by 47% of those in joint-stock companies), while by 28% in the public sector.
6. The impact of values on the system of management in an organization is most frequently stated to be important by the respondents. This particularly relates to the impact of values on the following:
   - external image of the organization (as many as 79.6% of respondents feel that is strong or even very strong);
   - motivating employees (72.9% indicate the impact as being strong, or rather strong);
   - strengthening the organizational discipline and work (72.5% of respondents evaluate it as strong);
   - overcoming crises (72.1% of such indicators);
   - growth of the effectiveness of the operations of the organization (71.6% of people state that it is strong or even very strong);
   - integrating people in the organization (66.3% of people indicated as above).

   There are certain, albeit not very significant differences between the impact of values on the management of an organization depending on the legislative and organizational form, while also the area of operations. Generally speaking, the impact of values on the management in joint-stock companies is slightly weaker than in the remaining enterprises and in organizations from the public sector.
7. The significance of values is not stable over time – some gain in terms of importance, while others lose it relatively speaking. The most frequently indicated growth in the significance of effectiveness(and profitability), which is possible to relate to the particularly high economic values in society, as well as the profile of education of the respondents (economics, management). Likewise, the following were also rated highly: creativity, knowledge, professional development and competitiveness. The rating of 8th place in terms of innovativeness and only 15th place in terms of honesty are surprising. With relation to innovativeness, this corresponds with the further responses (to question 20) from which a certain ambivalence is evident in the responses: in approximately 70% of cases, innovativeness is acknowledged to be important in organizations, but in 26% of cases of little importance due to factors of varying nature (type of business activities and products, monopolistic and oligopolistic positions and others). With regard to honesty, it is worth remembering that we are analysing a value list here, which has significantly grown.
8. Research has confirmed what was indicated by other researchers, namely the drop in significance of such values as trust (most frequently indicated), while subsequently: respect, social solidarity / solidarity, while moreover loyalty, understanding, justice, protection of health and life, amiabil-

ity, flexibility, empathy, discipline and patriotism (in 10th place on the list of dropped significance).

9. The concept of sustainable growth (and its value) is enjoying decisive support (93%), although twice more people claim that it is realized in a limited scope than those who express the opinion that it is implemented to a satisfying degree at present. The indicators of support are at the highest in the joint-stock companies, although the differences in the evaluation between them and the remaining types of organizations are not big.

10. Opinions relating to CSR are generally positive: 67% of respondents expressed the view that the approach to CSR by their organization is "universal and responsible", while 29% informed that their organizations did not differ either positively or negatively against the background of others. Nevertheless, organizations in which standardized ethical audits are applied are in the clear minority.

11. With relation to the dignity-based values (respect, respecting dignity, amiability, respecting human freedom and privacy, etc.) 48% of respondents are of the view that they constitute a real pillar in terms of shaping the relations with people both within the framework of the firm, as well as outside of it (in shaping the relations with clients, trading partners, local communities, etc.). 32% feel that they are generally declared, but not necessarily respected. 16% of those analysed are convinced that they are treated as second-rate. In the case of several percentage points (3%), in terms of the free description there were critical opinions on the issue of the lack of respect for human dignity and low personal culture and communication with the management staff. This is however a marginal matter.

12. Opinions associated with trust in their organizations are in general better among respondents than what was presented in nationwide research. This may be connected with the fact that educated people gave their opinions and did so in terms of human environments they are familiar with and not strangers where the level of trust is by nature lower. 61% of respondents stated that we can show trust and "enjoy trust ourselves", while 35% felt that trust should be strengthened, work on its improvement as it is not in the best shape. Research run by CBOS (2012), reveals that a mere 23% of Polish people think that the majority of people can be trusted, while trust in large enterprises was indicated at the level of 35%. Against this background, the results of the research outlined reveal a more optimistic picture.

13. Balancing professional work and other spheres of life is a relatively significant value in the context of the fact that Polish (those employed) belong to the group of people that work particularly hard against the background of the EU, while having a negative demographic growth,[22] while the civic and

---

[22] The indicator of female fertility in Poland is among the lowest in the world and amounts to 1.3 (GUS, 2012), with regard to 2.1 that is essential for simple reproduction.

political involvement of our fellow countrymen is low and a multitude of people are exhausted with work. Research indicated that only every fourth organization perceives this problem as requiring systemic activity on the scale of an organization. Half of the organizations deem this to be an issue to be resolved (solely) between the employees and their direct superiors, while in 22% of cases no-one from the framework of organizations was interested in this issue. Hence, there is a lot of work to be done.

14. In 65% of cases (79% in the case of joint-stock companies, whereas 49% in the analysed entities from the public sector) respondents inform that in their organizations common values (corporate) have been distinguished, acknowledged to be important and those which should be commonly respected. Most frequently, the number of these common values ranges from 3 to 7. These are relatively frequently as follows: effectiveness, quality, satisfaction of clients, responsibility, professionalism, business orientation, cooperation and teamwork, creativity and innovativeness, as well as entrepreneurship. In the majority of organizations (70%), there is no singular value that is acknowledged to be the most important of all. Familiarity with these values among managers and employees is widespread in 34% of entities, rather high in 51%, while low in 14%. Only 15% of respondents feel that the benefit of common values is meagre and does not lead too much.

15. Values are taken into consideration in personnel policy and management of human capital, particularly in terms of recruitment and selection of staff, in advanced policies, evaluation of employees, remuneration and intangible rewards. However, ties are most frequently fragmentary, moderately significant, while also visible in approximate terms with one third of organizations. Great difficulties are being caused by operationalization. Without doubt this aspect of the subject matter of research requires both more thorough research (this is our intention), as well as new ideas and research.

16. The established main thesis was as follows: **Management that respects the acknowledged values, not only economic ones, but increases the credibility and effectiveness of an organization, matches contemporary needs and expectations of managers at varying levels, as well as employees, favours the integration of people in an organization, while also facilitates the execution of personnel policy.** This thesis has been completely confirmed on multiple occasions in the results of the research.

17. Among the five complementary theses presented on pages 4–5, the first, fourth and fifth have been confirmed by research. The second and third theses have only been confirmed in part. This is mainly due to the resignation from the first version of the survey, which was more extended and had a separate set of questions directed towards confirming or rejecting

the second thesis. However, we decided that a survey numbering 14 pages in length had only a slight chance of being filled in by anyone, while the set of questions for the second thesis in the longer version of the survey was the most difficult in terms of providing responses.

The content of the second thesis was as follows: **It is not possible to manage professionally and efficiently only via values. Hence, it is necessary to search for compilatory and integrated techniques where values have a certain, yet by nature a rather limited role to fulfil, or also to apply management that respects values instead of MBV.**

In this situation, all that remains is for us to illustrate this issue in further research, which would be devoted to this issue in the future. Nevertheless, this subject-matter is not really suitable for survey research, thus it would be necessary to apply other research techniques.

18. The content of the third thesis is as follows: **It is not the deliberate absolutization and excessive promotion of any singular value or homogenous groups of value.** In part (as a whole it is large however), the confirmation of this thesis took place by means of the common recognition by the respondents of the necessity to respect a multitude of varying values from all their groups, not only economic values. The vast majority of respondents also claimed that in their organizations there is no singular value of key significance, as there are usually several of the most important ones.

This subject matter is still of practical importance as it is still possible to hear in many places the words of the "early Milton Friedman"[23] – that the main / only really important aim of the business activities of an enterprise is to increase the value for its owners. Research does not confirm this.

19. We express the conviction that the term Management by Values (MBV) is not the most appropriate as it is not possible to manage only via values. The values that were emphasized by among others, the previously quoted contemporary German philosopher Hans Joas, encounter difficulties when subject to operationalization (if at all), while management solely by means of values would have to be resemble management by appeal, which is difficult to accept for professional managers and indeed not recommended by us. Hence, in the title of this report under the formal name accepted for this research – "Management by values", we provided (in brackets) the title that in our view is more appropriate – "Management that respects and promotes values", which should not arouse any reservations.

---

[23] In the later period of his life, M. Friedman added that adherence to the law and ethics is also important.

Appendix 1. Survey research

VALUES IN THE SYSTEM OF MANAGEMENT SURVEY RESEARCH

Significance of values in management and priorities

1. **Economic values** – such as the value of a firm, effectiveness, profitability, competitiveness, the rate of return on the invested capital, innovativeness, the exchange rate, rationality, flexibility and others from this group – I perceive the company in the context of policies and the prevalent practices as: (*please choose and mark in one variant*):
    a) the most important alongside adherence to the law from the viewpoint of the management of the enterprise;
    b) values of key significance; adherence to the law is also of key significance, ethical norms and good practices;
    c) non-economic values – ethical, cultural, civic, those associated with development, ecology are deemed to be equally important by us as economic values;
    d) another response, namely ....
    ....

2. **Ethical and cultural values** – such as responsibility, honesty, justice, involvement, amiability, credibility, reliability, trust, respect, cooperation, solidarity, skill of achieving compromise, tolerance, generosity, empathy, understanding, civil courage, moderation, loyalty, others from this group – I perceive the company in the context of policies and the prevalent practices as: (*please choose one variant that is closest to your beliefs*)
    a) important for realization of the mission, aims and image of the organization, as well as the promoted culture; they are appreciated and sufficiently displayed in the system of managing the firm;
    b) important for realization of the mission, aims and image of the organization, as well as the promoted culture, although not appreciated and insufficiently displayed in the system of managing the firm;
    c) treated in general as second-rate in the set with economic values;
    d) another response, namely ....

3. **Competence and developmental values** – such as education and knowledge, experience and skills, leadership, creativity, activity, communicativeness, approaches and behaviour, health and psychophysical condition, professionalism, ability to achieve aims and realization of tasks, professional development, others from this group – I perceive the company in the context of policies and the prevalent practices as:
    a) neuralgic for its existence, competitiveness and development and treated so;
    b) significant values, although not always sufficiently displayed in the policies of the firm;
    c) in general rather secondary, although primary in some areas of activity;
    d) another response, namely ....

4. **Social and civic values** – such as civic involvement, activity for the common good (on behalf of restricting unemployment, environmental protection, development of culture, protection of health and life, sport and recreation, charity, etc.), social cohesion, adherence to the law, patriotism, others from this group – are in my opinion:
    a) equally important as economic values;
    b) significant, however less important than economic values;

c) perceived rather as secondary, taking on significance rather sporadically;

d) another response, namely ....

5. Please **scale the importance of values** in the management of an organization in accordance with your individual assessment. Legend: 1 – significance completely secondary; 2 – of little importance; 3 – of moderate importance; 4 – important; 5 – very important. (*marking with sign of "x"*)

No.	Significance / role of values in management of company	1	2	3	4	5
1.	Integrating people in an organization					
2.	Constituting a real element of the motivational system					
3	Enabling the overcoming of crises and difficulties					
4.	Increasing discipline					
5.	Having a favourable impact on culture of organization					
6.	Serving the higher effectiveness of organization					
7.	Favouring greater satisfaction among employees					
8.	Having a restrictive impact on pathology					
9.	Leading to the case whereby people expect their presence and adherence					
10.	Having an impact on external image of company					
11.	Other, namely					
12.	Other, namely					

6. Please indicate <u>up to</u> three values whose significance in your organization has grown most in the past few years in your opinion (at least three years)

(1) ....

(2) ....

(3) ....

(4) Please indicate <u>up to</u> three values whose significance in your organization has fallen most in the past few years in your opinion (at least three years)

(1) ....

(2) ....

(3) ....

Level of importance of chosen economic values

7. What is the **level of profit in the long-term** (at least 5 years) in terms of the aims and pursuits of your organization? Please mark in one response variant that is closest to the truth:

a) the greatest of all values;

b) it is placed in a group of several of the most important values <u>alongside</u> ....
    ....

c) high; although we rate more highly..

d) another response, namely ....
    ....

8. What is the **level of profit in the short-term** (for a given year) in terms of the aims and pursuits of your organization against the background of other aims and pursuits? Please mark in one response variant that is closest to the truth:
   a) the highest;
   b) it is placed in a group of several of the most important values <u>alongside</u> ....
   ....
   c) high, although lower than ....
   d) another response, namely ....
9. What is the level of importance of the **exchange rate / value of shares** in terms of the aims and pursuits of your organization against the background of other aims and pursuits of the Board? Please mark in one response variant that is closest to the truth:
   a) the highest;
   b) it is placed in a group of several of the most important values <u>alongside</u> ....
   ....
   c) high, although lower than ....
   d) another response, namely ....
10. **Competitiveness of organization is perceived in it** as a value:
    a) key, decisive to a fundamental degree in terms of the survival and development; strongly supported;
    b) significant, however we are oriented towards not only competing, but cooperating too (also with market competitors);
    c) with regard to your position (natural monopoly, oligopoly, etc.) we do not have to compete strongly;
    d) another response, namely ....
    ....
11. **Innovativeness of organization**, I perceive the products, technologies and activities in the company as:
    a) value of key significance, which is sufficiently strongly supported;
    b) value of key significance, although supported in a way that is frequently insufficient;
    c) significant value, although not of key significance;
    d) value of little importance in our case;
    e) another response, namely ....
12. **Effectiveness** (perceived as the relation of results to costs) is one of the key values in economics, the economy and management. Please provide the dimension of the various features and aspects of effectiveness in the organization with the use of the following gauges: 1 – significance completely secondary; 2 – of little importance; 3 – of moderate importance; 4 – important; 5 – very important.

No.	Feature or aspect of effectiveness	1	2	3	4	5
1.	Effectiveness as criteria for evaluating an organization					
2.	Effectiveness as criteria for evaluating particular areas / organizational units					
3.	Effectiveness as criteria for evaluating management team					
4.	Effectiveness as criteria for evaluating employees in areas where it is measurable /easy to enumerate					
5.	Effectiveness as criteria for evaluating employees in areas where it is not very measurable / difficult to enumerate					
6.	Effectiveness (work, activities) as competence of management team					
7.	Effectiveness (work, activities) as competence of employees					
8.	Increasing effectiveness in areas where it is deemed to be excessively low					
9.	Increasing effectiveness in areas where it is already high					

14. **Fair remuneration**[24] in an organization is a value which:
   a) is currently realized with relation to all those employed;
   b) is realized with relation to the majority of the professional-qualification groups and we are aiming for its full realization in the upcoming years (with relation to the total employed);
   c) is realized with relation to the key managers and specialists; in the case of the others this value is not realized, although it is in our plans for the future;
   d) is realized with relation to the key managers and specialists; in the case of the others this value is not realized and it is not in our plans for the foreseeable future;
   e) another response, namely ....

Level of importance of non-economic values

15. **Sustainable growth**, taking account of both all the stakeholders, as well as the natural environment and future generations, I perceive the company in the context of policies and the prevalent practices as (*please choose one response variant*):
   a) a precious value, which we treat seriously and are currently executing;
   b) a precious value, which we are however executing only in a limited scope;
   c) a controversial value; I do not think that the concept of sustainable growth would be appropriate in the case of our organization as ....
   d) another response, namely ....
      ....

16. **Corporate Social Responsibility** (*you may mark in several variants of responses*):
   a) is treated in a universal and responsible way; we are regularly subjected to external audits and we attain good results;
   b) is treated in a universal and responsible way; although we are not regularly subjected to external audits;
   c) we are not distinctive from a favourable or unfavourable viewpoint in this sphere in-terms of a group of organizations similar to ours;
   d) I feel that we are fulfilling the requirements well in terms of...............................
      however, we should work more intensively on..
   e) another response, namely ....

17. **Values associated with dignity** (trust / respecting dignity, amiability, respecting freedom and privacy, others from this group) I perceive as (*please choose one response variant*):
   a) real pillar in shaping the relations with people within the framework of the organization, as well as outside of it (in shaping the relations with clients, trading partners, local communities, etc.);
   b) a pillar that is more intentional than real in shaping the relations with people within the framework of the organization, as well as outside of it – in shaping the relations with clients, trading partners, local communities, etc.;
   c) treated as rather secondary, although in a way that does not violate good practices;
   d) another response, namely ....

---

[24] Its essence is defined in art. 4 of the European Social Card. Out of the five criterions mentioned, two of them are the most significant : fair remuneration should be sufficient to maintain an employee and his family at a level that is deemed to be dignified in the given local community (which signifies various levels in various countries and regions); remuneration should be similar for similar qualifications, types of work and their effects, regardless of sex, age, nationality, race, outlook, political convictions, etc.

18. Trust in our organization is a value that is (*please choose the one which is the closest to your beliefs*):
   a) is well-displayed both in internal relations (we know how to show this and we do so), as well as external (we also enjoy a high level of trust among our clients and other external partners);
   b) requires strengthening, mainly in terms of relations with ....
   c) another response, namely ....

19. Balancing professional work, personal life /family life and social /civic involvement not only depends on the employer (for sure not in the main). Nevertheless, you have a certain impact on this by means of the policies you run. Please mark in the response variant that is closest to the truth:
   a) the Board has an active and efficient impact in the direction of the afore-mentioned balancing particularly by means of the following: not imposing effusive requirements with reference to the quantity and pace of work, openness with regard to the wishes of employees relating to making the dimension and time of work flexible (in as much as possible), limiting work overtime and other activities;
   b) the Board requires adherence to the law and good practices, while apart from this it does not interfere in the aforesaid issues as a principle, by acknowledging that they are at the discretion of the employees and their direct superiors;
   c) we require a high level of effectiveness, great involvement in professional work and devotion to the good of the organization. the aforesaid issues are of less interest to us;
   d) another response, namely..

20. Quality – products, technology, qualifications, processes of work, procedures, work, co-operation, ties, etc. – over many of the past decades this has been of great and indeed, key significance. However, recently it has been possible to hear more frequently that the "excessively high" quality and durability of products is not in the interests of producers and service providers as it restricts the demand and revenue of enterprises. On the basis of your familiarity with the organization, please express your opinions on this issue by means of marking in one or several of the response variants that is closest to the truth:
   a) quality, also including the durability of foods and services, remains an extremely important value and its significance is by no means falling, but rather growing;
   b) quality remains very important, however its relation of durability / lifespan / time of use or utilization of products is undergoing change; the latter are deliberately restricted in terms of time and has little in common with the good of the client or indeed protection of the natural environment;
   c) quality is losing out to prices; despite political correctness, but in accordance with the truth it is necessary to state that mainly due to the barriers of demand and the expectations of clients that demand constant promotions and price reductions, we have a multitude of various tacky markets in Poland, a multitude of various tacky products and sub-standard quality at work (in spite of unemployment);
   d) another response, namely ....

21. Justice was deemed by Plato to be the most important of all virtues. The need for justice has constantly accompanied people down through the ages, while simultaneously a multitude of abuse and iniquity has been committed on its behalf. It is additionally a notion that is very subjective and potentially conflicting. What assumptions do you accept (even in silence)? (*please choose one variant out of those presented below*)
   a) we try to be fair in our decisions and managerial activity, relying on our socially and culturally educated perception of justice;
   b) we try to be fair in our decisions and managerial activity, relying on our socially and culturally educated perception of justice, but also considering what is fair and what is not in the company and communicating with others on these issues;

c) anotherresponse,namely...
....

22. **Honesty** – in business, management, mutual ties between employers and employees, intentions, etc. is the value that is commonly acknowledged to be important and expected. What assumptions and policies do you accept in terms of these issues?
   a) we show people trust, by restricting appeals and inspections to the necessary minimum;
   b) we show people limited trust, we apply inspections and monitoring in places deemed to be neuralgic;
   c) we feel that there is too much dishonesty and that it constitutes a serious problem; inspections and monitoring are applied on a widespread basis;
   d) another response, namely...

Common values for employees / corporate

23. In our enterprise the **values expected from managers and employees** have been defined – all of them or the majority of them:
   a) Yes;   b) No.
24. If the response to question no. 23 is negative, please move on to question no. 29. In the case of providing a positive response to question no. 23, please mark in **how these values are termed:**
   a) corporate values;   b) common values;   c) universal values;
   d) capital values;   e) other, namely ....
25. **Familiarity with common / corporate values** in our organization is:
   a) widespread;
   b) rather high, but not widespread;
   c) not very high /significantly varied in different areas;
   d) slight;
   e) other response, namely ....
26. **Common / corporate values accepted by us** are: *(please mark in all that are accepted)*
   a) high quality (products, processes, work, ties, etc.); b) business orientation;
   c) effectiveness; d) professionalism; e) responsibility; f) innovativeness / creativity;
   g) trust; h) cooperation; i) loyalty; j) honesty; k) other, namely .... ;
27. **The most significant common / corporate values** are deemed by us to be:
   a) ....;
   b) We do not set out one value that is the most important.
28. **My evaluation of the practical usefulness of the registered corporate values** for management in the organization *(please choose one variant that is closest to the truth)*:
   a) in essence they are of little use and not much comes from them;
   b) they are known and generally accepted; we encompassed them into the system of management (its various sub-systems), with varying degrees of effects however;
   c) they are known and accepted; we encompassed them into the system of management-to a generally good effect;
   d) they are known and accepted; we encompassed them into the system of managementwith a very good effect; we feel that it brings significant effects.

Respecting values in personnel policies of an organization

29. **Taking account of values during recruitment and selection of people** – evaluation of practices (*please mark in one response*):
    a) this takes place in the sphere that is dependent on individual knowledge, abilities and curiosity in terms of the particular personnel specialists and managers; we do not have the tools and procedures at our disposal that would facilitate the analysis of the candidates for work in the context of values in a credible manner that is credible in an organization, while also comparable and routine;
    b) as above, although with relation to some positions and professional and qualification groups, we have carried out a satisfactory operationalization and we can do this;
    c) we take account of values with relation to the majority of candidates for work and we have the methodologies at our disposal, which may be deemed to be appropriate;
    d) other response, namely ....
    ....

30. **Taking account of values during the evaluation of employees** – not necessarily only in the formalized periodical assessments; (*please mark in the most appropriate response variant*):
    a) in the evaluation of employees we do not take account of the declared and respected values by them; we are guided by the assessment of the results of work and qualifications;
    b) we take account of them in individual and rather exceptional cases;
    c) we take account of them in a routine way with relation to the chosen professional groups;
    d) we take account of them with relation to the majority of professional groups / employees;
    e) other response, namely ....

31. **Taking account of values in decisions relating to promotions:**
    a) we do not take account of the acknowledged values; we are geared by competences and the hitherto results / successes;
    b) we only take values into account with relation to some positions, especially managerial ones; we do not have any professional instrumentarium at our disposal;
    c) we only take values into account with relation to some positions, especially managerial ones; we have a professional instrumentarium at our disposal;
    d) we take values into account with relation to the majority of positions, we do not however have any specialized techniques or tools;
    e) we take values into account with relation to the majority of positionsand we havespecialized techniques, toolsand procedures at our disposal;
    f) another response, namely..

32. **Taking account of values during process of remuneration** of the management team and employees:
    a) we are not guided by the evaluation of the degree of conformity with the expected values in our company during the course of providing remuneration for managers and employees;
    b) we are guided by this sporadically, mainly with relation to critical events (very positive, sometimes involving rewards, or very negative, sometimes involving penalties);
    c) we take account of this rather often, particularly with the use of the system of rewards and penalties, although sometimes to increase the level of the basic salaries too;
    d) we apply a routine systemic relation in terms of the total number of managers and employees;

e) another response, namely...

33. Ties between promoting values and intangible rewards are as follows:

  a) none;
  b) rather sporadic;
  c) they happen rather frequently;
  d) they constitute an element of the system and are of a routine nature.

34. If such ties occur, the intangible rewards involve ....
....

35. Optional opinions relating to management by values in an organization: ....

Specifications

(1) Function fulfilled in the organization:

  a) member of the Board;
  b) personnel director / manager;
  c) HR specialist;
  d) other specialist
  e) other, namely ....

(2) Market sector (according to GUS), in which an organization achieves the largest revenue:

  a) industry;
  b) trade; repair of vehicles;
  c) construction;
  d) transportation and warehouse management;
  e) professional, scientific and technical activities;
  f) financial and insurance activities;
  g) accommodation and catering;
  h) information and communication;
  i) serving real estate market;
  j) other, namely..

(3) Number of employed workers:

  a) up to 49 people;
  b) 50–249 people;
  c) 250–499 people;
  d) over 500 people.

(4) Nature of organization:

  a) joint-stock company;
  b) other organization from private sector;
  c) organization from public sector;
  d) other, namely ....

SECTION TWO

CASE STUDIES

Contents

Tadeusz Oleksyn
Izabela Stańczyk

1. CAPGEMINI – VALUES ON THE GLOBAL MARKET
CASE STUDY

1. General information on the corporation

Capgemini is a global and multi-cultural corporation of French origin that operates in 44 countries. Its domain is that of services in the fields of consulting, IT technologies and outsourcing.

Consulting services relate to management. They are most frequently of a complex and integrated nature. They are by assumption to have an impact on the market value and competitive advantage of the firm and clients. Projects are frequently vast, of a restructuring nature and sometimes even transformational.

IT technologies encompass designing, development and implementation of IT projects. They take account of the complex integration of systems and development of IT applications.

Outsourcing relates to the total or partial support of clients in the field of IT systems, as well as designing and servicing business processes. The Sogeti company, which belongs to Capgemini Group, renders specialist services in the sphere of infrastructure and software, applications and testing.

The Corporation possesses vast experience in terms of cooperation with clients and has developed its own business model that is executed with a high degree of success.

Capgemini employs over 130,000 workers worldwide, of which the geographical dispersal has been presented in Table 1.

Table 1. Employment numbers in Capgemini distributed in terms of continents at the end of 2013

Region in the world	Number of people employed
North America	9,700
South America	9,500
Europe	60,300
Africa	800
Asia	50,700
Total	**131,000**

Source: Annual report 2013, internal materials of Capgemini.

The Board of Capgemini Group enumerates 12 directors and meet no less than 6 times a year. Its main aim is to mark out and supervise the realization of the strategies of the Group. A significant task is also the fact that, in view of the mission of Capgemini (including the domain), the strategic management in the sphere of human resources is inherent. The Board avoids any over-activity and excessive centralization, which is attested to by both the restraint in terms of the number of sessions of the Board, as well as the concentration on the relatively small group of issues of key significance.

The current personnel of the Board of the Group is as follows:[1]
- Paul Hermelin, Chairman and CEO;
- Serge Kampf (founder and long-standing chairman), currently Vice-Chairman;
- Daniel Bernard, Lead Independent Director;
- Anne Bouverot;
- Bruno Roger;
- Laurence Dors;
- Lucia Sinapi-Thomas;
- Phil Laskawy;
- Pierre Prinquet;
- Yann Delabriere;
- Xavier Musca;
- Caroline Matteeuw-Carlisle.

The commissions are of assistance in terms of the management of the Group. They do not have authorization for decision-making, however they provide considerable aid by means of research on the chosen issues and problems, preparation of the projects of certain resolutions, as well as submission of opinions and recommendations to the Board, both on request and from their own initiatives.

Four regular commissions are in functioning:[2]
- Audit Commission (Yann Dalabriere – Chairman);
- Commission relating to Remuneration (Ruud van Ommeren – Chairman);
- Commission relating to Ethics and Management (Serge Kampf – Chairman);
- Commission relating to Strategy and Investments (Anne Bouverot – Chairwoman).

The names of the commissions themselves speak volumes about the culture of the Group. An interesting fact is that Serge Kampf, the founder of Sogeti company (47 years ago), which in turn sowed the seed for the initiation of the whole Capgemini Group, still plays a significant role. He is not

---

[1] See: http://www.capgemini.com/about/governance/corporate-governance [10.01.2015].
[2] Ibidem.

only the Honorary Chairman and active Vice-Chairman of the Board, but also the Chairman of the Commission of Ethics and Management. The name of this Commission is characteristic (and most certainly rare), in which ethics is in first place, while management is placed in second.

Likewise, it is also telling that attendance at the sessions of the Board and the commissions is recorded and constantly published, both in terms of the particular sessions, as well as the average annual ones (expressed in percentage points that are usually very high; which incidentally would be a useful custom in the Polish Parliament).

2. Capgemini in Poland

The business activities of Capgemini in Poland commenced in 1996 with the takeover of the consulting firm Bossard. In 2000, Capgemini Consulting purchased the consulting activity of Ernst & Young in Poland, while in 2003 as Capgemini Ernst & Young it purchased the Centre of Outsourcing in Cracow (which had existed from 1996). Since 2004, the firm has been called Capgemini.

Capgemini is the second largest foreign investor from the sector of modern services for business in this country. The domestic branches of the company serve foreign clients (including stores of the largest corporations), as well as entities operating in Poland, mainly in the telecommunications, banking, insurance and energy sectors. Specialists from the Polish branches during the course of serving foreign clients and cooperating in the realization of agreements with foreign partners avail of 31 languages. The English language is naturally perceived to be the second mother tongue. A good knowledge of foreign languages is one of the fundamental conditions of employment for the majority of positions.

Almost 6,000 people are employed in our country, in offices in Cracow (the largest), Katowice, Wrocław, Warsaw and Opole. The level of employment in Polish offices is presented in Table 2.

Table 2. Level of employment in Polish offices of Capgemini at the end of October 2014

No.	Office	Number of employed
1.	in Cracow	3,650
2.	in Katowice	1,549
3.	in Wrocław	620
4.	in Warsaw	86
5.	in Opole	94
6.	**Total**	**5,999**

Source: Internal materials of the firm.

Board Management Team of Capgemini Polska:[3]
- Dariusz Mazurek (CEO, Application Services);
- Marek Grodziński (Vice-President, Director of BPO Centre in Europe);
- Daniel Habrat (Senior Vice-President, Director of Global Infrastructure Outsourcing Capgemini for the Central and Eastern European Region).

3. Genesis and development

Capgemini emerged from the foundations of Sogeti company, which was established in 1967 in Grenoble by an entrepreneur named Serga Kampf (born in 1934). The mission of Sogeti was to provide technical support for computer users. During a period of almost 8 years, Sogeti became the leading entity of the French IT sector and one of the most important in Europe. Subsequently, following the takeover of a range of enterprises up to the year 1975, particularly Cap and Gemini Computer System, the Capgemini company was established, which as a consequence of further takeovers and restructuring became the largest European firm in the IT sector. The restructuring particularly involved the withdrawal from dealing with IT hardware and specialization in consulting, IT technologies, while subsequently outsourcing. The restructuring is also associated with numerous and important mergers and takeovers, as a result of which Capgemini significantly increased its value and possibilities of operations. Takeovers included among others, United Research (1990) and Mac Group (1991) in the USA, while also in Europe, namely Gruber Titze and Partners (1993), Bossard (1997), a proportion of the business activities of Ernst & Yong (2000), Telekom and others.

Following the elaboration of an original concept of rendering consulting services termed the Collaborative Business Experience™[4] and entry into the US market, Capgemini found itself in a group of the five largest and most important consulting firms in the world. The Corporation pays particular attention to the experience of working with a client and developed its own model of rendering services, termed as Rightshore*.

---

[3] See: http://www.pl. capgemini.com/ o-capgemini/wladze/zarzad-capgemini-polska [20. 11.2014].

[4] Rightshore* involves the creation of teams of balanced high competences in terms of the people inhabiting and working in the various regions and countries. The composition of these teams in terms of the personnel is modified appropriately to the changing needs of the particular advisory-design teams, as a result of the issues and structures of the commissioned subjects / orders of clients.

In 2012, Capgemini Group noted revenue to the amount of 10.3 bn Euro. The shares of Capgemini are listed on the Stock Exchange in Paris, while since 2005, Capgemini has been a member of the consortium known as The Open Group.

Capgemini is a large corporation and time is required to become familiar with it. A diagram has been presented below taken from the film entitled: "Discover Capgemini Group in 10 steps."

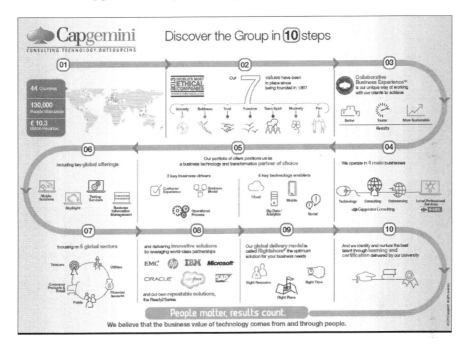

Illustration 1. Information about business activities of Capgemini in ten steps

Source: Internal materials of the firm, http://www.pl.capgemini.com/about-capgemini [12.11.2014].

4. Values in the system of management in Capgemini

Professed values are always of significance, while also have an impact on the motivation, procedure and behaviour of people, even when they do not think about it or are unaware of it.

4.1. Significance of values in Capgemini

Capgemini is undoubtedly an organization, in which values are acknowledged to be important and are placed in the centre of the system of management. Here it is deemed that values serve to as follows:

- facilitate business and relations with business partners, where they are known and respected by parties to the cooperation;
- integrate people in an organization;
- constitute a realistic element of the motivational system;
- have a favourable impact on the culture of an organization;
- serve the higher level of effectiveness of an organization;
- favour greater satisfaction among employees;
- have a restrictive impact on pathology;
- people expect their presence and adherence.

Over the past three years in Capgemini, the significance of the following issues has grown in importance:

- innovativeness and competitiveness,
- corporate social responsibility (CSR) and environmental protection,
- competences; a new competence model emerged, which is availed of in all HR processes of the firm.

4.2. Seven corporate values

The system of management in Capgemini is based on values. This was greatly influenced by its founder, Serge Kampf, by setting out the principle that the basis of business is that of seven values as follows:

(1) honesty;
(2) boldness;
(3) trust;
(4) freedom;
(5) team spirit;
(6) modesty;
(7) fun.

Honesty as a value does not require any particular justification. Even if it sometimes appears to be a tad old-fashioned, its evident lacking is most certainly damaging not only in business. It is well associated within a set of the three remaining values, namely trust, cooperation and modesty, which mutually strengthen each other.

Courage is important particularly when business is run so expansively and the market value of the company is increased so dynamically as in the case of Serge Kampf and his close associates. Likewise, courage is also expected in the expression of views and opinions, as well as the fighting against negative phenomena, attitudes and behaviour.

Trust, similarly to honesty, is binding both in terms of the relations of employer-superiors – employees, as well as with clients and business partners and with the local communities. Trust in Capgemini is at a high level, yet not implicit; as monitoring and inspections are applied in neuralgic areas.

Freedom is also appreciated in a corporation as a feature that favours creativity. Hence, internal ties are promoted, in which it may develop freely.

The spirit of cooperation is very important in an organization of such magnitude, or so multi-cultural and complex that is based on innovations and management of projects. Cooperation is advocated in a systemic manner with the aid of among others, the concept of cooperation in business known as The Collaborative Business Experience TM and the global model of rendering services known as Rightshore®, which has been previously referred to.

Modesty blends well with such values as cooperation, honesty and trust. This favours the direct and good internal relations. It is also the contradiction of such unpleasant flaws in both an organization and life itself as pride, insolence and arrogance. A lack of these flaws has a good impact on cooperation, creativity, trust and business. Modesty also facilitates listening to others, which is key to the perception of cooperation by Capgemini.

Fun and joy are certainly seldom mentioned among the corporate values. Nevertheless, they have their meaning in terms of professional work and the realities of a competitive market, while also having a favourable impact on the vibe of the working environment, reducing the level of stress at work (which in turn favours innovativeness and creativity), the level of satisfaction at work and with the employer. This relates to among other things, creating the environment of people whose work and association with each other leads to the sense of satisfaction and increases the level of satisfaction with work.

The seven principles mentioned above are binding for both the management, as well as for the employees, thus constituting corporate values. The founder of the company treated them very seriously and the fact that he ran the company for almost half a century and created a great impact on Capgemini means that these principles are deeply embedded. Actually, it is difficult to forget them as they are written in great metal letters in prominent places of the offices of the corporation. Likewise, they are also integrated into an array of organizational documents and programs, such as the following: *Our Ethical Code, Ethics & Conformance, Cooperation in Business, Style of our Work, Rightshore®* (treated as a global model of running a business). *Our Ethical Code* is handed to each employee, as well as the fact that everyone participates in training based on its sphere, in which the binding values of the corporation are presented.

There is no value that is stipulated as the most important as the aforementioned catalogue is binding. These values are generally known and integrated into the system of management to good effect. Newly employed workers are informed of this catalogue on the very first day of work and their period of adaptation in the firm starts from here.

In Capgemini, as a business organization, economic and managerial values are still of great significance, particularly the efficiency of activities, effectiveness and performance, viability of activities / profitability, creativity and innovativeness, competitiveness and flexibility. Nevertheless, of the values acknowledged to be organizational /corporate values, neither economic nor managerial values are listed at all, which incidentally rarely occurs in other business organizations. Only ethical, cultural and social values are listed here. Hence, this gives rise to the question as to whether this is due to the fact that there is a conviction that non-economic values are of a primary nature and their adherence is the preliminary condition for the achievement of economic success, or perhaps the absence of the economic values among the corporate values stems from other reasons. One of these other reasons may be the conviction that the necessity of efficient management and the "economic being" are so obvious in the market economy that there is no need to speak or write about that, thus they are not treated as values.

Capgemini is an organization of French origin whose culture was formed in France. The corporate values were also formulated there and were adopted in Poland without modifications. We did not have the opportunity to discuss with the Board members of Capgemini Group in France, thus this issue shall not be resolved on these pages.

Our partners from Cracow are of the opinion that corporate values are the basis and reference point for all activities, as well as being the framework for setting out the standards of work, although economic values appear in the vision and mission of the company by setting out its aim of activities. This issue would seem to require further exchange of opinions and reflection. However, there is no doubt that economic and managerial values are very significant in Capgemini and are also currently in its philosophy of management, as well as in specific systems such as Rightshore®, Collaboratore Business Experience™ and others.

4.3. Values included in the mission of the organization

There are various definitions of the mission of an organization. The one which is most appropriate in our opinion was once proposed by A.K. Koźmiński, in which the **mission** encompasses the following five elements:

(1) Notion and values, which an organization wants to serve.
(2) Domain, thus,
   – products;
   – markets which the organization operates on;
   – main groups of clients which the products are addressed to.
(3) Offer particularly aimed at the clients and trading partners.

(4) Offer particularly aimed at society / local community.

(5) Motto, or a catchy summary of the most significant intentions of the organization.

With regard to the **vision,** there is greater convergence of the views of the experts of management: it is a way to realize the mission and its operationalization. It is to answer the question how and in what way the given mission is to be fulfilled.

In Capgemini, the mission and vision are presented together and apart from this, both the mission and vision are separate. Such a triple notion is seldom encountered. The mission and vision of Capgemini combined are encaptured in the "promises of Capgemini" (Capgemini Promise): In Capgemini, **people and results count** – people matter, results count.[5] In these four words, there are certain inherent values which when combined, form an important credo.

Showing people in first place is not a novelty[6] – the slogan of "people are the most important" is commonly verbalized nowadays, although much more seldomly applied. Emphasizing the significance of results indicates a pragmatic approach, as well as business and professional ones. The claim that "people matter, results count" is appropriate: while saying that only people count would be banal, sentimental and flattering. The claim that only results count would be authoritarian and dehumanized. The fact that "people matter, results count" is balanced and makes both these elements realistic, while simultaneously not allowing the absolutization of either of them. Likewise, it is also important what has not been directly said (and should not be said), but may be deduced, namely, people should achieve results and the reverse: results are important but it is necessary to recognize the people behind them. Perhaps the "results are our gauge of the usefulness of people" and "we are not pursuing results at the (excessive) cost of people" – their overloading and professional burnout. One way or another, it makes an impression that is extraordinarily terse, minimalist even, while simultaneously being a wise message. We express our admiration for the author and for the people who have accepted it. Nevertheless, in our opinion this is neither a mission, nor a vision, while also not (all the more) one and the other combined. We claim that it is a motto – a good and useful one, but a motto all the same. Perhaps from a practical viewpoint this issue is of no great significance.

The **mission** of Capgemini itself was formulated as follows: "to provide specific business results. "However, it was not written as to who should be the recipient. Perhaps just as well, as the more broadly it is perceived, the better.[7]

---

[5] See: http://www.pl.capgemini.com/o-capgemini/grupa/misja-i-wizja-firmy [12.11.2014].

[6] In the period when Capgemini was founded, this was new.

[7] We understand that this relates to providing values for both the clients and trading partners, as well as for the owners / shareholders, societies /local communities, thus in essence for all stakeholders.

Following this sentence, the following elaboration is presented: "Capgemini enables the transformation of your business and the increase in efficiency. Our aim is to prepare clients for a faster and more intuitive reaction to the changing dynamics of the market. We support clients in the attainment of greater flexibility and competitiveness thanks to the utilization of new technologies. Cooperation is at the heart of our relations with clients and partners, which leads to the case whereby they are closer and more effective. Our approach to business is termed the Collaborative Business Experience™."[8]

Such a formulated mission is original and distinctive from others, which in fact is one of the general pursuits of the authors of the mission, which is so rarely successful, but it has succeeded here. However, several doubts remain as follows: Surely not all projects of Capgemini are of /must be of a transformational nature, thus radical and profound restructuring, as clients do not always wish to have this. Is "a more intuitive reaction" always an advantage? Indeed, intuitive management has been more appreciated of late, and even "instinctive" management (previously underestimated in general). If someone manages only or is primarily intuitive, is this good or bad? Is it always good?

With relation to the subject matter of the research, we are most interested in the values that are borne in the mission. These are the following:
- "specific business results" – factual and economic, while probably renowned too that translates to future orders and profits;
- competitiveness;
- speed of action / reaction to change;
- innovativeness and creativity, leading to new technologies;
- flexibility;
- cooperation;
- good of the clients.

These are almost exclusively economic values.

4.4. Values included in the vision of the organization

The **vision** of Capgemini has been registered as follows: "Capgemini understands that business values do not merely create technology. Everything starts with the people who reach the core of your business needs together and create the most appropriate solutions for them. We believe that the approach to technology that is oriented towards people is of significance for your business."

Such a formulated vision gives rise to several ascertainments as follows:

---

[8] See: http://www.pl.capgemini.com/o-capgemini/grupa/misja-i-wizja-firmy [12.11.2014].

- Technologies by themselves are not sufficient. People are necessary who "reach the core of business possibilities together" and create the solutions that are the most appropriate for the client.
- The phrase "reach together" indicates the intention of the close ties between the specialists of Capgemini and the clients, which is reflected in the application / preference by Capgemini of the technique of counselling, rather than consulting. This is not an accusation, but an expression of acknowledgement as counselling is in general terms a better technique. In this communiqué, the following thought is discreetly provided (in general executed in business) "You will probably not manage on your own; avail of our professional aid."
- The technology offered should take account of the specific needs, possibilities and preferences of people and should be "oriented towards people."

By translating the aforesaid vision into values, it is possible to distinguish the following:

- individualized approach;
- professionalism (in the background);
- activity; necessary and justified action;
- partnership, cooperation;
- flexibility.

However, the question arises as to whether what is presented as a vision is actually a vision. It would seem that it is a certain credo, display of intention, or defined philosophy of management (good, precious). We would not term this as a vision however, but rather one of the assumptions for the purpose of building this vision. Incidentally, the phrase "Capgemini understands" is an anthropomorphism. It is worth withdrawing this and replacing it with for instance, "We understand."

4.5. Professional development and professionalism as values

The organization, which holds such a high position in the international ranking of firms is so large and so strongly associated with the market / sector of knowledge that it must pay great attention to the professional development and professionalism of its employees and co-workers who are perceived to be still significant values of Capgemini.

Professional development is carried out in individual and team dimensions and is supported by the corporation. Support particularly depends on the preparation and execution of the programs which favour this. Some of them have been displayed in Illustration 2.

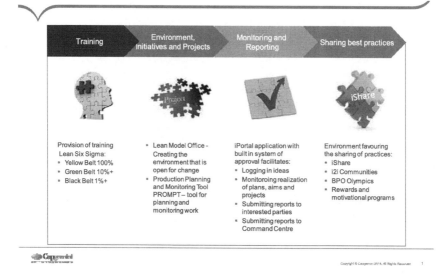

Illustration 2. Methods of constant development in Capgemini

Source: Internal materials of the corporation.

Effectiveness is a very important criteria in the evaluation of employees in areas where it is measureable. It fulfils a significant role as the criteria of the evaluation of the management staff and the employees even in areas where it is not so measureable. This constitutes an important element in the assessment of the competence of the management staff and the employees. This is what gives rise to such a large number of implemented projects improving the quality of work to varying dimensions and levels of the organization. A brief layout has been presented in Illustration 3.

Significant activities in the organization which favour professional development are insights into the employees from the viewpoint of their future development within the framework of the organization in accordance with the program *Career Employability Management*. The HR Business partner, together with the manager of a given department exchange information and opinions on the issue of all the employees by analysing their work experience in a given position, evaluation of the results of work, the potential of development within the framework of the department, as well as the possibility of designating a new role or promotion. Within the framework of the annual employee evaluation, apart from the realization of the business and development aims, the degree of sustainability between professional work and personal or family life is discussed, mainly from the viewpoint of counteracting workaholism and professional burnout that also threaten the good of the cor-

Statistics relating to Constant Development (August 2014)

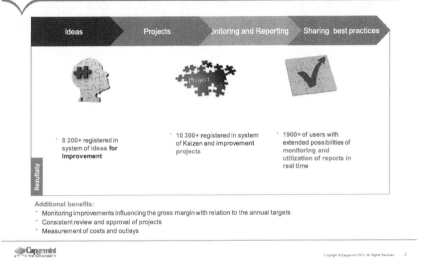

Illustration 3. Number of projects improving work in the firm

Source: Internal materials of the corporation.

poration. In the cases of demanding support for the employees, particularly key specialists, professional aid by a coach may be provided.

Regardless of the aid in overcoming the personal difficulties, training programs are executed that are oriented towards the acceleration of the professional development and faster and better social and professional adaptation of new employees.

Last year in Capgemini (2014) Kaizen Week was organized in Poland for the first time. It was a time for the exchange of knowledge, science, acquisition of new skills and discovering new perspectives. Likewise, it was also a time to meet extraordinary people. Last year's event was participated in by Masaaki Imai, the co-creator and great propagator of the Kaizen philosophy around the world. By way of summarizing the week-long event he stated the following: "In my life I have visited a multitude of service firms, but I have never seen any in which the operations of Kaizen and Lean Management are of such significance and of such a high level of importance as in Capgemini company (…). I am very impressed and I have great expectations with regard to their role in the future also."[9]

---

[9] Internal materials of the firm.

4.6. Capgemini in group of most ethical firms in the world

In 2014, Capgemini was honoured with the title of the most ethical company of the world for the second time. This type of classification is run by Ethisphere Institute from the USA. The winners of these titles are entities that form relations with business, ethics and renown in the best way by marking out new and higher standards of ethical leadership.

The criteria according to which the assessment of the Most Ethical Firms In the World is carried out on the basis of the Ethisphere Institute's Ethics Quotient – a complex methodology that was formulated over many years in order to serve as a tool that gauges the activities of organizations in a way that is conceivably objective, cohesive and standardized. The particular assessment of the ranking is grouped into five categories as follows:

(1) ethics and conformance with the standards (25%);
(2) image, directorship and innovativeness (20%);
(3) management (10%);
(4) corporate social responsibility (25%);
(5) culture of ethics (20%).[10]

The Program of Ethics and Conformance of Capgemini Group was implemented by the Group's Board in 2009. It is based on the culture of ethics which has been treated, as previously mentioned, as the foundation of the business operations of Capgemini since the moment of its establishment in 1967 by Serge Kampf. Within the framework of the implementation of the program, the following was created: the position of Directors relating to Ethics and Conformance, Code of Ethics, Policy of Anti-Corruption and Policy of the Right of Competition, which facilitate to consolidate the values in every country where they operate. The program is supported by the global program of training, in which training online may be found in the offer that is devoted to each of the policies, while also several options for full-time training.

The Code of Ethics of Capgemini, which is based on values encompasses the following aspects:
- <u>People</u>: health, safety, open dialogue.
- <u>Running a business</u>: honest competition, anti-corruption, avoidance of conflict of interests.
- <u>Bussiness relations</u>: close cooperation with clients, partners and suppliers.
- <u>Property of group and third parties</u>: protection of intellectual property and confidential information, appropriate utilization of resources and property of third parties.

---

[10] See: http://www.pl.capgemini.com/aktualnosci/capgemini-po-raz-drugi-z-tytulem-najbardziej-etycznej-firmy-swiata-2014 r. [12.11.2014].

- <u>Social responsibility</u>: involvement in the local communities and limitation of the negative impact on the environment.[11]

With the aim of strengthening and establishment of the culture of ethics and ethical behaviour, while also a better familiarity with the international regulations, national law and internal regulations within the framework of the Group, the **Program of Ethics and Conformance** was prepared and implemented. This also contains regulations and initiatives that strengthen the prevention and counteraction of pathology.

The Program of Ethics and Conformance in Capgemini at the level of the Group is run by the Chief Ethics & Compliance Officer, who is supported by the local leaders during the course of executing their tasks.

4.7. Fair remuneration, non-wage tangible motivators

Fair remuneration is the right of citizens of the EU member states that is signed and ratified by the European Social Card (art. 4). Remuneration (in essence – work income) may be acknowledged to be fair in accordance with varying standards accepted in particular countries, however in every location it is to facilitate the maintenance of an employee and his / her family. The right to fair remuneration is also stipulated in the Polish Labour Code (art. 13), but in that case it is associated with the minimum wage; fair remuneration is to be no less than the lowest level of remuneration. This assumption of the Code is in contrast with art. 4 ESC, where fair remuneration is different, more beneficial for employees and defined in detail.

As remuneration constitutes the main source of maintenance for employees and their families, birth rates in Poland are excessively low, while emigration for work reasons excessively high, fair remuneration is a value that should be treated seriously and supported. This is a task not only for the state, but even more so for the employers.

The levels of remuneration for the chosen positions in the sector of business services according to *Business Services and IT Sector in Małopolska*[12] have been displayed in Table 3. The data provided relates to the year 2013.

---

[11] See: http://www.pl.capgemini.com/nasz-kodek.s-etyki [12.11.2014].

[12] Source: Business Services and IT Sector in Małopolska, p. 11, http://absl.pl/documents/10186/26940/Business+Services+and+IT+Sector+in+Ma%C5%82opolska.pdf/1cef8a57-81d1-4784-8d5e-fbf5e03b6b3b [11.11.2014].

Table 3. An average monthly gross salary in the business services sector in Cracow for employees with knowledge of English

Financial and accounting processes: General Ledger (GL)	Min	Optimum	Max
Junior Accountant (1–2 years of experience)	2,800	3,500	4,500
Accountant (2–3 years of experience)	4,200	4,800	5,500
Senior Accountant (over 3 years of experience)	5,000	6,500	7,000
Team Leader (team of 5–15 employees)	7,000	8,000	9,500
Process Manager (team of up to 50 employees)	11,000	14,000	17,000
Financial and accounting processes: Accounts Payable and Accounts Receivable (AP/AR)	**Min**	**Optimum**	**Max**
Junior Associate (0–1 year of experience)	2,300	2,700	3,500
Accountant (1–2 years of experience)	2,700	3,500	4,300
Senior Associate (over 2 years of experience)	4,000	4,300	5,000
Team Leader (team of 5–15 employees)	6,500	7,000	8,000
Process Manager (team of up to 50 employees)	9,000	12,000	15,000
Sales	**Min**	**Optimum**	**Max**
Junior Specialist (no experience)	2,700	3,000	3,500
Specialist (over 1 year of experience)	3,000	3,500	4,000
Team Leader (team of 5–15 employees)	6,000	7,000	9,000
Process Manager (team of up to 50 employees)	11,000	13,000	15,000
Customer service processes	**Min**	**Optimum**	**Max**
Junior Specialist (no experience)	2,300	3,000	3,500
Specialist (over 1 year of experience)	3,000	3,500	4,000
Team Leader (team of 5–15 employees)	6,000	7,500	8,000
Process Manager (team of up to 50 employees)	9,000	12,000	15,000
IT processes / technical support	**Min**	**Optimum**	**Max**
1st Line Support (0–1 year of experience)	2,800	3,500	4,500
2nd Line Support 4,500 6,000 8,000			
Team Leader (team of 5–15 employees)	7,000	9,000	11,000
Process Manager (team of up to 50 employees)	12,000	14,000	17,000
Purchases (order management)	**Min**	**Optimum**	**Max**
Junior Specialist (0–1 year of experience)	3,000	3,500	4,000
Accountant (1–3 years of experience)	4,500	5,000	5,500
Senior Specialist (over 3 years of experience)	5,500	6,500	8,000
Team Leader (team of 5–15 employees)	7,000	8,500	10,000
Process Manager (team of up to 50 employees)	10,000	14,000	16,000

HR processes	Min	Optimum	Max
Junior Specialist (0–1 year of experience)	3,000	3,300	4,000
Specialist (1–2 years of experience)	3,800	4,000	4,500
Senior Specialist (over 2 years of experience)	4,500	5,000	6,500
Team Leader (team of 5–15 employees)	6,500	7,500	9,000
Process Manager (team of up to 50 employees)	9,000	12,000	14,000

Source: Business Services and IT Sector in Małopolska, p. 11, http://absl.pl/documents/10186/26940/Business+Services+and+IT+Sector+in+Ma%C5%82opolska.pdf/1cef8a57-81d1-4784-8d5e-fbf5e03b6b3b [11.11.2014].

As it would seem, the conditions of salaries and social benefits offered are relatively good with reference to the Polish conditions, although there are employers in Poland that offer conditions that are significantly better (for certain positions). Similar work and positions in the wealthier EU countries or in the USA are paid significantly higher levels, but this does not only relate to Capgemini. If it were the reverse, such workplaces would not be created in Poland.

Various opinions are expressed on Internet blogs on the issue of work and remuneration in Capgemini; although there are good opinions expressed. In particular, it is noted that it is a good place to start for people after studies and with a good familiarity of foreign languages, aid provided by the corporation in terms of socio-professional adaptation and in development. Promotions are realistic and relatively fast, particularly in the case of project managers. A multitude of people had positive views about the atmosphere at work and nice colleagues.

Capgemini offers a rather rich package of additional benefits, which is differentiated depending on the position occupied. Packages of medical care are also offered for employees and their families, as well as life assurance. There is a possibility of purchasing employee shares once every two years. Managers receive personally selected company cars to the value of the amount allocated for this purpose.

The conditions of premises are good; in Cracow, where we had the possibility of staying and running talks, people work in beautiful and comfortable offices of class A type.

Source: Internal materials of the firm.

4.8. Balancing professional work, personal and family life, as well as other areas of human activity as value

This issue has been the subject of increased interest worldwide, primarily in highly developed countries for several decades. The reasons for this are varied as follows: a change in the perception of work and overwork, the excessively high personal and family price paid for the excessive involvement, workaholism, stress at work and professional burnout, neglecting family duties, crisis of the civic society caused by the lack of time and other aspects.

In Capgemini, this problem, specified as work-life balance is observed and confronted. Simultaneously, this is executed while maintaining the principles of taking account of and supporting the various initiatives of employees. This relates to both the convenient and individualized working time (in as much as possible), by taking into consideration the needs of employees and their families, as well as taking account of the individual preferences with regard to the frequency and duration of travelling. Each employee specifies his/her mobility at least once a year in a system utilized for the management of business aims and the development of an employee. This information is taken into consideration in the planning of careers, as well as long-term and short-term projects. Supporting the balance of professional and personal life takes place by means of the program termed Business Parent, which from this year is dedicated to not only (future) mothers employed in Capgemini, but also fathers and their superiors. The main aims associated with this program are as follows:
1. Informing future parents of their rights and obligations in such an important moment.
2. Activation of women on maternity leave to return to work.
3. Provision of all necessary information necessary for a business mum.
4. Educating Team Leaders and managers in the sphere of law and essential information associated with maternity / paternity leave, as well as every aspect connected with the Labour law.

Thanks to the program, the employees (regardless of sex type) may count on the following:
   - ensuring the help offered by the employer to his/her employees;
   - ensuring a return to work;
   - support of development during the course of maternity leave for mothers that have such expectations;
   - provision of a guidebook relating to the procedural complexities in the sphere of redundancies, leave, subsidies, etc.

Thanks to this program, the superiors of working parents are aware and informed with relation to the legal regulations associated with motherhood and receive information on the issue of what Capgemini offers parents as an employer.

Within the framework of the project, the following has been prepared:

1. Guidebook for parents.
2. Guidebook for superiors.
3. Website Business Mum available from home, which has been divided into 3 parts:
   - *I am pregnant.*
   - *I am on maternity leave.*
   - *I want to return to work.*

In each section, there is information that is utilized at a given stage.

Each mother may see the company updates that may be of significance to her and helpful in terms of contacting the company during periods of her absence. Likewise, the Internet bookmark may also be useful, as it includes useful information for parents.

In Capgemini, conditions are created for the realization of various non-occupational passions in the case of the employees. It is worth mentioning the following in particular:

   - **Theatre Project**. This was met with a large reaction as it breaks the schematic and negative image of a corporation and actually gives it a warmer feeling.
   - The program **"We invest in good ideas"** is for enthusiasts, social workers and local leaders.

The Theatre Project was initiated in 2008 and has become the pride of the company, as well as an undertaking that makes a multitude of employees get involved every year. Specialists from the branch of outsourcing turn into actors, producers and stage designers, while the effects of their work may be seen on the stage of the theatre usually before Christmas. Prior to this for a period of approximately 3–4 months, dress rehearsals are performed up to the moment of the premiere, during which the amateur actors under the watchful eye of an experienced director become familiar with the techniques of acting. In their own words, it is hard work that requires the sacrifice of free time, but which provides plenty of joy. Following the long preparations, an interesting and well-prepared play is watched by children from the Society of "Siemacha", the employees of Capgemini, together with their families and guests every year.

So far, the actors from Capgemini have played in the following plays: in 2008 "Śnieżka Spółka z.o.o.", in 2009 "Zła nocka", in 2010 "Peter Pan", in 2011 "Ychu-Dychu", or in other words,"Tytus, Romek and Atomek", in 2012 "Little Red Riding Hood"; in 2014 "Oz", or in other words, "Quarrel over Toto" – a play with audio description. The receipts from the tickets are utilized for social aid for the needy. In 2014, a play was made available for an audience with a hearing impediment by availing of the technique of audio description.

Grant program "We support good ideas"

In 2013, an exceptional grant program was launched under the name of "We support good ideas". This program is the response to the multitude of bottom-up initiatives of the employees of the company who regularly draw attention to the significant social problems in their environs. This involves the involvement of the employees of the company in the role of volunteers for activities on behalf of resolving social issues that are important to them and for their environs. Simultaneously, the company provides financial, substantive and organizational support for the employees that submit the best social projects.

In 2013, 27 original ideas were submitted, while in 2014, there were 10 times more. Their realization attracted over 200 employees or volunteers, as well as over 130 people outside of the company that are ready to help others. Among those submitting their ideas were as many as 19 "new" leaders of projects, or in other words, those who apply to become leaders of the *Program for the first time*. A proportion of the submitted projects was the continuation of the initiatives commenced in the previous year. The majority of the projects submitted related to running various types of development workshops – ranging from artistic ones, to languages, development of communication competences to sports workshops. Some of them were aimed at renovating rooms, improving the conditions of the functioning of the organization, while also better integration of people. The most numerous group constituted children and the youth, while subsequently the elderly. A proportion of the initiatives referred to providing care for animals.

The Competition Jury of the Program selected 15 projects, which, in its opinion, was the best response to the social and environmental problems, while also proposed innovative action, activated local communities and fulfilled the formal requirements of the program. The projects distinguished are in the course of execution all over Poland.

We are writing about all of this with a deep sense of pleasure as the activities enumerated here certify to the actual, multi-directional and dignified acknowledgement of the realization of the concept of balancing professional work, personal life and family life, as well as other areas of human activity. In Capgemini, the realization of this concept is specific and serious activity and not just pleas and postulates.

5. Awards for Capgemini

Respecting values in the management and formulation of organizational culture has been noted by way of the environment, the effect of which has been numerous awards bestowed on this corporation. The following are just some of these that have been received over the past two years:
- Gold Medal and Pearl of Quality for the year 2013; award for quality awarded by Rada Biznesu (Business Council).
- Leader of managing human resources and award for strategy of Employer Branding 2013.
- European Outsourcing Award – the most desirable employer 2013.
- Award of "Next Generation" Process Excellence for "creating a friendly place for change" "Lean Model Office", awarded by Process Excellence Network, 2014.
- Award of "Most ethical firm", awarded by Ethisphere Institute in 2014.
- Silver Cross for the Director of BPO Centre for philanthropic activities in 2014.

We would like to take the opportunity to thank Mrs. Agnieszka Jarecka, Head of HR Services, Capgemini Poland and Mrs. Dominika Nawrocka, Talent Acquisition Manager – Cracow, for their discussions, time devoted and material made available, while also the actual co-writing of this work. We are truly grateful.

Materials availed of:
1. Business Services and IT Sector in Małopolska, http://absl.pl/documents/10186/26940/Business+Services+and+IT+Sector+in+ Ma%C5 %82 opolska.pdf/1cef8a57-81d1-4784-8d5e-fbf5e03b6b3b [12.11.2014].
2. http://www.pl.capgemini.com [12.11.2014].
3. Internal materials of firm.

Tadeusz Oleksyn
Izabela Stańczyk

2. QUMAK S.A. – VALUES IN AN INNOVATIVE FIRM
CASE STUDY

1. Genesis and history

The company Qumak S.A. is one of the greatest integrators of the Polish ICT market. This was formulated as a result of the two-stage merger of several firms, which had been cooperating with each other for a long time prior to this.

In 2000, the following enterprises were encompassed into the structure of the Warsaw-based company Sekom S.A.: Blue Bridge Sp. z o.o. and Gandalf Polska Sp. z o.o. Subsequently, three firms (Sekom S.A., Qumak International Sp. z o.o. and Pulsar Electronics) created Sekom Group.

The second stage (in 2002) involved the transformation of Sekom Group into the listed company Qumak–Sekom. Currently, the headquarters are located in Warsaw, with a branch in Cracow and a subsidiary in Bielsko-Biała. Since 2006, this company has been listed on the Warsaw Stock Exchange.

The merger of partners that had known each other well prior to that led to the case whereby it increased their potential and capacity, while also being able to realize greater orders, significantly increase sales and profit and also increase the level of competitiveness. A very significant factor that had an impact on the development of the company was to become listed on the Stock Exchange and utilize the capital gained. Within five years (2005–2010), the turnover of Qumak–Sekom S.A. grew threefold – from 113 m PLN to 329 m PLN. Since January 2013, the company has been called Qumak S.A.

The company implemented a system of quality management for the services rendered by it for which it received the EN ISO 9001 certificate in 2005 (in 2011 this was extended by a further three years in the second process of recertification in a row). The certificate encompasses all the services rendered within its scope. It is currently headed in the direction of the philosophy of Total Quality Management and combining the philosophy of HRM into a standardized system of TQ HRM. The orientation towards a high level of competences and distinctive quality is well-associated with the orientation towards clients and the pursuit of their satisfaction, as well as the ever more complex servicing. The effect of the realization of the strategies of the company is the constant strengthening of its position by means of increasing its share in the chosen market segments of new technologies. The strategy of the company also assumes the achievement of synergic effects within the framework of IT solutions. The fundamentals of the strategy were prepared in 2003 with the aid of the renowned consultancy firm, AT Kearney. At present, a significant element in the strategy is the preparation of new and original solutions.

The mission of the company is formulated as follows: "We help our clients to achieve their business aims by means of providing the highest quality of services and solutions in the area of new technologies. We realize projects that support the flow of information, management and organization, while also guaranteeing the security and comfort of work in modern firms and institutions. Our aim is to build long-lasting relations based on the harmonious cooperation with clients." http://www.qumak.pl [25.11.2014].

2. Domain

Qumak S.A. is a highly innovative engineering enterprise that specializes in the **imposing extensive problematic issues**. This encompasses designing, implementation and servicing of modern technologies (in a systemic notion) in twelve areas, which constitute the following:

(1) Airports, radars. Buildings associated with the technical servicing of airplanes, as well as serving passengers are both designed and modernized. The following may be particularly mentioned:

- FIS system (Flight Information System), radio navigation and radio communications, as well as controlling the navigational lighting for airports and landing areas;
- AWOS system (Automated Weather Observing System);
- BHS system (Baggage Handling Systems);
- complex realization of helipads for helicopters – ranking from the concept, design and construction and registration with the Civil Aviation Authority.[13]

An interesting example of the project realized by Qumak is that of the radar station, which shall be installed in Góra św. Anny in the province of Opole. In this area, a technologically advanced **magnetronic meteorological radar shall be located**, which with the aid of the waves sent shall facilitate among other aspects, the detection of clouds, definition of their structure and speed of movement. Thanks to this, **weather forecasters shall be able to pre-**

---

[13] See: http://www.qumak.pl/rozwiazania/infrastruktura-lotnicza/uslugi/ [25.11.2014].

pare the weather forecast for the region with greater precision, while first
and foremost specify the location of occurrence of violent meteorological
phenomena. Furthermore, this shall be the 9th device integrated into the network of radars of Poland managed by IMGW. **This radar shall also become
integrated with the military network of meteorological radars.** Moreover,
Qumak, in cooperation with Selex company, the producer of the equipment,
shall integrate both of these systems, thanks to which the range of the radars
shall cover the area of the whole country. This is the first project of this type in
Poland. The information gained shall serve both civil and military aims. The
contractor shall also be responsible for designing and the complete construction of the installation, while also the provision of the required software of
the radar, as well as the training of the personnel.

(2) **Management of the resources of enterprises and capital groups**,
particularly with the utilization of the following systems:

- Enterprise Asset Management / EAM (inventory and passporting
  of resources; planning and settling budgets; serving the purchasing
  processes; contract management; planning renovation, maintenance,
  overhauls, inspections, elimination of breakdowns);
- IT Service Management / ITSM (registration and searching for resources; configuration associated with the IT infrastructure; management of
  licences; management of orders, problems and incidents; management
  of shifts and despatches; management of knowledge database; management of contracts; monitoring of critical time of execution of services).

In the afore-mentioned fields of EAM and ITSM – Qumak SA identifies
the needs, prepares the concepts and strategies of development; installs the
systems, manages the projects and runs training.[14]

(3) **Building Management System / BMS and building technologies**
– modern solutions streamlining the management of a building premises,
the optimization of its costs of maintenance and guaranteeing a high level of
safety. They ensure the integration of the particular elements of a building.
Energy-saving and ecological solutions are availed of here thanks to which,
the buildings are both modern and environmentally friendly.

The building is equipped with a set of equipment, sensors and detectors,
while also creating a central system integrating all the existing technological
solutions in the building, as well as facilitating reactions to the changes in
both the internal and external environments. This ensures the maximization
of functionality, comfort and safety with the simultaneous minimization of
the costs of utilization and restrictions in the emissions of pollutants.[15]

---

[14] See: http://www.qumak.pl/rozwiazania/zarzadzanie-infrastruktura-utrzymaniem-i-ser-
wisem/uslugi/ [25.11.2014].

[15] See: http://www.qumak.pl/o-firmie/strategia/ [25.11.2014].

This type of realization is exemplified by the modern 15 storey office building of class A+ type, known as Eurocentrum Office Complex, which is situated on Aleje Jerozolimskie in theWarsaw district of Ochota that was designed in accordance with the demanding norms of sustainable construction, which received the pre-certificate – LEED at the level of Gold. The building has a range of ecological solutions, among other aspects, water-saving fittings, external screens on the elevation restricting the excessive access of the sunshine inside the building, or the system of ventilation and air-conditioning with maximum heat recovery. The applied technologies facilitate among other aspects, the saving on the utilization of drinking water by even up to 50% and restriction of the consumption of electric power. Furthermore, there are various facilities in Eurocentrum for cyclists (showers, changing rooms, self-serving repair stations and renting of bicycles), the implementation of systems of safety: fire alarm system and access control, voice alarm system, cameras monitoring buildings (CCTV) and system of CO detection. The installed solutions are inspected and managed with the aid of the BMS system installed by us. The Warsaw head office of the company is currently located in this office building.

(4) Business Intelligence / BI – a group of methodics, processes and technologies that exchange large quantities of data into information that is useful for business aims. This information is also presented in graphic form in order for managers and specialists who deal with strategy to avoid the necessity of browsing through a welter of numbers. The widely perceived BI also encompasses the following:

- processes of ETL, encompassing cooperation with data warehouses and their preparation and presentation to clients in the necessary sets and arrangements;
- systems of Big Data, thus solutions for firms whose reported data is featured by large volume, great variety and variability;
- planning applications for the preparation of plans and budgets;
- application of Data Mining, enabling the detection of hidden patterns and correlations.[16]

(5) Integrated systems of customer service – designed to streamline and improve contacts between the client and the firm, as well as the coordination of the processes associated with reacting to the questions coming into the institution. Thanks to this, among other aspects, the advanced systems of customer service are becoming modern centres serving all the channels which the firm avails of to make contact with the clients.

Their task is to streamline the customer service, while also to reduce the costs of the functioning of the firm and the costs of its turnover by means

---

[16] See: http://www.qumak.pl/rozwiazania/business-intelligence/uslugi/ [25.11.2014].

of the following: increasing the effectiveness of cross-selling and up-selling, providing the appropriate and associated information accumulated by various business applications, intelligent management of applications based on priorities, skills of the consultants, the costs of services and availability of resources.[17]

(6) Intelligent Transport System (ITS) is a solution that avails of various IT technologies, telecommunications, automatics of movable facilities in the sphere of road transportation. These encompass infrastructure, vehicles and their users. They serve the management of traffic, management of mobility, charging fees and notification. In turn, they may cooperate with similar systems applied in other types of transportation, e.g. railways.

ITS systems are executed in a complex manner by taking account of the creation of all the stages of the investment process, including the following:
- analysis of the needs of the client and the conceptual projects;
- preparation of the architecture of the technical system and specifics of the equipment and sub-systems;
- executive, construction and technical projects, as well as projects for IT applications;
- training of employees and aid in the servicing of the completed system;
- maintenance services;
- integrating of the new ITS system of the existing elements of the infrastructure, e.g. the controllers of traffic lights.

In the realization of the projects, the experience and competences of the company are availed of, which encompass an extensive computer network, centre of data processing, technologies of intelligent building, integration of sub-systems derived from various producers, remote monitoring of the whole ITS infrastructure, service provided in the mode of 24 hours a day, 7 days a week.

The implementation of ITS is aimed at improving the effectiveness of traffic by shortening the duration of a journey, restricting the nuisance such as pollution or noise, as well as increasing the safety in transportation.[18]

(7) IT systems for public sector. IT systems designed for the public sector are the answer to the needs of administration, thanks to the support of the EU funds they dynamically create and develop ICT resources.

The aim of the projects is to increase state security and streamline public administration, as well as improving the service provided for citizens availing of the services of public administration. In this sense, the beneficiaries are all the citizens of the country. The ICT needs of the state are executed on the

---

[17] See: http://www.qumak.pl/rozwiazania/zintegrowane-systemy-obslugi-klientow/uslugi/ [25.11.2014].
[18] See: http:// www.qumak.pl/ rozwiazania/ inteligentne-systemy-transportowe/uslugi/ [25.11.2014].

basis of the law relating to public procurement within the framework of the tender proceedings submitted.

Qumak S.A. realizes among other aspects, the following: an intelligent system of controlling traffic, which would streamline municipal communication, the system of protecting the country against meteorological threats whose aim is to predict and warn citizens of for instance the dangers of floods, regional information platforms for the inhabitants and self-governments of the particular provinces.

Complex work encompasses the following:
- analysis of the needs of the orderer;
- designing;
- building the dedicated IT systems;
- implementation of solutions based on the SOA, WorkFlow, DMS, CMS, BI systems;
- installation of the IT hardware infrastructure (e.g. servers class x and RISC, matrix, libraries);
- installation of the IT network infrastructure (routers, switches, equipment for transmitting data over large distances – WDM, others);
- ensuring security of IT (firewall, IPS, SIEM, DAM, Guardium, others);
- data base and data warehouse on the basis of IBM, Oracle products (among others, DB2, Netezza, Exadata);
- solutions dedicated to the Pure Systems type (new trends on IT market);
- filing data and digitalization of archives;
- training;
- maintaining systems and servicing solutions.[19]

(8) Data Centres – Centre of Data Processing. Data Centre is a modern technological centre consisting of an expanded server room and a range of devices that supports its functioning. It serves the storage and processing of sometimes enormous amounts of information and enables the execution of operations with confidential data in a secure IT environment.

The realization of the modern building of the Data Centre encompasses the entire designing and construction work: the architecture and construction adjusted to the needs of IT infrastructure, power systems, sanitary infrastructure, together with precise air-conditioning, telecommunications systems and equipment of the IT sector. The certainty of the functioning of the building is guaranteed by the security systems as follows: physical (among others, the system of CCTV cameras, system of Access Control), fire safety and IT security (firewall). In the sphere of the Data Centre the following are

---

[19] See: http:// www.qumak.pl/ rozwiazania/systemy-it-dla-sektora-publicznego/uslugi/ [25.11.2014].

executed: new building premises, modernization work on the older building premises, adaptation of existing office space of the Centre of Data Processing, as well as relocation of IT equipment.

Buildings of this type are mainly constructed in sectors where huge sheets of information are utilized, e.g. in the telecommunications sector, as well as the banking and financial sectors, while also orders from the institutions of the public sector: government agencies and military institutions. Due to the constant growth in the market demand for computing power and data storage, the sector of the Data Centre is one of the most rapidly developing market sectors worldwide.[20]

(9) Integrated systems of customer service. The integrated systems of serving clients are designated for the streamlining and improvement of contacts along the lines of client and the firm, with the utilization of various forms of media, as well as coordinating the processes associated with reacting to the inflow to a given organization. Advanced systems of customer service are becoming more and more frequently modern centres, utilizing all the channels that the firm uses to make contact with the clients of their services.

The task of such systems is to streamline customer service and in effect, reduce the costs of the functioning of the firm and increase its turnover by the following, among others: increasing the effectiveness of cross-selling and up-selling, providing the appropriately related information accumulated by various business applications together with the enquiry of the client, intelligent management of enquiries on the basis of priorities, the skills of a consultant, the costs of service and the availability of resources.

Qumak offers complex systems and tools for the professional servicing of interactions with clients. These consist of products that are derived from renowned suppliers and availing of the latest ICT technologies including the following:

- software for Contact Centre;
- application of Interactive Voice Response (IVR) based on the standard Voice XML;
- systems for quality management and registration of contacts with clients;
- copyright applications adjusted to the specifics of the sector (applications of an agent, modules of scripting supporting the work of an agent, call back, management of "outgoing campaigns";
- intelligent knowledge base, IVR applications (facilitating among other aspects,the execution of payments by credit cards, execution of debt collection, self-service, as well as serving loyalty programs).

---

[20] See: http://www.qumak.pl/rozwiazania/data-center/uslugi/ [25.11.2014].

(10) Systems supporting management associated with CRM are among others, as follows:
- centralized management of contacts with clients;
- effective, multi-channel processing of orders;
- process of smooth realization of orders (reservation or allocation of tangible stocks, management of queues and tasks in all transactions);
- controlling price and promotion policies;
- management of loyalty programs;
- management of complaints;
- complex management of supply chain and optimization of supplies;
- complete tracking of product lots and container supplies;
- analysis and processing of the costs of goods;
- extended control of warehouse management, full control of the whole lifecycle of series and lots;
- complex solutions supporting management of chain of shops, including the copyright system of serving retail sales termed as "salon";
- serving customs warehouse.

(11) Business Continuity & Data Security encompasses the scope of data that is critical for the functioning of the business. Its theft, loss or temporary lack of availability may have a negative impact on the operations of the firm and expose it to high losses. The solution of Business Continuity & Data Security serves the protection of data when it is processed, transmitted or stored.

Business Continuity is a solution of a wide perception of business continuity. It includes among other aspects, the physical infrastructure, operational systems, database, applicational servers, systems of managing and monitoring, as well as concentrating on the provision of a high level of availability for the business services and processes of a client. In the case of the occurrence of an unplanned break in operations, they facilitate the rapid restoration of the production to workability.

Data Security consists of ways to protect confidential information from becoming available to, used, modified, stolen and utilized by unauthorized people. Currently, when firms and institutions store key business information and data of consumers in virtual space, their effective defence against cyber-attacks is particularly important.

(12) Outsourcing of IT specialists is a modern solution that facilitates the temporary increase in the IT team by additional experts without the necessity of employing them in the organizational structures of the client. The appropriate provision of services is monitored by a team dealing with the recruitment and a team responsible for the execution of contracts.

The recruitment team acquires the appropriate candidates who shall be rendering services in the projects of the client. These specialists shall be encompassed in the care of personnel, administration, logistics and legislative, although the service itself is usually rendered in the headquarters of the organizations of clients. A client acquires the copyright rights to the assets created by the recruited experts.

The executive team however, deals with maintaining constant contact with the specialist provided, as well as the coordinator on the part of the client. The tasks of the team involve, among other things, settling for the work of the consultant, taking care of all formal and legislative issues, as well as issuing income invoices.[21]

Clients of Qumak S.A. constitute70 out of 100 of the largest enterprises operating in Poland. The company is also present in the public sector executing projects on behalf of government and self-government administrations, among others.

Qumak S.A. cooperates with the world leaders from the IT sector. Likewise, it also cooperates with multitude of scientific centres AGH, Technical Universities of Warsaw and Cracow, as well as the Jagiellonian University.

3. Results of business activities, employment

Revenue from the sales of IT products and services in 2013 amounted to 530 m PLN, which places the company in the first three in terms of integrators operating on the Polish market. Charts 1 and 2 presented below illustrate the dynamic development of the company over the past several years.

In December 2014, approximately 720 people were employed on contract basis, while approximately 150 cooperated within the framework of civil and legislative agreements. With such a number of employees, restructuring was necessary as a result of which the following departments were created: Trading (50 people), Support (50 people), Realization of Contracts (230 people), Financial and Organization and Promotion (46 people). This structure has been added to by the service of outsourcing (175 contracts with a further 120 employees acquired by Hewlett Packard).

---

[21] See: http://www.qumak.pl/rozwiazania/outsourcing-specjalistow-it-body-leasing/uslu-gi/ [25.11.2014].

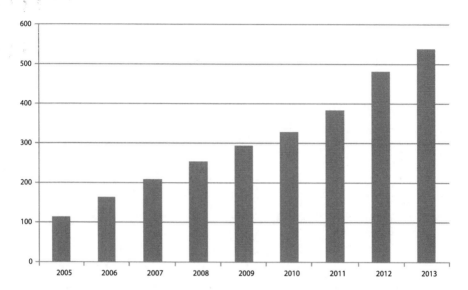

Chart 1. Revenue of Qumak S.A. in millions of PLN in the period 2005–2013

Source: Self-analysis on the basis of annual reports of the firm, http://www.qumak.pl/gielda/raporty-roczne [25.11.2014].

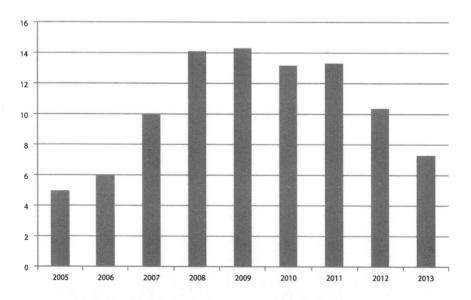

Chart 2. Net profit of Qumak S.A. in millions of PLN in the period 2005–2013

Source: Self-analysis on the basis of annual reports of the firm, http://www.qumak.pl/gielda/raporty-roczne [25.11.2014].

The average age of employees amounts to 35 years of age, while work seniority shall be presented in the Table 1.

Table 1. Differentiation in numbers of employees with regard to seniority in Qumak company

No.	Work experience	Percentage of employees (%)
1.	up to 3 years	36.6
2.	from 3 to 5 years	30.35
3.	from 6 to 10 years	19.6
4.	Over 10 years	13.5

Source: Internal materials of firm.

As may be observed, the majority of employees (67%) have been briefly associated with the company, namely up to 5 years. The enterprise tries to retain the employees for longer and with this aim in mind they build loyalty programs and work out career paths.

4. Respecting and promoting values

Attempts at the sustainability of values are visible in the company in terms of their various groups as follows: economic–managerial, competence–development, ethical–cultural, as well as civic ones. Economic values and adherence to the law, ethics and good practices come to the foreground, although it is not possible to state that other groups of values were of a secondary nature.

Qumak as an engineering firm must take account of the fact that as perceived by Janusz Urbański[22], the world of values permeates techniques, technical activities and their effects. Technical activities require axiological order. This order is essential in order to fully understand the sense of techniques and have the criteria of its appropriate evaluation for executing the rating of engineering activities and its effects. Performing the profession of an engineer gives rise to numerous and significant moral problems, both for the engineer himself and for other people. The facts are that the fate of mankind depends to a great extent on the good and conceivably safe functioning of techniques.[23] he development of both the organization, as well as the people associated with it is of a high level of importance. Development (research and development) is the displayed strategic aim. The subject matter coordi-

---

[22] Urbański J., *Zasady etyki inżyniera i ich funkcjonowanie*; http://www.simp.pl/gsk/doc/Konwersatorium/SIMP%20abstrakt%20wykładu.pdf.

[23] Ibidem.

nating the development of an organization is the Department of Research and Development, which directly co-creates and realizes the strategic aims of the firm as follows: by supporting the strong trademark and innovative technological solutions. The market of modern technologies is created. Almost thirty years of experience of the firm is availed of and the wide range of possibilities of the specialized department are combined in order for the cooperation with scientific institutions and innovative ICT firms to create and commercialize innovative technological projects.

Qumak was classified in second place among the firms with the greatest potential of development in Poland in 2014 by the monthly magazine called "Bank". Its ranking in terms of the potential of development as defined on the basis of the absolute magnitude of sales, its growth of value, the dynamics of outlays on research and development and their relation to turnover, while also the number of products offered. In the ranking of the best IT firms in Poland in 2014, Qumak took first place.[24]

For over ten years, Qumak has been actively involved in the educational sector, executing projects for higher level colleges and scientific centres. In accordance with the report on the IT market prepared by **IDG–TOP200** (edition of 2014), the firm occupied fifth place as a service provider for the scientific and research sector and education. Today, the effects of this cooperation are obvious. Thanks to the acquired trust of the partners, effective cooperation with the research sector is possible. The firm adds its own value to joint ventures– a team of experts with broad practical knowledge gained during the execution of the extended implementation of IT and ICT.[25] The high class of the specialists is certified to by the specialist certificates that amount to as many as 1,543.

In Qumak, the principle of fair remuneration has a high degree of success. The average salary in the firms almost twice higher than the national average and amounts to approximately 7,000 PLN gross, while the specialists earn significantly less more. The appropriate differentiation of salaries while taking account of the differences in terms of content / difficulties of work, its quality and effects, as well as quantities is the subject matter of professional analysis, qualifications and assessment of work.

The firm tries to involve the employees in joint activities, not only professionally, but also in a social and recreational form. These activities integrate, but also have an impact on the level of satisfaction of the employees and facilitate the devotion to various non-occupational passions, constituting a form of relaxation and having a beneficial impact on the level of satisfaction of the employees and the culture of the organization. This may be exemplified

---

[24] http://www.qumak.pl/qumak-nagrodzony-przez-miesiecznik-bank/ [26.11.2014].
[25] http://www.qumak.pl/o-firmie/badania-i-rozwoj [3.10.2014].

by the annual company calendar made with photographs of the employees. This is formulated from the award-winning and distinguished work of the employees submitted for the photography competition. During the course of 5 years of the aforesaid competition, 1,700 photographs have been submitted. All the employees are invited to participate in the competition and the main themes are strongly varied as follows: Our Passions, Colours of the World, Contrasts, etc. Joint starting events are also organized for the employees and their families.

Activities that are significant in social terms are undertaken. Qumak is involved in educational projects supporting and promoting science, talented youths and students, as well as subsidizing culture and art. In cooperation with social partners, it is involved in resolving social problems and builds good neighbourly ties with the local communities in areas where it operates.

For many years it has taken care of the foster children of Dom Małego Dziecka w Krakowie (Orphanage of Small Children in Cracow), by supporting it, not only in financial terms. The firm runs numerous activities in which both the employees and their families have the opportunity to participate. These activities are exemplified by the following:

- Project entitled „Bajki o magicznych wartościach" (Fairy tales of magical values) – aimed at the employees and their families, particularly children;
- Centre of Medical Rescue – training the employees in Warsaw and Cracow on the sphere of procedures relating to saving lives in emergency cases. The training is run by a specialized unit of medical rescue teams. It is financed by the funds of the City Offices that are allocated for this purpose. The participants of the training courses are employees who applied to participate as volunteers.

Simultaneous to the demarcation and realization of plans of business strategy[26] the concept of sustainable growth is advanced, whereby not only tangible benefits and economic activities are taken into account, but also the requirements of protecting the natural environment, the necessity of saving electric power (which to a significant degree depends on the quality and modernity of the project), the restriction of the emissions of greenhouse gases, as well as greater balance in terms of the lives of the employees in the relation of professional work and personal life and family life – health care, rest and recreation, social and civic involvement.

The firm is the leader of the *Sector of Green IT*. Qumak wants to be a firm that is responsible for the environment, buildings constructed according to its own designs and area utilized. Designs of *eco-offices*, *Green code*, eco-education for employees, recycling and saving water are all just some of the ways

---

[26] A plan for the period 2013–2016 is currently being executed.

to achieve this goal. It is still important to develop some new products and services for clients and invest in new and better technologies.[27]

The better balancing of work and other roles in the lives of employees is attained to a large degree by means of making the working time flexible, while also restricting overtime work. Teleworking is of additional significance, albeit in a restricted sense.

One of the most important aims is that of strengthening the level of trusting a firm, as well as its activities and possibilities. The objective is to build a culture based on trust and responsibility for the tasks entrusted.

Likewise, the efforts of safety and hygiene of work, as well as the practical utilization of the indicators and achievements of ergonomics are significant and necessary. This is served by the project entitled *Safe and convenient workplaces*. The Health and Safety Commissionare in operation here, while the assessment of professional risk is carried out, as well as the procedures of health and safety that are stipulated in the sphere of training courses, preventive measures, procedures in the case of accidents at work, the principles of cooperation with sub-contractors and others. Information materials are presented on the company Intranet system on the following issues:
- accidents at work;
- pre-medical first-aid;
- ergonomics;
- fire prevention and evacuation;
- stress and counteraction.

A particularly significant contribution in terms of increasing safety is made by one of the subsidiaries of Qumak S.A. – Star ITS.[28] Qualified maintenance engineers, as well as analysts and IT specialists work there by dealing with Intelligent Transport Systems. Star ITS is in charge of complex implementation, calibration and maintenance of the systems of controlling and management of traffic.

The solutions created here increase the level of road traffic in terms of its fluidity, while also the associated comfort for travellers. They also reduce the costs of maintenance incurred by the city. This organization deals with both individual and collective transportation in all its forms, ranging from cycling routes to railway lines in the suburbs.

At present, the company is executing one of the largest tasks relating to Intelligent Transport Systems, not only on a domestic scale, but a European-wide one. This is the Integrated System of Traffic Management TRISTAR encompassing Gdynia, Sopot and Gdańsk.

---

[27] http://www.qumak.pl/o-firmie/zrownowazony-rozwoj/ [3.10.2014].
[28] http://starits.pl/o_firmie.html [3.10.2014].

The strategic partners are leading software firms, namely PTV, Gevas and the Foundation of the Development of Civil Engineering and technical colleges. The subject matter of the activities of **SKYLAR** company is that of designing, implementing and maintaining navigation systems and meteoradars; the modernization and servicing of the systems of radio-communication, servicing heliports and military and civil landing areas, while also the assembly and servicing of baggage systems (BHS) and detection systems (EDS). Skylar is a firm that deals with the realization of airport infrastructure, radar meteorological stations and warning devices.

The driving force of the development of the firm has been partly described earlier as innovativeness. The firm invests in its own development structure and searches for strategic partners representing research and development centres. *Organizational innovativeness* is aimed at free dialogue in terms of the issues of the improvement and development of creativity. The tools for this purpose are the following in particular: platforms of innovativeness, think-tanks and workshops of creativity.

The broad perception of quality are of high level of importance in terms of products, technology, qualifications of the employed staff and the work processes. In the area of the acquisition and maintenance of the highest class specialists, the appropriate packages of remuneration, premiums, etc. have been created. In Qumak S.A. the philosophy of TQM and the modern management of human resources in the megasystem of TQM-HRM are combined.

By paying attention to values such as professionalism and high competences of employees, while also taking account of employment, a reorganization of the personnel functions in the firm has taken place. Three areas have been distinguished as follows:
- recruitment and development, as well as external and internal formation of the image of the employer;
- the so-called "hard" HR encompassing the personnel administration, as well as calculating salaries, taxes and insurance, while also reporting on this sphere;
- internal communications and running a website and Intranet service, as well as creating a base dedicated to employees and managers.

Common values for employees

In the organization, values expected from managers and employees have been defined. They are termed common or universal values. The level of familiaritywith them is differentiated in the particular areas of the firm.

Common / corporate values are as follows:
- high quality (products, processes, work, relations),

- professionalism,
- responsibility,
- innovativeness /creativity,
- trust,
- cooperation,
- loyalty,
- honesty.

Recruitment is based on the structurized analysis, while taking account of values during the recruitment and selection of people takes place in a sphere that is dependent on individual knowledge, abilities and curiosity of the particular personnel specialists and managers. The firm has created a profile for the candidate for work.

Currently, the firm does not have the tools and procedures at its disposal, which would facilitate the analysis of candidates for work in the context of values in a credible manner, while also commonplace, comparable and routine by nature. Nevertheless, for some groups of positions there are already profiles of candidates for work and their scope of duties prepared. In the future, it is planned to encompass all the employees with these activities.

At present, a catalogue of common competences is being prepared by the HR Department with the support of the managers for the whole organization and for the particular areas in the organization. A new system of periodical assessment of the employees is also being prepared, which is to have an impact on promotions. During the course of remuneration, values are taken into consideration rather sporadically.

The firm has a code of ethics and its entries are out of the workshops that encompass the representatives of all the groups of employees. This code consists of three parts as follows: Code of the Employer Qumak S.A., Code of the Employee of Qumak S.A. and Standards of Ties with External Stakeholders.

Values and culture of Qumak

Qumak was established in 1986 by a group of colleagues (mainly graduates of AGH), who were connected by a long-held friendship that emerged from their days as boy scouts, while also activities in student organizations, university chaplaincy centre and also a fondness for mountain hiking that was initially in their own group, but later with their families also. Since 1991, the company has operated as joint-ventures, with the participation of the Polish–American Entrepreneurial Fund, under the name of Qumak International.

In the Cracow-based Qumak, it was decided to create an organizational culture by basing on camaraderie, partnership and trust, which is free of unnecessary internal rivalry and with the participation of managers and employees in the economic results of the firm and this succeeded.

Following several numerical increases in the organization and the connection with the Warsaw-based Sekom, maintaining this type of culture became difficult, the more so as the colleagues-founders and their friends from youth became the minority in the enterprise that was now dominated by young people with a low level of experience and who only knew the history of the company from stories. Despite this fact, certain features of the early Qumak company survived, such as the emphasis on cooperation rather than internal rivalry and the spirit of a community, the go-ahead for creativity and creative freedom, camaraderie and trust, although the emphasis was moved towards professionalism, entrepreneurship (also internal entrepreneurship), as well as effectiveness. Undoubtedly, the management of such a large company as Qumak has taken on a different form nowadays than in the case of the small enterprise which it was at the beginning of its journey.

The authors would like to express their sincere gratitude to the director Mr. Adam Bunsch DEng and Mrs. Joanna Duliban M.A. for the time they devoted and the great creative contribution to the preparation of this study.

Izabela Stańczyk
Tadeusz Oleksyn

3. FIVE O'CLOCK – VALUES IN A FAMILY FIRM
CASE STUDY

Genesis of firm

The company Brzezicki & Siess – administrator of the trademark Five O'Clock – commenced business activities in 1994. The company was established by the following: Magdalena and Marek Brzezicki and Bartosz Siess, and was separated from a trading firm of the sector B2B–EIH Marek Brzezicki into one specializing in the importing and distribution of high quality tea and coffee. The experience gained beforehand led to the decision to develop activities in Lublin and Legnica where the first retail stores of the copyright trademark Five O'clock were opened. Since that time, the activity of the organization which is currently operating in the role of a coordinator in the supply chain has concentrated on the following: designing, marketing (including branding activities) and direct sales of products bearing the trademark Five O'Clock. As stated by one of the initiators of the trademark, Bartosz Siess,"Chcieliśmy stworzyć miejsce, gdzie z herbatą harmonizuje atmosfera. Znane do tej pory koncepty były, w moim odczuciu, niewystarczające. Brakowało w nich syntezy i prostoty (We wanted to create a place where the atmosphere is harmonized with tea. The well-known concepts up to that point had been, in my opinion, insufficient. There was no synthesis or simplicity in them)."

In designing the identity of the trademark Five O'Clock, it was decided to go with a minimalistic, yet elegant and rather nostalgic image by evoking the once cultivated custom of tea-time of Great Britain – afternoon meetings with a cup of good tea.

Domain, competition and market position

The development of the trademark based on the network of authorized sales and exclusive distribution accelerated following the signing of several long-term agreements for renting premises in shopping malls. The retail stores of

Five O'Clock which were formed in chronological order are as follows: M1, Poznań (1998), Janki, Warszawa (1999), Galeria Dominikańska, Wrocław (2001), Galeria Łódzka (2003), M1, Kraków (2001), Blue City, Warszawa (2005), Galeria Krakowska (2006), Złote Tarasy, Warszawa (2007), Galeria Bałtycka, Gdańsk (2007), Port, Łódź (2010), Galeria, Rzeszów (2012), Galeria Katowicka (2013), Stary Browar, Poznań (2014). The portfolio of the company includes a second trademark with a similar assumption to Five O'Clock, but aimed at the sale of coffee – Skład Kawy. This firm was founded in the City Centre (Poznań) in 2013, while the further expansion of the network of retail stores is being planned. In addition, there are three licenced stores of Five O'Clock: in Kołobrzeg, Szczecin and Poole (UK). Granting the licence to Five O'Clock comes with the obligation of close ties and respect for the policy of the image of the trademark. Prestigious outlets located in the largest and popular shopping malls, painstaking and exclusive image, while also the specialist and well-thought out assortment in terms of the gourmet category have all embedded the strong position of Five O'Clock in the premium segment –luxury goods of wide availability. By analysing the share of sales of classic tea against the background of the assortment as a whole, it is possible to observe the steady upward trend that is illustrated in Chart 1.

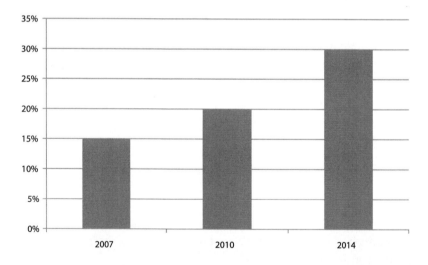

Chart 1. Percentage of sales of classic tea

Source: Internal materials of firm.

In 2007, the afore-mentioned indicators of share in combined sales reached the level of 15%, while 20% in 2010 and 30% in 2014.

High quality tea is gaining a wider group of connoisseurs. Classic tea such as black, green and special flavours (luxurious types) are natural, rare and limited types of tea. They are rigorously classified and provided with a special stamp specifying the precise gradation of the leaves. It is possible to purchase these products only in specialist shops and they are not available in distribution channels of mass markets. An example of the interesting types of classic tea that are available in Five O'Clock are as follows: Japanese Shincha Kirisakura, Yunnan White Silk, Darjeeling White Happy Valley WFTGFOP1, Thai Jing Shuan Oolong, Yunnan Golden Bud, DJ 15 Darjeeling Namring Lot. FF FTGFOP1. The combined collection enumerates approximately 81 varieties.

In Poland, apart from Five O'Clock there is also a trademark of Austrian origin – Demmers Tea House on the market of high quality premium tea. It possesses four franchising shops in Warsaw, Wrocław and Cracow. Demmers Tea House in comparison with Five O'Clock offers a poorer range of natural classic tea. The price level of both trademarks is similar, thus the quality of products in both cases is placed under rigorous certification.

In gauging the range of the networks on the local market, Five O'Clock possesses thirteen retail shops and may count on wider recognition, the more so as the shops of the trademark Demmer Tea House belong to several owners, which may hinder the cohesive strategy within the framework of the network as a whole.

In the segment of high quality tea the premium trademark is Mariage Freres, a chain of French teahouses of over 300 years of tradition. In Poland, their products may be purchased in the multi-brand boutique called Horn & More (Warsaw) in limited quantities (12 varieties). Despite the great popularity of the trademark among connoisseurs (traditionalists, experts), it is still not well-recognised in Poland. The barrier is most certainly the high prices, while also the market for luxury tea food articles which is not mature. In Mariage Freres, it is necessary to pay approximately 65–75 PLN for 100 g of aromatic tea (with additional aroma) in an elegant tin. In Five O'Clock, the analogical product costs between 24 and 30 PLN.

Specifics of behaviour of clients of high quality food products

The specialized and frequently luxurious food products belong to the relatively new category of luxury goods, the so-called **luxury experience**. This emerges with the need to experience unique feelings and emotional states such as: joy, happiness and pride. Products of the premium food sector help to compensate for the sphere of "being" by satisfying the sophisticated **emo-**

tional needs of a client such as: aesthetics, prestige, tradition and ecology. The segmentation of clients takes account of the broad psychological motivations that match the systems of value, approach to life and lifestyles.

The purchasing motivations of consumers may be divided into two groups. The first one is the so-called external motivation – a set of behaviour types of conspicuous consumption, in which the purchaser chooses renowned products that constitute symbols of status. Their choices fall on prestigious trademarks or specialized and frequently well-recognised products. An example of tea that enjoys respecting the aforesaid purchasing group is Japanese tea, which is promoted thanks to the trend of sushi bars or coffee that is to be found high on the rankings, e.g. Kopi Luwak.

In accordance with the technique of segmentation VALS, the purchasers with external motivation are termed **Achievers** and **Strivers**. This is a significant, dynamic and developmental group in Poland and in 2013 it encompassed approximately 2 m people (KPMG 2013). At the opposite extreme, there are purchasers who are guided by internal needs such as: ideals, principles and sensitivity. It is possible to distinguish the **Thinkers** among them – experts and traditionalists, conscious and educated buyers who appreciate the values of specialized products. Their choices fall on trademarks with a sense of history and tradition. The internal motivations also include hedonistic pursuits that are appropriate for seekers **of experiences**. In the case of a client of these preferences, a product constitutes a way of expressing personality. During the course of making a choice, they are guided by novelty, innovation, yet they are an unstable purchasing group that yields to varying consumer trends. An important group of consumers of qualitative food products is the so-called **Dreamers**. These are occasional trippers to the world of luxury and who spend money on luxury food products sporadically. The act of consuming good tea is for them a moment of discreet luxury which they can afford festively. A large percentage of these occasional purchasers may be observed around Christmas time, while also to a lesser degree on other festive occasions. Then the increased activity of *purchasing as a present* may be noted.

Portfolio and strategy of development of a product

Five O'Clock offers a rich and varied collection of tea and coffee of the highest class of quality, which are frequently types that were previously unknown in Poland. The company has cooperated with only tried and trusted business partners since the outset, such as a tea-tasting distributor from Hamburg as the direct importer. It takes responsibility for the tests, certification, technology of production by issuing a certificate of guarantee of quality. Due to the safety and protection of quality, the firm avoids short-term agreements with other producers, while also rejecting offers of direct distribution from plantations. The stage of inspections on behalf of the firm are tests on tea based on the assessment of the taster. Apart from ensuring high quality perceived as formal adherence to the norm and certificate, the source of customer satisfaction is the emotional and symbolic benefit of availing of the product. In marketing communiques, there are frequent references to history, as well as the cultural heritage of tea. The advertising campaigns are strengthened by the creative assumptions that facilitate the building of a message of an educational and informative nature.

The selection of the product portfolio of the trademark of Five O'Clock and its systematic expansion with new product lines and elements that are complementary with regard to tea and coffee is possible thanks to the cooperation with other administrators of trademarks on the principles of individually established marketing alliances, frequently of a very wide scope of cooperation. The criteria of selecting a business partner assumes the compatibility of the mutual assumptions of the mission and vision and convergent priorities which facilitates the penetration of the core competences of trademarks. In practice, it is the case whereby the trading partner is a family firm similar to Five O'Clock which is favourable to both mutual understanding, as well as displaying the personality and pursuits of the founders. Thus, it is of cultural significance and is favourable to the development of conflict-free and long-term cooperation. The marketing cooperation assumes the following: enrichment of the assortment with interesting niche and unique products, while also broadening the associations with the trademark, as well as strengthening the quality of the product. Thanks to these activities, the very high quality of the products offered becomes credible within the framework of the whole assortment line. It is possible to distinguish the following joint activities: creating a limited series of products such as chocolates for special occasions or unrepeatable compositions of festive tea launched during for instance, the Christmas period, short variable series of tea and coffee whose implementation into the offer is part of the policy of "managing unavailability" and an important element in surprising the client with novelties. The history of the cooperation with the acclaimed leaders of the market and delicatessen products displays that the partners acquired added value via among other aspects, in the form of image transfer, which realistically translates to the increase in the competitiveness and strong market position. Cooperation at the level of building intangible values is an important part of the strategy of Five O'Clock. By way of demonstrating mutual agreement, which frequently transgresses the priorities of pure business, the significance of maintaining good relations is communicated while remaining above mutual competition.

In the desire to indicate the values that are important and appreciated by the firm, it is essential to underline the priority of sustaining the symbolic placement of the trademark of Five O'Clock. All the internal processes of the organization– administrator of the trademark of Five O'Clock are dominated by marketing and have a real impact on the perceived external image. The current result and reputation of the trademark is the effect of many years of the processes of creating values, science and drawing conclusions, as well as shaping the culture of the organization, which is decisively influenced by the individual motivations of the direct creators of the trademark who since the very beginning of the existence of Five O'Clock on the market right up to today have maintained direct contact with the employees and clients. The advantage of branding activities and the expansion of them into the various areas of activities of the organization such as personnel management, planning services and procedures, internal communication assumes the goal of sustaining the set of desired associations with the trademark in the eyes of the purchasers. The strength of the trademark of Five O'Clock has always been its asset of intangible values: identity, culture, reputation and the distinctive image.

Mission and vision

The mission of the trademark of Five O'Clock is that of building the custom of tasting good tea. Providing a product of distinctive quality is also developing the contexts associated with the "tea style of life", which may be summed up as the aestheticization of the short everyday moments connected with the dinner table, celebration of moments of relaxation and providing frameworks of rituals for mutual encounters. „Miejsce w którym zatrzymał się czas" (places where time has stopped) is the motto of the trademark. This inspires a client towards the "aesthetic experience". This is an added value that emerges during the course of availing of products. A significant role in the process of "experiencing", which coincides with the perception of the reality of the trademark is played by the employees who are bearers of key values similar to the tangible testimony of the trademark such as the following: characteristic design, colours used and compositions. The common principle of the firm is the fact that everyone: the owners, the management staff, creative employees and others responsible for customer service are obliged to be ambassadors of the trademark. It strives towards a situation whereby the employees testify to the values that are important to the trademark. This relates to the working style, behaviour, the norms of outward appearance (discreet elegance). The employees are to give the impression that they are in love with brewing tea and this is not to be false pretences.

The tea style of being is perfectly reflected in the Japanese philosophy of tea cult. This is an approach towards discovering beauty in the surrounding reality and raising awareness to a triviality. In Five O'Clock, the tea cult has served as an inspiration, in order to display the British ritual of serving tea.

The nostalgia for the times from which the custom of Five O'Clock is derived from and in which it experienced its heyday also has a Polish connection. Despite the fact that Poland did not have any overseas colonies between the wars, *colonial shops* were very popular. Likewise, firms emerged that made the tea and coffee branch the main profile of activities. One of the more innovative in terms of the approach to the product, while also "the modern view" of business was a firm called Pluton – a coffee roasting plant and chain of shops prior to the outbreak of the Second World War that had a nationwide chain of as many as 30 shops in Warsaw, Lwów, Łódź, Poznań, Gdynia and Lublin. Pluton, the leader on the Polish market, had written in its mission the propagation of the culture of drinking tea and coffee and decisively led to their spread in Poland between the wars. Great popularity was enjoyed then by the afternoon *invitations to tea (fives)*. The display of not only the "dream of power", but also personal ambitions associated with good coffee and tea, as well as the accompanying culture was possessed by certain aristocratic families who had their own plantations of tea and coffee (e.g. Sapieha family had one in Congo).

2. Values important to Five O'Clock

The activities of the whole company are regulated by the four most important principles that shape the culture of the company and style of management. These principles have not been registered or formalized yet. Due to the jointly prepared agreement and insightful training, they have however created and are still creating the division of work since the beginning of the existence of this trademark. Nevertheless, with relation to the dynamic development of the network with the number of showrooms increasing from year to year, the necessity to describe and operationalize the culture of the company (commencing from 2015), as well as ethical issues and procedures that are associated with taking on employees, their development and first and foremost, maintaining the high standards of work.

With regard to the specifics of the domain, thus products, markets in which the company operates and the clients for whom the products are designed for, the **cultural and humanistic values** come to the fore, which are in particular as follows:

beauty and aesthetics; good tea, the skill of brewing and serving indicate a certain affinity towards art; it is no wonder that this is the subject of several years of studies in Japan;

- being together, here and now; making and strengthening interpersonal and personal ties;
- restraint, silence, mindfulness – to use the Buddhist terms to which the ritual of the preparation and consumption of good brands of tea and coffee lead to;
- respect, trust.

Nowadays, tea is an everyday product, however the mission of Five O'Clock is the promotion of the custom of tasting of good tea and inspiring the savouring of tea tasting in the atmosphere of silence.

Employees at sales outlets should express a sense of style and class, composure and a balanced way of behaviour. To a large extent, clients that visit a teashop possess such features, thus similar attitudes are required from the employees in order for communication during the process of sales and after-sales stages to be run smoothly (to which special attention is paid), in an atmosphere of trust, understanding and empathy.

The activities of the team are concentrated on the arrangement of the surroundings and atmosphere of sales in order to favour the perception of the preferences of a client that may bear fruition in the future by means of the desire to develop the element of tea and further tea adventure. A more business aim of such activities may be termed as the building of long term ties with a client that are based on trust. However, in order for the interaction along the lines of employee-client to run in an appropriate manner, the sellers must pay attention to the good and harmonious ties between them. Potential conflicts, disagreements and deconcentration of the team push the realization of the aims associated with an exceptional service to the background. The same relates to the style of management and relations between managers, employees of sales and other people of further levels of regional and central organization-coordination.

Further values and principles that directly result from the ideals and motivations of the creators of the trademark and relate to key competences are those of **passion and involvement**. The unique experience of the trademark is among other aspects, the wide knowledge referring to the specialized sphere of tea and coffee. The genesis of the formation of the trademark is directly connected with among other aspects, the personal involvement of Mr. Bartosz Siess, who is personally an expert and connoisseur of tea. The natural ambition of the creators of the trademark was the desire to select co-workers who indicated a similar level of interests. By no means does this refer to the recruitment of a fully qualified employee with a background of the necessary knowledge, nor the selection of people who are susceptible to becoming infected by this passion. Observation reveals that clients make purchasing decisions relating to niche and new brands of tea (previously unknown) as they perceive the actual and unforced attitude of the seller who recommends them in a suggestive and discreet manner, yet full of passion. If the employees like what they do, broadening their knowledge brings them personal satisfaction. This very fast attitude translates to the quantitative results of sales and has an impact on the product differentiation of the trademark on the market.

Another value and principle that is associated with passion and involvement is that of the **pursuit of perfection**. In the case of the employees of Five O'Clock, the achievement of perfection is the constant process of improvement in terms of gaining the competences of a taster. The use of the "tea language" in the descriptions of expressions of sensory brews, the skill of the correct brewing of tea and the selection of mixtures for the times of the day and dishes consumed.

The perfect execution of the everyday duties is the basis of the openness to the broadening of knowledge, maximum concentration on what is here and now, while also the concentration on the elements and rejection of routine.

In Far Eastern descriptions of the tea ceremonies, the description of a guru frequently appears, who alters the seemingly simple action of selecting and preparation of a brew into an artistic performance by transporting the participants into a world of beauty. The arrangement of the shops of Five O'Clock is toned down and aesthetic, while also referring to the classic canons of beauty. The sellers, by playing the role of guides around the tea arcanas discussing tea with the utilization of sophisticated vocabulary, frequently very poetic in fact, thus strengthening the experience of beauty for the client. There is an artism in itself in terms of these activities that provides more added value for the products at hand.

The afore-mentioned outlined values/principles serve the following key values: **high quality** products, processes, qualifications, relations and cooperation. Each employee is personally responsible for the high quality of execution in terms of the duties entrusted. The notion of management that is close to the philosophy of TQM (Total Quality Management) has illuminated the gesture of the trademark since the beginning of the activities of the network as the priority of building a strong trademark assumes the process of constant development in every area of the activities of the firm. This is a demanding process that is calculated over years and it is not possible to "take shortcuts" here by focusing on interim effects. Thanks to the basis of the complex management by means of quality, the trademark of Five O'Clock has registered a high level in terms of the level of innovation of their products.

This is exemplified by the high quality tea of the limited series of "Prestige" that is packed in convenient pyramid-shaped bags for brewing.

In the name of the principles of constant improvement, the employees illustrate great activity and desire in order to relay their suggestions and frequently very valuable observations. In Five O'Clock, the observations of the *front line employees* are particularly appreciated (coordinators, managers, sellers). They have the possibility of regular contact with decision-makers, namely the owners and their closest co-workers, while first and foremost with clients. Regular programs have been implemented where sales teams carry out thorough analysis of the previously painstakingly selected issues. Each employee should have and most frequently has in fact, the awareness that the decisions taken also depend on him/her, including those of strategic significance, as well as the prosperity of the firm and his/her own.

The structure of the firm is of a horizontal and matrix nature, which has been illustrated in Figure 1.

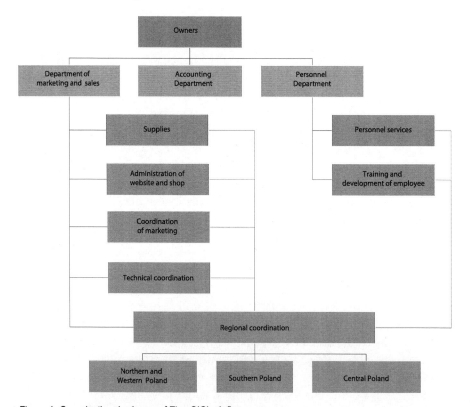

Figure 1. Organizational scheme of Five O'Clock firm

Source: Materials of company.

This is not entirely a reproduction of the organizational structure. The employees of independent entities cooperate closely with each other, thus supporting the work of direct sales. Relations are not dominated by hierarchy and both sides are gauged by the same criteria as the quality of cooperation. The sales outlets remain autonomous to a significant degree with regard to the units of the central organization.

The managers are directly responsible for the work of the team and have a great degree of independence in their activities, while also adjust the way and method of realizing these aims. The majority of these authorizations are delegated to the sales outlets. Cooperation is based on partnership, respect for the law and dignity. The model of partnership culture is binding.

A wider range of duties has been defined with regard to managers and are stipulated in the so-called frameworks of positions. These are also prepared layouts for monitoring the results of their work. Detailed activities relating to merchandising are encompassed within the so-called checklists. There is the possibility of modifying the instructions, as it is possible to implement the suggested solutions following prior agreement. The assessment of the quality of services is sometimes analysed by means of the tool termed Secret Shoppers.

The high level of culture of work in sales outlets is the effect of both the proper selection of people, as well as the impact of the management team and the care paid to having a good atmosphere. Disciplinary factors are of an auxiliary significance and are somewhat in the background.

Thanks to such a formulated style of management, Five O'Clock has acquired and maintains a multitude of talented employees. This is exemplified by students who after graduation decided to remain in the structures of Five O'Clock. During the course of the breakthrough moments, e.g. the opening of a new premises, they took on the function of a manager or coordinator in the rebuilding of the structures. Likewise, they also had an impact on the strategy of professional development, including plans for training, while also marketing strategies and plans.

Designing and realizing the individual career development paths that are adjusted to the skills and talents is so much easier and more realistic that taking on more advanced roles in the structures of Five O'Clock only takes place by means of internal recruitment.

An indirect link between the manager, the central coordination and the owners is that of the employees, namely regional coordination. They hold managerial functions in the sales outlets and know the specifics of the work in the area of direct sales very well. Due to the long work experience, they have a rich and wide-ranging knowledge with reference to products. The nominations for the position of coordinators are decided by the following factors:

- degree of identification with the assumptions of the mission and vision;
- distinctive perception of and skilful promotion of the philosophy of the trademark;
- creativity;
- experience;
- hitherto professional success in the firm;
- trust of the owners.

It is a frequent occurrence that the managers of the flagship products register high levels of sales, together with their teams of understudies. Moreover, they are featured by the skill of testing and implementing innovations and improvements in the system of work. All these advantages are decisive in terms of expanding the duties within the framework of the positions held.

The main tasks of the employees of regional coordination is to support the activities of managers in difficult situations, as well as crisis and conflict situations, while also the function of training. Employees of the coordination personally participate in creating the sales team of a newly opened shop by placing it under its direct guardianship. It happens that this is associated with the exclusion of the current roles and temporary allocation. The range of competences of a coordinator include routine visits, which constitute an important part of the final assessment of the employee and the team. A significant component of the evaluation is the impression of the general atmosphere and the vibe that prevails in the team. This evaluation is equally important as the effectiveness of sales and other business factors (costs, analysis of the market, predicted profits). These elements are served by surveys that are completed by the employees several times per year, among others following the period of Christmas (the season for the tea sector) and marketing campaigns launched.

In the history of the development of Five O'Clock, it has happened that a young team achieved success in terms of sales, however they did not respect the assumptions with relation to image, which was sufficient for the implementation of corrective programs. The range of the activities of coordination is set out by the territorial units, albeit when the situation requires decisiveness and the undertaking of decisive reaction, or when it is excessively intricate, then the team of coordinators searches for the appropriate solutions collectively and always with the participation of all the interested parties.

Processor recruiting and selecting staff, introduction to work

Building the trademark and the quality of customer service is the fundamental factor in building customer loyalty. Recruitment, selection, development and maintenance of employees are of particular significance here. They possess a nationwide network of authorized sales that is essential for running the joint personnel policy and coordinating activities on the scale of the whole organization. There are approximately 70 people employed in the sales outlets (together with the managers and coordinators working in the field), as well as approximately 14 at headquarters (Lubin).

The selection of employees for the sales positions in Five O'Clock is multi-staged and is associated with a long process of adaptation for a new employee. The candidates are faced with a range of requirements due to combining the function of a salesman with that of a specialist of a sphere that is more distant than it seems, namely the problematic issues of products. The predisposition of a taster is also significant. The fact that the common view of the position in the area of direct sales does not enjoy a good reputation on the labour market hinders the acquisition of the appropriate candidates.

By availing of the will to undertake paid work on the part of students, they are drafted in as part of the sales teams. Due to the restricted availability in terms of time, students seldom take on full time work and their working time is agreed on individually with the managers or coordinators of teams in terms of monthly or annual cycles. The availability of students is varied – the amount of hours increases in the summer period, while it happens that students go away on trips and come back to work in the autumn, thus are excluded from working during this period. The proportion between employees in sales outlets amounts to as follows: 45% full-time employment (work contracts), while 55% working on temporary contracts. This model has been functioning for many years.

The structure of sales teams depends on the results of the sales outlets. In the profitable outlets, there are 3 people employed on work contracts, including the manager and 2–3 students. In the remaining entities these teams are 1–2 people fewer. In 2015, the firm is planning to separate the position of the tea taster, who shall be a leading person in the sphere of running tests on tea, training in the field of tea tasting, while also creating descriptions of taste profiles.

The obligation of recruiting new employees for the position of sellers lies with the team managers who receive substantive support from the coordinators. External firms are not availed of. The preliminary evaluation of the candidate concentrates on the recognition of whether he/she would be capable of combining the values that are important for the brand with his/her own personal goals. From a practical point of view, the attempt to convince a candidate to respect principles if he/she does not identify with them is troublesome and over a long-term perspective increases the risk of rejecting the work. The selection of the appropriate tools, schemes or procedures that would objectively check the degree of identification of the convergent priorities is very difficult.

During the first stage of recruitment, the evaluation of the substantive skills is secondary. Multiple interviews are applied here by the representatives of the firm (the owners included) with the candidate, as well as sensory tests for the assessment of the tea tasting predisposition. The decision to accept a candidate is based to a large extent on the individual experiences, knowledge and astuteness of the recruiters. Additional training is organized for the permanent employees that is connected with an integration trip.

It is worth emphasizing that the process of forming the desired attitudes in an employee is frequently easier if he/she has no sales experience. On the other hand, this is associated with vast outlays on training. If the applicant displays personal predisposition – a high level of personal culture, curiosity, optimism, while also paying attention to aesthetics and has clear aspirations that are in accordance with the philosophy of the brand, then he/she qualifies for the training process.

At the training stage the firm has a multitude of tools that facilitate this process. The first aid tool is training material that is formulated as a compendium. This defines the framework and range of topics, as well as grouping the most important information in a substantive and legible manner. Tips relating to segmentation accruing from the systems of values of clients are attached to the information of a theoretical nature. Sets of exercises for the purpose of testing tea are also run that develop the sensitivity and essential skills in this field. Thanks to this fact, an apprentice is prepared for the sales process as early as at the stage of becoming familiar with the theory that is based on the individual identification of the needs of a client.

The first stage lasts approximately 2 weeks which is run by a manager independently or with the support of a coordinator. The process of becoming familiar with the knowledge is also about gaining a command of the specialized vocabulary and becoming familiar with the everyday duties. This is served by a detailed illustration of the routine activities that are stipulated in the form of a checklist, while also instructions explaining the assumptions of marketing campaigns that are enriched with detailed technical hints, e.g. the arrangements of the decor of the shop.

The complete process of adaptation of an employee lasts for approximately 3 months and is organized in the sales team, which facilitates the process of integration by means of sharing knowledge and common work. The employees that the firm plans to associate with in terms of cooperation are directed to the training centre that is located in one of the showrooms representing Five O'Clock company. This additional course fulfils the complementary function with regard to the complete preparatory process and accelerates the process of becoming familiar with the key people of the firm, including the owners, while also enabling the familiarity of the culture of the organization.

Education, system of training

Five O'Clock specializes in the sale of classic brands of tea. They have a particular impact on the image of the brand that is shaped and associated with the assumptions of the mission. The employees are required to display proficiency in the utilization of the context of knowledge in the procedures of sales. Taking the necessity of ensuring the high quality of the product into account, among other aspects, the freshness, the collection of brands of tea must be replaced several times a year. This is an opportunity to vary the assortment with new interesting types.

From the perspective of twenty years of existence of the trademark Five O'Clock on the market, it is possible to observe that it has come a long way in terms of its development. At the very beginning, bold attempts were made to launch very basic variations of mainly black tea. With the passing of time, an increasing number of more interesting and niche variations were made available for sale. At the beginning of the 21st century, when knowledge about tea in Poland was still not sufficiently propagated, a line of green tea was developed in Five O'Clock. Nowadays however, collectors' items of tea brand collections are formulated that are preciously unique on a worldwide scale.

The presence of rare tea brands provides the pretext to synchronize the marketing action with the seasonal access to some of them. These activities reinforce the position of Five O'Clock as a leader and expert on the market that has a large impact on the preferences and tastes of its clients, as it creates them to a large extent. Likewise, these activities give rise to a wide group of trusting and loyal clients that have an opportunity to develop and mature together with the brand.

The dynamics of change and turnover of tea are forcing the constant process of learning. The delicate sphere of the art of tea tasting, which is filled with nuances requires both experience and expertise. This is difficult to translate to a simple training scheme. The best specialists of this branch are people with many years of experience. In order to inspire employees to increase their qualifications and hone their competences, it has implemented a range of various innovations associated with training programs. One of the tools of activation are the so-called theme panels (personal or online). A range of issues are described here, from the participation of randomly selected people from various positions, empirical experience to tests of tea brands. These trainings are not restricted to the verification of knowledge alone, but are also of assistance for the enrichment and expansion of horizons and arousing creativity.

Brand managers also put in a lot of effort in order to ensure that the conditions for the development of their employees are provided. Every seller has the duty to test the tea brands systematically, which are frequently luxury and very expensive, to which a useful description is created with the aid of auxiliary materials that are useful in the sales process, which are sent as a report for the attention of the owners. If within the firm there is a unit that is more capable and involved, it is invited to the marketing project or training. A similar principle of the organized *cup-tasting* is binding for the coordinating employees, who on an everyday basis do not have direct contact with a client. They reserve at least one hour of their working time in order to jointly taste the brew. This custom then enables the building of mutual understanding, while also integrating employees of various organizational cells and sales outlets, as well as reminding us that the market success of Five O'Clock is based on the useful knowledge of tea.

Reports on the casting process run serve to prepare training scripts. These are prepared by a team of highly involved and educated specialists, whose materials are also applied in the edition of high quality marketing communiques, topical leaflets and descriptions of taste profiles of flavoured tea published in the company shop window. These are issues that are difficult to describe, thus require specific knowledge and creativity.

Rituals

The most mobilizing and integrating custom of the enterprises is that of the meeting of the employees with one of the owners – Mr. Bartosz Siess. He organizes the aforesaid meetings several times per year, or if they are to take on a more ceremonial form in an appropriate place away from the shop. For instance, jubilees of the firm are celebrated in this fashion, where cards and presents are awarded.

During the course of chamber-style visits in a group of an individual sales team, the employees may find out about the following: about the plans and successes of the firm, while also having the possibility of personal talks and joint work. These meetings are not formal visits and do not have an established schedule or plan. In general terms, the manager hosts the main boss as a partner and friend, while paying attention to a friendly atmosphere.

Once a year the managers of the brand Five O'Clock travel to the regions of tea cultivation with the aim of expanding knowledge and experience and becoming familiar with the production processes applied at the plantations. It is very frequent that trips are organized to the tea garden from which the tea was imported to the shops. This exclusive tea reconnaissance is organized by a tea distributor that cooperates with Five O'Clock, thus honouring its strategic business partners. These trips serve to make personal ties with the plantation owners, the employees of the plantation, while also other owners of European tea shops. Up to now, trips have been organized to China, Malaysia, Indonesia, India, Japan. In the edition of 2014, a tea shop expedition was organized to Sri Lanka and Taiwan, in which apart from Five O'Clock, the owners of the Spanish teashop Te Sans & Sans also took part.

Following the subsequent trip, meetings are organized with employees who taste the imported tea, while also watching video recordings, interviews and photos.

Policy of sustainable growth

The company Brzezicki & Siess is a Polish family firm, in which the owners take an active part in the processes of management by providing a wide basis of traditional values. The firm is not subject to external audits and certificates that monitor the implementation of the policy of sustainable growth, or corporate social responsibility (CSR). The creation of the image of the brand, for instance, the model of *before profit obligation* involves the significance of some elements of the concept of CSR which are key and respected in the sphere of building heritage and reinforcing the attributes of the image of the brand as follows: firm with class, while respecting and satisfying clients and being friendly towards employees.

Ethical responsibility lies at the basis of the individual decisions of the managerial staff, while the family-based origins of the firm takes account of the social aspect which shapes the ethical business behaviour, which in turn translates to the relations with the closest stakeholders of the brand: the suppliers, clients and employees. The most important principles include transparency in passing on feedback with relation to the assortment: the labels and direction of the product.

Notifications and requests received from clients are dealt with as priority, while in the case of doubt quality control is resumed immediately. Thanks to the symmetric communication that is binding in the firm, it is possible to provide a client with comprehensive answers and comments in the sales outlets.

Five O'Clock has enjoyed an impeccable reputation and prestige for many years. Recently the firm has been awarded with the certificate „Dobra Marka – jakość, zaufanie, renoma" (Good Brand – quality, trust and renown) in the editions of 2013 and 2014.

The enterprise has developed good relations with the employees, which has borne fruit in terms of the long-term harmonious cooperation. The level of employment is stable, as people seldom resign from work. Unforeseen resignations sometimes occur following the opening of a showroom and are a natural risk that is associated with the expansion of the network.

Rewarding employees

The personnel policy of the firm assumes the building of long-terms relations with the employees. Due to the large requirements, it strives to establish an attractive remuneration system. The firm is of the assumption that by setting high expectations, it must ensure an adequate level of remuneration. Employees that are employed on work contracts may count on higher levels of remuneration with relation to the competition.

The system is simple and is mainly based on the basic salary that is relatively high, which is dependent on the profitability and location of the sales outlets. The effectiveness and norms of work do not constitute the main criteria of evaluation. The application of varying elements of remuneration is avoided as it is acknowledged that a regular salary, by taking account of all the previously generated level of results, builds the feeling of security, while simultaneously implementing harmonious relations in the sales teams. An active salary policy particularly takes the relatively frequent pay rises into consideration, only when there is an objective basis for this.

The remuneration in the case of students is established on an individual basis by the managers and this depends on their level of involvement, creativity, general assessment in terms of cooperation and disposition. The flexibility of procedures enables the establishment of satisfying and fair remuneration.

Apart from the basic remuneration, individually awarded prizes are practiced. Up to now, they have been awarded in the following situations:
- preparation of a training module on a chosen theme (coffee, tea group);
- edition of professional articles, image promotion articles, granting interviews in the media (topic of high level tea and coffee brands is popular, hence the employees are asked for expert opinions);
- representing the firm at meetings with business partners;
- rewarding distinctive attitudes acquired by means of the analysis of secret shopper;
- winning internal competitions.

Awarding such prizes is associated with expressing acknowledgement and distinction for an employee on the part of the superior, thus in essence it is not only of a tangible nature, but an intangible one too.

Some of the employees receive premiums that are dependent on the level of sales. This stimulus is applied in the newly opened and "developing" shops.

There is also the practice of material prizes, which are frequently exclusive brands of tea that the employees receive for, e.g. occasions of a jubilee. The non-financial stimuli are of a supplementary nature, yet are important as they build a tie with the employer. These particularly include the following: a congratulatory letter, a public expression of acknowledgement, allocating ambitious tasks that are frequently individually tailored to the abilities and expectations of the employees, while also a display of respect. In the case of students, there is an arrangement of the work shifts, so as not to disrupt college studies.

Granting people trust and independence at work is motivating, as well as good relations with the superiors.

Good practices

If an employee decides to leave his/her workplace, notification must be made sooner than the statutory period of notice, which provides the superiors with time to prepare the process of recruitment and become involved in its execution. If the decision to resign has been caused by a change in the place of residence, there have been cases of internal transfer in which the firm created the possibility of reconciling individual pursuits and work by helping with the relocation to and equipping of the new place of residence.

The necessary changes accruing from the reorganization (generally speaking rather seldom), the relocation is run in such a way as for the employee not to lose any privileges, including the reduction of remuneration. In fact, it usually remains at least at the hitherto level. Similarly, when a weaker period of time is noted by low results in terms of sales, if there are objective reasons that justify this downward trend and if it is temporary, then the level of the basic remuneration for employees remains the same.

In the case whereby the failure to execute duties is observed, or recurring conflicts, the corrective programs are always initiated if the need arises, which is sometimes preceded by external training assistance (i.e. in the sphere of management or communication). Dismissals are very seldom in terms of action taken by the employer.

Guiding the employees through change (implementation of organizational change, new systems of work) is preceded by long talks and meetings.

Discussions or mediations are continued to the moment of gaining an agreement. Solutions are not imposed top-down, if the employees neither accept them, nor understand them.

The sales teams have their own stabilized and set work tempo in the arrangement of shift work. Periods requiring greater efforts and overtime (e.g. months of the high season) are known in advance. Decisions relating to the need for additional support are left to the discretion of each employee and he/she most frequently declare such a need.

In the periods requiring more intensive work, while also the implementation of overtime, for instance before Christmas, employees are asked to present their possibilities and preferences two months previously (number of hours, preferred shifts, etc.). following thorough analysis that is carried out jointly, it is usually possible to solve the problem together. Thanks to this, work is run in an atmosphere that is undisrupted by conflict.

In the face of the challenges of the future

"A brand is built slowly, over many years" – is a saying by Bernard Arnault[29] which is an accurate reflection of the motto that is illuminated by the tasters of the brand of Five O'Clock. The development of the firm is determined to a significant extent by very competent and creative people who build the "*brand personality*". Such people have been and shall continue to be supported as they exert a great impact on the market position and sales.

A certain challenge is that of the style of management. In the preliminary and early phase of the development of the firm, the owners had a dominating impact on the management, integration of people, trust, culture and vibe of the working environment. Everything, particularly the success of the firm indicates that they did this well. In terms of the growth of the firm Five O'Clock, by transforming from a small enterprise to a medium-sized one, by the nature of things this influence should be on the wane. It should be reducing as the amount of work, tasks, problems, etc. are becoming excessively large given the possibilities of even the most capable and most hardworking owners and management. It should also be reducing due to the fact that adult people have been employed by them and have been professionally prepared (at least some) for more ambitious tasks with greater creativity and independence;

---

[29] A French businessman, who was born in 1945 and whose career started in family firms. Since 1984, he has been running the LVMH group, while possessing shares in the company Christian Dior S.A. According to "Time" magazine, he is listed among the Top 100 Most Influential People in the world.

whereas if they do not display such competences they shall be frustrated, while some may resign or at least stagnate in terms of development.

In every organization that transforms from a small enterprise to a medium-sized enterprise and later to a large one, there are the so-called crises of growth which occur that are frequently caused by the difficulty of the owners and managers to refrain from the tactic of deciding about everything and controlling all the details to the gradual empowerment of the best and most reliable people. This may signify the gradual restriction of self-involvement in strategic issues and those of neuralgic significance, but not all issues as there may be people in the organization who could do it better, if not now, then perhaps in the near future. If such people appear, this is obviously a real reason to be proud in the case of the founder/owner, as it is to his/her merit. Nevertheless, now is the time to be consistent and move forward. This does not mean that the hitherto pillar of the firm may rest on his/her laurels. This may signify that he / she deserves to work less, following the change in the division of work, competences and responsibilities.

In no firm do all the changes become implemented in an entirely smooth manner. In Five O'Clock, the example of implementation that reveals certain (natural) tensions against the background of professional ambitions and the division of competences was the policy in the sphere of standardizing the *visual merchandising*. For several years, the arrangement of the decor of the shops has been regulated by written guidelines, while their correctness in terms of execution and the final results have been thoroughly analysed. The aim was the cohesive identification of the brand in the physical environment. Nevertheless, these directives were perceived by several employees as being a restriction on creative freedom. Convincing them towards the new principles required time and a multitude of compromises.

In the face of the intricacy of the processes of management, it became a necessity to reorganize the professional roles in the organization, as well as the optimization of the coordination of the sales network and further professionalization of management. This process is still continuing. However, the decision to appoint managers and specialists from the external environment was not taken, but rather the closest co-workers were promoted to the key positions (outside of the family), who are familiar with the niche domain of the firm by investing in their education (studies, workshops, training).

In the development of the network, the policy of *small steps* was applied, while each opening was associated with the efforts of the entire organization and a high level of uncertainty. In the new sales teams resignations from work occurred more frequently than in the implemented sales outlets. Likewise, it was also observed that the new employees find the perception of culture and acceptance of the binding customs particularly difficult.

Due to the further plans of expansion for the network, it is planned to implement a code of ethics that shall sum up all the issues that have been elaborated on and which are significant for the brand up to now. Its implementation is planned for the current year of 2015.

We would like to express our gratitude toms. Ania Sroka, PR Manager in the firm Five O'Clock, for the discussion and materials made available, while in particular for the excellent contribution to the preparation of this case study.

Izabela Stańczyk
Tadeusz Oleksyn

4. DELPHI AUTOMOTIVE S.A. – DRIVE VALUES
CASE STUDY

1. General information on concern

The concern of Delphi Automotive is a leading worldwide supplier of electronic solutions and systemic technologies that have numerous applications, mainly in the automotive sector. The mission of the concern is to make their products (in particular passenger cars and trucks) safer, stronger and more efficient, while also better at communication with drivers and the world by means of equipping them with advanced technologies that serve these purposes. Products and technologies are prepared and the production of electrical and electronic appliances are executed that are particularly associated with the following: petrol and diesel driver engines, systems of safety for drivers and passengers, systems controlled from the steering wheel and from a console, electrical equipment, switches and fuel steam absorbers, ventilation systems, air-conditioning, cockpit heating, theft prevention systems, while also charges (alarms, immobilizers). Advanced technologies are prepared and tested that facilitates the improvement of the technical parameters, as well as miniaturization and the extremely long product life of the elements manufactured here, which in the case of car electronics is a particularly worthy acknowledgement.

The concern possesses over 100 production plants and 15 technical centres in 33 countries that employ a combined total of 100,000 workers. The headquarters are located in the town of Gillingham in England, while there are subsidiaries in Luxembourg (Bascharage), Brazil (Sao Paulo), China (Shanghai) and in the USA (Troy, Michigan).[30]

The modern technological solutions provided by Delphi may be found in all the leading brands of cars in the world.

As Rodney O'Neal, the Chief Executive Officer says, "Delphi is exceptionally focused on creating value for the shareholder by means of ensuring safe,

---

[30] See: http://www.delphi.com/about/; http://www.delphikrakow.pl/ [27.11.2014].

ecological products that fulfil the needs of our clients via the high quality of production and operational perfection."[31]

The data relating to the net revenue from sales and net profit have been presented in Table 1.

Table 1. Financial indicators for Delphi Automotive for the period 2011–2013

Specification	2013	2012	2011
Net revenue from sales (millions of dollars)	16.463	15.519	16.041
Net profit (millions of dollars)	89	83	78

Source: http://investor.delphi.com/investors/financial-information/financial-overview/ default.aspx [27.11.2014].

Delphi Automotive pays particular attention to the quality and reliability of its products and this value is placed in first position among the most highly valued. Delphi is an engineering and highly innovative firm. In December 2007, the American Chamber of Commerce distinguished Delphi for its "Perfection in Innovations".

Personnel team of Board of Concern:
- John A. Krol – Board Chairman (since 2009),
- Gary L. Cowger,
- Nicholas M. Donofrio,
- Mark P. Frissora,
- Rajiv L. Gupta,
- J. Randall MacDonald,
- Sean O. Mahoney,
- Rodney O'Neal,
- Thomas W. Sidlik,
- BerndWiedemann,
- Lawrence A. Zimmerman.

2. Delphi Automotive in Poland

Delphi Automotive has invested over 380 bn USD dollars in Poland both in terms of production, as well as in R & D technologies. Delphi currently employs over 4,000 workers in four manufacturing plants – in Jeleśnia, Błonie, Ostrów Wielkopolski and Gdańsk, while also two modern technical centres that have been operating for over ten years in Cracow and Ostrów Wielkopol-

---

[31] See: http://www.delphi.com [27.11.2014].

ski. Polish engineers have been listing Delphi as one of the leading employers they would like to work in for years.[32]

As opposed to a multitude of foreign concerns that moved their production to Poland from the 1990s without engaging Polish engineers in the designing work, construction and technological work, Delphi creates conditions for them for this type of activity.

Delphi Poland S.A. is a laureate of the award for the Best Foreign Investor. In 2003, it was awarded with the honorary emblem of "Investor w Kapitsa Ludic" (Investor in Human Capital).

Plant in Jeleśnia

The production plant in Jeleśnia (province of Silesia) is located near the town of Żywiec in the south of Poland, which is close to the borders with the Czech Republic and Slovakia. It was established in 1994. The main activities involve the production of electric cables and wire harnesses, as well as module for fire-optic cables for the automotive industry and the medical industry, in the majority of cases for export. The plant is in possession of the ISO 14001 and ISO/TS 16949 certificates. They have received honourable distinction from Volvo for the quality of its products and the implementation of the latest technological solutions, as well as the Q1 certificate from the Ford / Volvo concern.

Plant in Błonie near Warsaw

The plant in Błonie near Warsaw has existed since 1998. Its main products are as follows: systems of powering an engine, shock absorbers, braking systems, exhaust systems, fuel power systems and fuel vapour canisters, as well as air filters.

The plant is in possession of the ISO/TS 16949 and ISO 14001 certificates, while the factory also received the Q1 quality certificate from the Ford / Volvo concern.

Plant in Ostrów Wielkopolski

The plant was established in 1997 and manufactures modules for engine cooling (CRFM), modules of air-conditioning (HVAC), coolers, capacitors, radiators, condensers and charge air coolers. The products of the plant are assembled into the car models of the leading brands. An important client is also the market of spare parts.

In the Delphi plant of Ostrów Wielkopolski, there is a group of stores of engineers that deal with the designing and testing of heat exchangers. Within

---

[32] Research was carried out on the engineers in the period of 2005–2011 by the Databank of Engineers.

the last few years, these engineers have submitted over 25 patents. The plant which possesses both the ISO 14001 certificate, as well as the ISO/TS 16949 certificate received the Q1 quality certificate from the Ford / Volvo concern.

In 2012, the condenser prepared by the innovative team of the plant at Ostrów Wielkopolski was based on the technology of Multi-Port Folded Tube Condenser (MFTC), which was honoured as the laureate of the prestigious PACE award that is awarded by Automotive News. This new technology enabled producers to avail of the greater offer of materials forth production of more reliable condensers that are light, resistant to corrosion, while also featured by better thermal properties.

Plant in Gdańsk
A plant that was built on a greenfield site that became part of the organization of Delphi in 2001, which produces a wide range of electrical and electronic appliances for vehicles, including switches for many producers of cars. The plant in Gdańsk, which within the last few years has expanded its surface area and also possesses the ISO 14001, ISO/TS 16949 and OSHAS 18001 certificates.

3. Research and Development Centre in Cracow

Cracow has long been perceived by the management of the Delphi concern as a significant scientific and academic centre, which it acknowledged was worth availing of the potential of Polish engineers. Following the opening of the centre in July 2000, the headquarters of Delphi in Warsaw, Poland were also moved to Cracow. Currently, the centre employs over 1,000 workers, mostly engineers, of which many of them have undergone training in the Delphi centres abroad.

The R & D centres are constantly expanding, while more and more new research projects are being executed. The leading field in the Cracow Centre of Delphi is advanced car electronics. In November 2000, the Centre of Software Development was established where engineers design software for the automotive industry as the car of tomorrow shall be even more computerized. This assumes a significant increase in the number of engineers and software programmers in this centre in the near future. Further areas that are being intensively developed and modernized in the Cracow R & D Centre are the engineering of wire harnesses, switches and fuel vapour canisters.

"Today we do not have to prove that it was worth moving the R & D work to Poland. Having the trademark that we have built up over the past ten years or more, we are ready to take on further projects and bring new technologies under the roof of the Cracow Centre. The Technical Centre of Delphi is in search of both the best graduates, as well as candidates with experience from different fields" – such a statement may be read on the main website of the company.[33]However much Delphi is a firm that is deeply rooted in the automotive industry, candidates for a particular position also come from outside this sector.

3. System of quality assurance in Delphi

Producers of cars while wanting to ensure the appropriate quality of their goods, demanded the components and technologies, as well as tight qualitative norms that are characteristic for the automotive industry for many years from their suppliers. The suppliers that have many clients, gained the required certificates in the particular countries, which was a complicated process. Hence, in agreement with the world producers of the automotive industry, the technical specifications of ISO/TS 16949 were prepared, which combines the norms of the automotive sectors of particular countries in unison. Possessing the system of quality management in accordance with the aforesaid specifications certifies to the high quality of goods and prestige of the company. The Polish entities of Delphi (plants, technical centres) have implemented the system of ISO/TS 16949 over the past few years. Since 2013, the Technical Centre in Cracow has an integrated system of quality management that encompasses the requirements of ISO/TS16949 (system certified since 2002); ISO14001 (Environmental Management – system certified since 2006) and implemented in 2013 with the system of Work Safety and Hygiene according to OHSAS18001.[34]

4. Constructive statement and less unequivocal practices

The Cracow branch of Delphi has prepared a "set of reasons", for which it is worth commencing cooperation with them. It is possible to find the following entries in this set:

1. We are a strong, stable and prospering firm that has powerful know-how resources at its disposal, while also an experienced and talented team.
2. We run innovative projects forth leading world producers of cars.

---

[33] See: http://www.delphikrakow.pl [27.11.2014].
[34] Material from the website: http://www.delphikrakow.pl/5,o-nas,71 [2.11.2014].

3. We rely on Polish technical thought – we have been investing in Polish specialists for years.
4. We offer competitive remuneration and modern working conditions.
5. We ensure ongoing contact with the latest technologies.
6. We take care of new challenges for our employees.
7. We ensure an attractive social package that includes among other aspects, additional health insurance, vouchers for cultural events and sporting activity.
8. We create a modern culture of work that is based on professional communication with employees and mutual trust (flexitime).
9. We take care of the appropriate and friendly atmosphere of work.
10. We belong to the group of firms that are "socially involved."[35]

In the opinions of bloggers that comment on websites, they are more differentiated in terms of their tone and purport.

5. Apprenticeships and training periods in the firm

Due to the type of activities and the location of the Cracow branch, Delphi Corporation offers special apprenticeships and training periods for students from various colleges and specializations. In the past few years, first and foremost during the summer months, apprenticeships in the Technical Centre in Cracow were participated in by scores of students and pupils. Similar programs are run each year. Every person that is accepted for apprenticeships is allocated a specific task to execute within the framework of the commercial projects or R & D projects realized. The apprentice has his/her own mentor, who assigns the tasks, supervises their execution and offers support in technical and organizational issues. The mentors are experienced employees of a given department that are well informed about the structure of the firm as a whole, as well as the characteristic managerial competences at a high level.

Examples of apprenticeships realized in the firm are as follows:
- expansion of the functionality of the low level for DPS (Digital Power Supply),
- universal tool for communicating via serial port,
- fast monitor of IIC bus,
- EMC scanner,
- universal environment for automatic generation of test scripts based on the MOST bus and CAN bus,
- application monitoring GPS parameters facilitating navigational tests while driving a car with the prototype multimedia system.

---

[35] See: http://www.delphikrakow.pl/co-oferujemy [27.11.2014].

Apprenticeships are offered to the following teams:
- designing software,
- designing electronics,
- designing mechanical elements in CAD system,
- testing and verification of software,
- research laboratory and product validation,
- departments relating to products,
- departments relating to quality,
- other teams when vacancies arise.

Conditions of realization of apprenticeship training are as follows:
- apprenticeships last a minimum 1 calendar month,
- the possibility exists of undergoing apprenticeship both during the academic year and during vacations,
- following completion of the apprenticeship a certificate is issued confirming its realization and references.

If a person that is searching for apprenticeship has not found a place that is appropriate and wants to undertake cooperation with a firm, then he/she may apply for the so-called "General apprenticeship". If possible, the places are searched for which match the profile of the candidate.

Current offers of apprenticeship and training periods:[36]
- Student apprenticeship – generally;
- Student apprenticeship – corporate function;
- Programmer – training period;
- Trainee in Software Designers team;
- Supply Chain Team Trainee;
- Purchasing Assistant;
- Trainee in team of engineers and mechanics;
- EMEA Customs Trainee;
- Trainee of DFMEA;
- Business Analyst Assistant.

6. Significance of values in management and priorities

The firm indicates the importance of economic and non-economic values in the management of an organization to an identical degree. Ethical and cultural values are acknowledged to be significant for the realization of the mission, aims and image of the firm, as well as the promoted culture; they are appreciated and sufficiently displayed in the management system of the firm. The direction of activities and procedures in business are driven by the

---

[36] See: http://www.delphikrakow.pl/205,praktyki-i-staze [16.12.2014].

so-called Absolute Perfection, which specifies the goal, achievement, method of activity, while also defining control, the way of activity of people and their style of work, as well as specifying the awards.

Delphi possesses the code of ethical procedure in business, which is a set of principles of honest proceedings that are binding for employees of Delphi worldwide. It is termed DRIVE; and this acronym is read as follows:

- D – Diversity: perceiving the success of a firm in terms of both the diversity of the skills of the employees, as well as the creation of various teams.
- R – Respect: trust and respect are (and are to be) maintained at every level of cooperation between the employees, clients, suppliers, the interested entities on the basis of the legislative regulations.
- I – Integrity: each task is to be realized in the spirit of the values of ethics, honesty and integrity of activities.
- V – Value: the values of a firm constitute the foundation of cooperation at various levels, both within the firm and outside.
- E – Excellence: the success of a firm in the future depends on the uncompromising adherence to the vision of a firm and pursuit of absolute perfection.[37]

Nevertheless, although according to the declarations all the values are important, it would seem that <u>a particular significance is attached to quality and innovativeness, as well as the chosen economic values in Delphi</u>.

As regards quality, the priority in this sphere is confirmed by the hard facts – the certificates. The Polish entities of Delphi (factories, technical centres) have implemented the ISO/TS 16949 system over the past few years. Since 2013, the Technical Centre in Cracow possesses an integrated system of quality management encompassing the requirements of the ISO/TS16949 norm (this system has been certified since 2002); ISO14001 (Environmental Management – this system has been certified since 2006), as well as the system of Work Safety and Hygiene according to OHSAS18001, which was implemented in 2013. In addition to this, it is possible to mention the certificates from Ford and Volvo, the awards received for both quality and innovativeness. The most important confirmation of high quality is the continuation of the cooperation with the entire worldwide motoring elite.

Quality and innovativeness are placed at the top of the pile of economic, competence and managerial values. References to the perception of economic values in Delphi are presented in a few sentences below.

---

[37] See: http://delphi.com/pdf/Delphi-Code-Of-Conduct.pdf [27.11.2014].

7. Importance and preferred economic values

The significance of profit over both long and short periods of time is placed in a group of several of the most important values in the company, alongside customer satisfaction (in Delphi there is an indication of the purposefulness of "exceeding the expectations of clients").

Competitiveness and innovativeness are perceived as values that are equal to the former. It is acknowledged here that they are decisive to a fundamental degree in terms of survival and development and are strongly promoted. In this firm, the improvements proposed by the employees are supported and availed of, including the field of work safety and hygiene. One of the examples of the so-called program of suggestions is where each employee may alert to the threat of accidents, as well as provide suggestions relating to the improvement of work safety and hygiene by putting them into a special box. Suggestions that are implemented lead to the employees receiving awards.

Efficiency is obviously of neuralgic significance in the automotive industry, as even the largest concerns and prospering concerns may find themselves on the verge of bankruptcy in a short period of time. This has been experienced by even General Motors of late, which for almost 70 years was the unquestioned world leader of the automotive sector, from which in fact 1998 Delphi separated in 1998.

From the viewpoint of efficiency, the concern itself is evaluated, as well as the particular plants, teams and managerial staff. It is striving towards the increase in efficiency in all the areas, which may be controversial. In the opinion of the authors, increasing the efficiency where it is already very high may not be a good idea and may pose a threat to the future. It is better to concentrate on the "narrow passages / bottlenecks" and on areas where it clearly too low.

8. Chosen non-economic values

Competence and developmental values – such as in particular professionalism, knowledge and skills, professional experience, skill of preparing and undertaking shrewd decisions, efficiency of activities, ability and propensity towards professional development are perceived as important, albeit their significance is varied for the particular groups of positions. The significance of these competences rises in the case of key specialists and managerial staff, especially in the areas of key significance. In the executive positions, particularly where work is relatively simple, they are of clearly lower significance.

In the production plants of Delphi, there is a challenge that is generally known in similar environments–counteracting the monotony of work and ensuring the professional development of people that perform relatively simple and repetitive work, albeit frequently at a fast pace that requires skill and certain psycho-technical predisposition. In theory, people should not perform this kind of work long, but rotate in terms of positions and become oriented towards work of richer elements, while also more difficult, better paid, changing the work no less than every three years and increasing qualifications on multiple occasions. In the opinion of the authors however, in practice difficulties occur on both the side of the employers, as well as on the side of the employees. In the case of the employers, such an "ascending rotation" may be hard to fulfil due to the structure of all the work that is to be done in a factory. If a robotized or automated job is unprofitable or difficult for technical reasons, the amount of work is usually more complex than simple, which naturally speaking restricts the possibility of running such a personnel policy in the plant. Furthermore, running planned rotation requires a certain organizational effort and goodwill.

Likewise, on the part of the employees difficulties may occur as not everyone treats professional work as a primary concern, nor does everyone want to develop or participate in management, etc. There are those for whom the real and fascinating life starts from the moment of leaving the factory, in which work is merely treated as an economic necessity and do not want to devote more attention to it.

A certain compromise may be the increased share of teamwork, in which people rotate in terms of work positions, thus avoiding the constant over-exertion of the same body muscles, tendons and joints, while also breaking up monotony and developing from a professional viewpoint, at least to a certain degree. Within the framework of our project, we did not visit the production facilities of Delphi, during the course of which there would have been a possibility of running talks with the employees and leaders of the teams, or analysis of the scope of autonomy of these teams and development intentions associated with them. Hence, we do not know to what extent this direction of evolution is possible in the plants of Delphi (where teamwork is applied anyway) and how realistic the opportunities of professional development are and the execution of the concept of a learning organization on a greater scale. Undoubtedly, certain possibilities provide changes to products and technologies rather frequently, which signify the necessity of science, even without rotation in terms of the positions.

The issue of the autonomy of work and the insufficient professional development does not exist and is at least significantly less in the scientific and research centres.

The determination in terms of the sphere of environmental protection in Delphi would seem to be great, which is confirmed by the possession of the certificate for the ISO 14001 norm. However, the issue of involvement in environmental protection was not analysed in closer detail.

9. Sustainable growth and corporate social responsibility

Sustainable growth in Delphi Polska is perceived as running business activities in a way that is not in contrast to the requirements of environmental protection and the interests of the local communities. Environmental protection is perceived in a pragmatic way as respecting the standards of the ISO 14001 norm. Such a norm was implemented together with a formal certificate, while the production plants and the R & D centres are subject to external audits.

Sustainable growth may be understood in a broader context as not only care for the good of the natural environment, but also the pursuit of greater sustainability between professional work and personal and family life of the employees and their social involvement, which in turn, requires first and foremost time and strength; whereas if the employees devote themselves to their work to an excessive degree (also in a dimension that is longer than the nominal one), then the time and strength would not suffice to practice the non-professional roles appropriately.

The scope of work in terms of overtime in Delphi is not wide, thus the threat on the part of the employer associated with the violation of this balance is generally speaking, slight at best. Another neuralgic area is that of the norm of work-temporary and efficiency-wise. We did not have the possibility of checking whether they have a technically justified norm. Several people expressed the opinion on blogs that the norms are overly strict, but not all bloggers share this view. This is of course not evidence in itself, but no more than an indication that it is worth analysing the norms of work from time to time from the viewpoint of adherence to norms that are technically justified with regard to changes in the products and technologies that are rather frequent in this sector.

Social responsibility is also involvement on behalf of the local communities, including among other aspects, people in need. Delphi company has been running operations in support of the local community for many years. In the period of 2010–2013, it was a partner of the Foundation "United Way" Polska and joined the program of Partnership for Children, whose aim is to support the development of young people coming from poor families. Thanks to the involvement of teams from the plants of Delphi company in Poland, as well as the implementation of the voluntary service, it was possible to help scores of children that are charges of the branches of the partnership foundation.

10. Common values for employees

In the company, there are values specified which are expected of the general group of managers and employees, herein referred to as corporate values. We did not analyse to what degree they are known among the managers and employees.

The following corporate values have been adopted:
- high quality of products, processes, work, relations;
- effectiveness;
- responsibility;
- innovativeness /creativity;
- trust;
- cooperation.

No particular value has been stipulated as the most important in Delphi Polska. Surely the value which is nearest to the first position is that of quality.

In propagating the systems of values, the corporate tools of communication are of assistance, which include the following: the Intranet, newsletters and letters to employees.

11. Respected values in personnel policy of firm

The ties between values and the personnel policy in Delphi Polska look different in its various areas.

With relation to the recruitment and selection of staff, apart from competence requirements that are expected for a given position, the people running the process of recruitment and selection of candidates for work also take into consideration the values known to them that are expected in Delphi. There are no elaborated and tested tools that would be a facilitation in terms of such procedure. During the course of periodical assessment and promotion of values they are taken into consideration with reference to the majority of professional groups and employees.

The relations of value with the system of remuneration are presented depending on the values. The strongest is surely the value taken into account, which is justice. The majority of managers try to manage professionally and have a developed sense of justice, while the system of remuneration, especially the part called the tariff system is so constructed as for the relations of payment with the type and results of work to be as objective and fair as possible. A lot depends on the appropriate system of work evaluation; it is always something which is not necessarily analytical, nor in point form, which is frequently associated with work evaluation. However, we had the possibilities of a closer view into these systems in the particular workplaces and the correctness of work qualification. This would require a separate and quite time-consuming research.

Premiums and awards are usually not (and actually should not be) associated with values, but rather mainly with the results of work and the real merits. However, sometimes rewards and penalties are influenced by <u>critical events</u>(particularly positive and particularly bad attitudes, behaviour and neglect), which result from the defence of the acknowledged values, or their clear violation. In such cases, the supervisors may feel discouraged or provoked to take tangible action.

Some activities of Delphi are oriented towards the promotion of added values. These are as follows:

- the annual "Week of Perfection" combines the promotion of the values of the concern with the integration of the employees; integration outings/trips take place here, various types of sporting events, entertainment events, etc.;
- events directed towards the employees and their families: a family picnic, events of the type of "Santa Claus", etc. may be noted in terms of strengthening common values, balancing professional work and family life;
- organizing and supporting sporting events, as well as the participation in competitions are a stimulus for a healthy lifestyle and care for the psycho-physical condition;
- deliberate auxiliary action (frequently initiated separately by the employees and supported by the firm) strengthen the values, which are subsidiarity, kindness and solidarity.

12. Final comments

Delphi Poland S.A. is an interesting example of an engineering firm that respects and promotes values, while also applying their advanced operationalization. This is particularly visible in the sphere of values which is the broadly understood concept of quality, especially products and technologies, while also the organization of work, relations, competences, etc. The particular importance of quality is understandable in the automotive sector, where the safety and reliability of the operations of the products are of key importance.

High quality is associated with (and supported by) innovativeness. Numerous awards and other displays of acknowledgement from the car producers and other organizations from all around the world attest to the high level of importance of this value in Delphi – not in terms of declarations, but in reality.

A key value is also efficiency. The economic results attained confirm that it is successfully promoted and executed both in terms of the scale of the concern (albeit in the past there were certain crises), as well as in Poland.

Striving towards high quality and efficiency may be easier in conditions of the simultaneously efficient endeavours towards good working conditions and the level of satisfaction of the managers and employees. This requires the harmonization of activities in both of these spheres – in tangible and economic, as well as humanistic–psychological areas. Large concentration on the former may draw attention away from the latter. Naturally speaking, the good working conditions alone and care for people do not guarantee good tangible and economic results. It is worth viewing the former and the latter, as well as striving towards the mutual connection of both of these spheres.

The objective and great difficulty is to ensure professional development and satisfaction among employees (from work, its conditions and atmosphere, earnings) in conditions that involve a large number of work tasks that are relatively simple and repeatable in production plants in conditions of the necessity of adhering to the technological regimes. The satisfaction of the employees of course depends on a multitude of factors – both easier and more difficult to accomplish. The following are relatively easy and possible to fulfil without large outlays: the style of managing an organization, as well as the styles of running the particular line managers, which has an impact on the feeling of employees and the general vibe at work. Perhaps it would be better to evaluate the state of affairs and possibly support the managers in terms of moderation of their individual styles of leadership, where it is indicated and where they see such a need themselves. On the other hand, it is worth reinforcing the ties between the content and results of work and the earnings of the employees– thus avoiding the creation of systems that are excessively aggressive, or disintegrating for the environment.

We would like to express our gratitude to the experts of Delphi Automotive Polska for actively participating in the formation of this study program, particularly Mrs. Anna Bodzioch, Recruitment Specialist and Mrs. Izabela Kaczyńska, HR Manager.

SECTION THREE

CHOSEN AXIOLOGICAL ISSUES

Contents

Andrzej Herman

1. CONTEMPORARY ECONOMIC AXIOLOGY AND ITS RELATIONS WITH THE MANAGEMENT OF ECONOMIC VALUE

Nowadays people know the price of everything and the value of nothing.
Oscar Wilde, *Portrait of Dorian Gray**

1. General and economic axiology

Axiology is a notion that is derived from the Greek language and consists of two parts as follows: the first one that is defined as *axios*, namely something which has value and thanks to this it is valuable, while the second one is derived from the word *logos*, which signifies reason, but also theory and science. Axiology is a theory of values that however have strong relations with life and practice, both in a singular dimension and in a wider notion. The values that we profess, how we perceive them and what significance they hold for us are a reflection of us in terms of who we are, what we do and why we do not do other things, what we aim for, how we react, what we accept and what arouses our dissent, etc.

The division into general and economic axiology is not accepted on a wider scale. For the purposes of this work, it has been acknowledged that as there is a multitude of various values that may be arranged in different groups, while the subject of detailed interest shall be economic values, it would be convenient to apply the division of "general axiology," relating to the values as a whole, whereas the "economic values" are narrowed down to the economic values. In our era, economic values such as efficiency, profitability, effectiveness, performance, competitiveness, innovativeness, as well as others are perceived to be very important. The economy, employment, economic activity and prosperity are deemed to be particularly important. In other eras, both earlier and perhaps later ones, the hierarchy of the groups has been and per-

---

* Quote from Raj Patel, *Wartość niczego. Jak przekształcić społeczeństwo rynkowe i na nowo zdefiniować demokrację*, Muza S.A., Warszawa 2010.

haps still is different. Of course, in the search for these answers it is worth adding "important for whom". It has always been the case that the defined values are more important for some people, social stratum or societies as a whole, whereas less important or even quite unimportant for others. This aspect is variable over time and is dependent on the constantly evolving way of perceiving the changing world by means of the changing people and their experiences.

The historical view of axiology indicated its relations with ethics ("ethos" – a Greek custom, analysis of morality). It is also necessary to mention here that economics as a science also arose out of the basis of morality and ethics (assuming that ethics is the science of morality). The subject matter of the research on axiology is the general theory of values and valuation. In precise terms, its analytical scope relates to the search for the essence of all values (including economic ones), the criteria of values and their gradation, as well as methods of valuation, including the attempts to quantify them.

Axiology is a science that borders on the theoretical and applied sciences, while all the added value viewed in terms of its perspective is the fundamental criteria for the assessment of the human attitudes, behaviour and activities. Likewise, it also relates to the theoretical and practical axiology, while also the axiological technologies. In the nature of things, it is a category that is of a varying nature as it is to an enormous extent dependent on the constantly evolving manner of perceiving the changing world by people.

Axiology is the general philosophy of values, by means of which the attempts to acquire the most adequate experience/image of the changing world in terms of reality are undertaken. As it is not of a static nature, thus the principal development trends should be illustrated and accounted for.

Axiology is an important part of philosophy. Since the times of Plato to contemporary times, it has been distinguished within the framework of three overriding types of values (*summum bonum* from Latin, which means the greatest good): good, beauty and the truth. Simultaneously, two types of existence may be distinguished as follows: (1) those that are part of nature and are not dependent on mankind; (2) those that are dependent on mankind and have a practical and social dimension as they are the result of its varied activities.

The processes of managing undoubtedly lead to the latter category. Their foundation in the axiological layer is the fact that only recently has the general notion of the philosophy of management began to be used. As acknowledged by Tadeusz Oleksyn, this is a multi-dimensional definition and constantly controversial. "Filozofia zarządzania wyraża stosunek zarządzających do kluczowych kwestii, takich jak istota i sens zarządzania, efektywność, zysk i dywidenda, relacje z interesariuszami i menedżerami nawzajem. Jest to pewna ogólna orientacja. Sprawia, że zarządzanie staje się bardziej wy-

raziste, a jego kierunek określają nie tylko cele. Stanowi wyraz wartości wy-
znawanych przez zarządzających, ich wewnętrznych przekonań, stosunku do
ludzi i do siebie. Ukazuje priorytety – to, co dla zarządzających ma szczegól-
ne znaczenie"[1] (The philosophy of management expresses the relation of the
management staff to the key issues such as the essence and sense of management, efficiency, profit and dividends, the mutual relations between the
stakeholders and the managers. It is a certain general orientation. It leads to
the case whereby management becomes more clear and its direction is not
only defined by its aims. It constitutes an expression of the values professed
by the management staff, their internal beliefs, relations with people and to
themselves. It illustrates the priorities – what is of significant meaning for the
management staff).

Economic axiology is a certain base for the theories and practices of management. Thanks to this, it is possible to speak of philosophy or the philosophies of management, which by means of the experiences drawn from the
practices of management are becoming the foundation for further theoretical
generalization. Hence, we are faced with feedback in itself that translates to
the relation between what is to be found at the higher levels and what is to
be found at the micro-economic level, while also the relations between economic theory and practice.

It is worth drawing attention to the fact that it is most frequently the practice of management at all its levels which overtakes theory. This is a situation
whereby the theoretical generalization moves in time as it comes to pass only
after the accumulation of sufficient empirical material.[2] Thus, as a result, the
movement in time of the academic theoretical generalization with relation
to practices. This is in accordance with the observations of Max Weber who
stated that the practical evaluation of any phenomenon as in its merit for rejection or approval/valuation is only possible to execute after a certain period
of time.

Up until recently, axiology developed in terms of conditions of acceptance
of the fixed values, criteria of valuation and norms that arose out of philosophy and ethics, thus initially constituting unity. During ancient times the two
most brilliant minds of Europe of the period – Plato and Aristotle, undertook
attempts to create all syntheses in which values were of significant meaning.[3]
The synthesis of Plato was the result of the humanist orientation in terms of
the notion and spirit he saw in the structure of existence. Plato distinguished

---

[1] *Filozofia a zarządzanie*, red. T. Oleksyn, Wolters Kluwer Business, Warszawa 2013,
pp. 44–45.
[2] Consulting firms have the fastest and best access to this material, but are not inclined
to make this accumulated knowledge and experience available to the academic world very
quickly.
[3] Values were expressed by such notions as ideas and virtues.

many notions and their worth was perceived by him to be hierarchical, while the highest notion was that of good in his opinion, while virtue the highest justice.[4]

In the case of Aristotle the greatest good was *Eudaimonia*, which may be understood both as perfection, as well as the greatest goal and happiness associated with rational activity and reason. The happiness of man has a close relation with his choices, albeit choices illustrate the relation with precious values. Eudaimonia was a notion that referred to the unit level and not the wider social one. This was associated with the pursuit of attaining such an optimum that a given man is able to attain. Nevertheless, a man cannot live on notions alone and the needs of the spirit must also give way to practical activities. This refers to the fact of doing this sensibly and in accordance with ethical virtues.[5]

The bond of the values and the practical side of life, as well as usefulness was not frequent among the Greek philosophers. Nevertheless, certain relations of this type were possible to find, as apart from Aristotle, there were also those among the sophists, epicureans or stoics. In terms of the sophists, especially Protagoras, drawing attention to usefulness was associated with their practicism, sensualism, conventionalism and conviction that the ethical norms are mainly the result of social agreements. Epicureans evaluated moral values from the viewpoint of the usefulness achieved, particularly pleasure. They emphasized the natural joys of life, more spiritual pleasures than carnal pleasures, while postulating on the restraint from such pleasures that could lead to bad consequences for a person and others. Stoics broadly defined virtue (both as good and happiness), by postulating involvement in good things and those within the sphere of our possibilities of activity and indifference with regard to the events which we have no influence on. They emphasized the necessity of life in harmony with nature, both in terms of nature with its laws, as well as the natural course of events and fulfilling our obligations.

The obligation and responsibility were particularly displayed by Immanuel Kant in the 18th century when he advocated the deontology and its specific motto – "Do what you should, because you should". He felt that the fundamental axiological dilemma is not associated with instrumental values (usefulness), but with values that he termed "inbred". Indeed, he was of the opinion that the morality of a given deed was decided by selflessness (obligation), which was connected with the "imperative duty".

In the18th century, the trend associated with usefulness was strengthened by utilitarianism, particularly by Jeremy Bentham and John Stewart Mill. Utilitarianism was to a significant extent the continuation of the epicurean

---

[4] W. Tatarkiewicz, *Historia filozofii*, PWN, Warszawa 1982, t. 1, pp. 82, 87.
[5] W. Tatarkiewicz, *op. cit.*, pp. 118–119.

culture, albeit the emphasis was primarily placed on a broader social context and not only a unit level. The search for a possibly favourable proportion between the good and bad effects of various decisions and activities, which is close to the perception of the economist that avails of the balance so willingly, but which is more difficult to accept via ethics.[6]

In the aftermath of Kant, the level of interest in the philosophy of values weakened and the significance of the naturalist ethical trend began to increase, which reduced values to the subjective emotion. Such a perception of values had and still has its practical consequences. As a result, it could for instance develop as a behavioural trend in social sciences, which even nowadays increasingly emphasizes its presence in terms of the theory and practices of economics, management and finances. It would seem that it is one of several significant reasons that led to the case whereby behavioural finances are currently experiencing such a great boom.

In contemporary times, there is an increasingly strong and fast implementation of the relativization of values, criteria of valuation and ethical norms. This relates to both its content and the ways of its interpretation. Just as in the ancient times, when at a preliminary stage the sphere of the interest of philosophy encompassed the entirety of knowledge about the world in order to gradually separate from its area to the particular detailed sciences with the passing of time, this same process took place and is currently taking place in the area of contemporary axiology.

What was hitherto the basis of traditional ethics and axiology is changing and disappearing. The progressing dispersal of the theory of values in terms of the various specialized areas has taken place, which in fact is continuing to disperse. Nevertheless, an increasingly lower number of researchers search for the answer to the following question: What is any value? (What is its nature?). Do the universal values exist and to what extent? In what way is it possible to undertake attempts at integrating these dispersed areas?

The eco-philosopher Wiesław Sztumski, pays attention to the turnaround that has taken place in the field of ethics. He emphasizes that the relativization of ethical norms is taking place increasingly frequently and faster, both in terms of its content, as well as in the ways of interpretation. In his words, „w ciągu stuleci aksjologię budowano na bazie podstawowych wartości etycznych, które charakteryzowały się powszechnością (uniwersalnością), absolutnością i niezmiennością. Jednak doświadczenia dwudziestego wieku

---

[6] Jenny Teichman expresses the view that in terms of morality, it is not possible to be guided by a simple calculation of the number of people happy and unhappy by a defined policy, decision or deed. History teaches us that this may be dangerous for instance in the case of national ethnic minorities, political opposition and democracy, as well as the creation of totalitarian systems (J. Teichman, *Etyka społeczna*, Oficyna Wydawnicza, Warszawa 2002).

pokazały, że takich wartości nie ma.[7] W związku z tym teraz mamy do czynienia z etykami fundowanymi na wartościach zmiennych i dostosowywanych do wymogów aktualnie panujących ideologii, wyznań religijnych oraz polityki, a także na użytek różnych grup społecznych, w szczególności korporacji"[8] (within a hundred years axiology was built on the basis of the fundamental ethical values that were featured by commonness (universality) absoluteness and permanence. However, the experience of the 20th century showed that such values do not exist. With relation to this, we are dealing with the ethics founded on the varying values and adjusted to the requirements of the currently existing ideology, religious beliefs and politics, while also for the use of various social groups, particularly corporations).

The choice of values not only defines the direction of cultural development, as well as political, social and economic development, but also has an enormous impact on adopting aims for realization, as well as the contradictions and conflicts emerging between them. This decides to a large extent on the ways and methods of their realization. Due to these reasons, among others, the axiology among the branches of philosophy belongs to one of the most important. This has a growing influence on any practical activity of man, as it translates to the attitudes, human behaviour and activity, as well as on the world outlook.[9] This occurs on the one hand, in terms of the acceptance of a certain set of desired values and not any other. On the other hand, it is expressed by means of the processes of valuation – establishing the hierarchy of importance of these values.

Valuation by its nature of things, requires not only various types of practical decisions with regard to the choices made in specific situations, but also decisions of an ethical nature. These decisions are becoming the criteria of evaluating the attitudes and behaviour, as well as defining the nature of interpersonal ties in the processes of management. Identifying with specific values to a greater or lesser degree is associated with the responsibility for their adherence and realization in practice. Responsibility, both in terms of formal and informal types is a value in itself. Its very existence increases the transparency of the market transactions, the predictability of the reactions of the entities operating on the market, as well as the general feeling of trust. All

---

[7] No doubt it is possible to ask the following question: Are such values really not there, or are they not widely respected?

[8] W. Sztumski, *Transformacja nowym paradygmatem ewolucji społecznej*, „Transformacje. Pismo Interdyscyplinarne", Centrum Badań Ewaluacyjnych, Akademia Leona Koźmińskiego, Warszawa 2013, pp. 58–59.

[9] Alongside ontology, gnoseology, epistemology, historiosophy, ethics, aesthetics, the philosophies of nature, law, politics, management, creativity, culture, medicine, pharmaceuticals, everyday life and philosophical anthropology.

[2] T. Sedlacek, *Ekonomia dobra i zła. W poszukiwaniu istoty ekonomii od Gilgamesza do Wall Street*, Audiobook 2012.

of this together leads to the reduction of the transaction costs in the processes of management.

2. Neoliberalism and economic axiology

Neoliberalism is an economic doctrine (also partly in terms of ideology), which is responsible for the market economy, freedom of economic activity and minimal state intervention in the economy. Other key words associated with this direction are privatization and deregulation. This was created by the economists of the Chicago School, including Milton Friedman in particular (laureate of the Nobel Prize in 1976), albeit a significant contribution was also made by the economists from the Austrian School too, especially by Friedrich Hayeck. Neoliberals eagerly refer to the "father of modern economics", Adam Smith, who also spoke about the market economy and the freedom of economic activity, although he was an opponent of laissez faire, which weighs down on neoliberalism.

In accordance with the neoliberal doctrine, which is still placed in the mainstream economic trend, the market mechanisms should not only be the driving force of the economy, but also the decisive criteria in the choice of economic, social and ecological values. To a large extent, such a perception is the result of a hugely simplified liberal model of the market economy. In this model, an enterprise is treated as a machine whose aim is the generation of profit for its owners and investors. The greater these profits are achieved over a shorter period, the better. Simultaneously, the power and effectiveness of the market self-regulation is over-estimated, in terms of the metaphoric "invisible hand."[10] Albeit no sensible person would negate the processes of self-regulation in the market economy, nor its power, the market economy is not however a perfect homeostat and requires certain legislative-institutional protection, without which it undergoes degeneration.

Without questioning the role and significance of either the market or owners, investors or profit, it is thus, not possible to accept the fundamentalist approach and apologetics of the market mechanisms. It is difficult to share the conviction that the market is a universal type of institution that also ensures the necessary social self-regulation. There is no way to accept the over-valued position of the financial markets and the financial-banking institutions, the large and constantly increasing social stratification that is the effect of implementing neoliberal methods, the weakening (some even refer

---

[10] Adam Smith, whom this definition is attributed to, wrote about the "invisible hand", thus treating this phrase as a metaphor. The "invisible hand of the market" appeared later, subsequent to his death.

to this as disappearing, which is surely an exaggeration) of the middle class, the increase in indebtedness of both the citizens and the states.

Neoliberalism became and still stands in opposition to Keynesism and state interventionism. Nevertheless, the tension and antagonism between them should be at least partly outmoded as in the era of globalization, the national states are losing their significance and have restricted possibilities for the effective regulation of economic issues and not only economic ones. State interventionism has a significantly lesser causative power than in the past, while the sensible and responsible intervention on a regional or global scale much harder from an intellectual viewpoint, as well as organizational, financial and political viewpoints. As a matter of fact, it is still not known how to do this well.

At the turn of the first and second decades of the 21st century, the criticism of the neoliberal doctrine and ideology intensified, including the similar orthodox view of the processes of creating and managing economic value. More and more frequently, not only economists, but also researchers from other social sciences underline the fact that a long-term view is essential for the creation of fixed business values and taking account of the social and cultural conditioning of their creation. Likewise, there is also an indication of the significance of the "cultural capital" and "cultural creativity", while also the "capital of relations". This differentiated analysis is subjected tote significance of the relations between the implemented models of running economic activities and the ethics in business associated with the social responsibility of a firm. Attention is also paid to the need to combine the "hard" and "soft" elements in management – not only in an enterprise, but also in other organizations.

A practical question arises here as to in what way is the thinking about the economy possible as a social system to transfer from the level of macro-economic solutions to a micro-economic level, namely entities managing enterprises and households. How to make the economic policy, not only in terms of its economic dimension, but also in a social, ecological and institutional sense not subject to ideology and the "only rightful" doctrine, but based on the search for solutions in specific situations and be of a pragmatic nature?

In contemporary times, we are faced with the departure from the level of theoretical reflection among some researchers, or from the orthodox way of thinking about the processes of management. Not only are the drawbacks gradually displayed, while in some areas the social harmfulness of the neoliberal paradigm, but also a search is run with reference to the possibilities of changing this. A significant proportion of the attempts made are aimed at not only restricting and mitigating the effects of the malfunctioning free markets and repairing the situation by means of various types of regulatory solutions undertaken by the state. Their intention is most frequently however the implementation of changes in such a manner so as not to violate the fundamental principles of the neoliberal paradigm. Simultaneously, attention is paid to the necessity of executing certain regulations on a supranational scale as the national regulations are insufficient in the realities of regionalization and globalization.

At the end of the 1990s this issue was undertaken by among others, Joseph Stiglitz, sometimes inaccurately referred to as one of the dissidents of mainstream economics. In fact, his aim is not the pursuit of change in the system, but merely the removal of some of its significant shortcomings. Stiglitz aims to increase the role of state intervention, but in a manner whereby the changes implemented by the state could be removed from the social cost.

The creation of another paradigm than the neoliberal one first and foremost requires a fundamental reorientation in the broad perception of the axiological sphere in contemporary theories of economics. It is difficult to overestimate the growing power in terms of the relation between the economic and general axiology and the management practice, as well as its social effects. All managerial decisions are based on some values whose source results from the defined world outlook and paradigm.

The significance of values depends to a large extent on the context in which it is viewed. The failure to take the growing significance of this conditioning into account leads to the case whereby "ekonomia, której nauczamy, nie uczy nas najistotniejszego – tego, jak konstruować cele rozwoju w nowym kontekście zmiany technologicznej, deregulacji i zmiany instytucjonalnej"[11] (the economics which we teach, does not teach us the most important aspect, the fact of how to construct the aims of development in the new context of technological changes, deregulation and institutional changes).

From this viewpoint it is possible to suppose that the changes in the hitherto binding paradigm of the theories of management of economic value shall soon become more significant. It is possible to expect that by means of implementing a new set of macro-economic, global and eco-system values into the sphere of the practices of management, they shall have a stronger impact on the ways of management at all its levels.

The awareness of this type of upcoming change in management and first and foremost the rapidly growing dysfunction of the neoliberal doctrine requires the expansion and enrichment of the scope of the subject matter cognitive areas of interest in terms of axiology, while also economic areas and their relations with the methods of gauging values. The changes made in the hitherto binding and traditional paradigm of theory and practices of management of values shall certainly have a clearly growing influence on taking

---

[11] L. Dowbor, *Demokracja ekonomiczna*, Instytut Wydawniczy Książka i Prasa, Warszawa 2008, p. 43.

other values into account in the processes of management, instead of only a narrow economic view. This requires the search for the possibilities of eliminating the existing loopholes in the theory, which from the viewpoint of the needs of the practices of management are becoming more significant.

In thinking about the "other values" that are neglected, it would be necessary to first and foremost distinguish such values as justice, dignity, solidarity, activity, participation in socio-economic life (and restriction of social exclusion), protection of the natural environment and health. The dysfunctionality of neoliberalism occurs to a significant degree in the case whereby in essence it does not have composite mechanisms that would promote, or at least take account of the aforesaid values at an essential level. There is a new and growing number of employees who are termed "precariat", or in other words, those employed on the basis of uncertain conditions.[12] Income inequality has been undergoing profound intensification – in Europe 10% of the richest people possess 65% of assets, whereas in USA 70% of assets, which arouses the rising social opposition.[13] Even in the wealthy USA, as many as 19% of their society lives in poverty according to their statistics.

Counteracting this problem is to a certain degree (and should be more energetically and effectively so) run by particular internal organizations by means of developing the appropriate IT and analytical systems, which are partly refocused by the policies of employment and remuneration, the fight against corruption and other pathologies, the increase in the morale of the management staff and the employees, while also the growth in the level of trust, etc.

What is at least controversial and frequently immoral relates to the mass redundancies of employees in enterprises that are in good economic condition in their pursuit for even greater profits. These practices should therefore be placed under greater legislative and social control.

However, it is not possible to expect that while operating at a micro-economic level, even if streamlining would be sufficient. Of the multitude of reasons for the growing dysfunction, the withdrawal of the state from its protective functions is still significant as the realization of many values to a significant degree depends on this. The restriction of the role of the state in such areas as: health care, education, social welfare and social aid lead to the case whereby the social differences and the phenomenon of pauperization have become intensified.

Even worse results are induced by the **rarity of the planetary method of perceiving the world and the weakness of the global impact**. The restric-

---

[12] J. Urbański, *Prekariat i nowa walka klas*, Książka i Prasa, Warszawa 2014.

[13] T. Piketty, *Capital in the Twenty-First Century*, Belknap Press World, Cambridge, Massachusetts 2014.

tion of activities to the faith in the efficiency and almighty power of the free markets, individual entrepreneurship and free trade are insufficient. There is a growing awareness of the need for another direction for the fundamental aims of development. This shall not be possible without the contemporary reinterpretation and reconferring of new significance to values, including economic values.

Including the problematic issues of the economic values in the empirical research generally starts with the attempts to gauge their varied attributes – their parameterization and quantification, in order to move towards some kind of systematization. It is often forgotten that the precision in terms of measuring the economic values with the aid of various indicators not only depends on their perfection, but also their selection and honesty and accuracy of interpretation, which to a large extent also depends on the professional qualifications and systems of values of the interpreters themselves.

In this very context, Ladislau Dowboraptly observes that "Sprawą zasadniczą jest przezwyciężenie fałszywej obiektywności nauk ekonomicznych, tak, jakby miały one ograniczać się do liczenia (…). Ekonomia jest tak skomplikowana dlatego, że różne prądy ekonomiczne po prostu służą różnym interesom, a gdy interesy są sprzeczne, mamy do czynienia ze sprzecznymi analizami"[14] (the fundamental issue is to overcome the false objectivity of the economic sciences in such a manner as for them to be limited to calculations […]. Economics is so complicated as the various economic streams simply serve various interests and when interests are contrasting, we are faced with contrasting analyses).

Therefore, there are potentially significant fields that exist here within the framework of which it is possible to not only make a multitude of costly mistakes, but it may also lead to a lot of abuse and manipulation, which is exemplified by the so-called "creative accounting". It is necessary to also emphasize that the measuring of economic values, their valuation, or perhaps in broader terms, their measurement (not only in quantitative terms, but also in qualitative terms), have become in contemporary times *conditio sine qua non* of all rationally executed processes of management. As a result of this, in economics a clear and strengthening relation is emerging between one of the many fields of axiology, namely economic axiology and the pursuit of finding and improving the various methods of measuring the economic values. Likewise, it is worth noting that such a relation opens up new research areas and cognitive possibilities in economics, management and finance.

In the sphere of the choice of specific values, the majority of people prefer transparent instructions that relate to their possible procedure with reference to the profession executed. The creation of unequivocal norms and regula-

---

[14] L. Dowbor, *op. cit.*, p. 31.

tions of behaviour within the confines of a specific profession may also be necessary when there is a desire to avoid various types of pathology that may take place. With this aim in mind, various types of codes of ethics are created.

In Poland, it is currently possible to count up to over forty different kinds of codes of ethics for groups of professions. These are primarily moral norms of a given environment and principles that should be adopted in order to fulfil a mission or task associated with the occupation in question with dignity and in a proper way. They are also the benchmarks of the desired attitudes and regulations of *fair play* that refers to how to proceed in the appropriate manner. Another group of this type of regulation are the codes of ethics of organization, also referred to as the codes of good practices of "our credo" and otherwise. Maria Szyszkowska,[15] who is the propagator of the new trend within the confines of the philosophy of values – the philosophy of pharmacy, proposes the name of the "code of honour" that was applied in Poland in the period of twenty years between the world wars and to increase its importance.

With regard to the codes of ethics, various reservations have been put forward.[16] Nevertheless, "byłyby one bardziej przekonywujące, gdyby ogólnoludzka uniwersalna etyka była faktem, a nie jedynie, jak dotąd postulatem. Pragnienie, by taką utworzyć, nie może przesłaniać jej braku"[17] (they would be more convincing if the general human universal ethics was fact and not as up to now merely a postulate. The desire to create this cannot cover its shortage).The codes of ethics, regardless of their various weaknesses are an expression of the specific needs of various environments and to what extent they complement economics, which is sometimes accused of being scientific and in practice devoid of morality.

In practice, legislative norms are of greater significance. It is worth realising that the relations between the constituted law and morality are dominated by the former. The norms (good) of law also constitute a certain minimum of ethics. However, on the other hand, ethics and morality may pose greater requirements as in many cases where the law is not violated (yet), the action is specified as to whether the behaviour or negligence may be deemed to be inappropriate or reprehensible from an ethical viewpoint.

---

[15] In 2005, she was nominated for the Nobel Peace Prize.

[16] A severe critic of them is among others, Zygmunt Bauman who opines in favour of morality and against ethics, particularly against the code of ethics. The code of ethics preaches the acceptance of the externally imposed principles and procedures, which are frequently prepared in a rather incapable manner, while renouncing the individual "compass" and moral sensitivity, which is perhaps even more valuable. It is also not technically possible to register the whole intricate material well that is supposed to be regulated on umpteen pages, the more so as the codes are frequently prepared by people who are insufficiently prepared from a substantive and literary point of view, thus utilizing the word matter incompetently.

[17] M. Szyszkowska, *Każdy bywa pacjentem. Zarys filozofii farmacji*, Dom Wydawniczy Elipsa, Warszawa 2010, p. 77.

3. Multiplicity of various axiological practices and their economics

An interesting attempt to overcome the contradiction that exists between ethics and usefulness was made not by an economist, but by an outstanding French sociologist named Pierre Bourdieu, who proposed a new methodological approach and with relation to this implemented the new research notion of the "economies of practices" (*economie unifiee des practiques*). As a result of this innovation in terms of notions, the connection of the material sphere and the symbolic sphere has become much easier. He wrote as follows: "Ortodoksyjna ekonomia nie bierze pod uwagę faktu, że praktyką ludzką mogą rządzić zasady odmienne od przyczyn mechanicznych albo świadomych dążeń do maksymalizacji użyteczności, a jednocześnie może owa praktyka być poddana ekonomicznej logice. Praktyki też mają swą ekonomię, swą immanentną rację, niesprowadzaną do racji ekonomicznych, ponieważ ekonomię praktyk określa nieskończenie wiele funkcji i celów"[18] (The orthodox economy does not take account of the fact that human practices may be governed by principles that are different to the mechanical reasons or conscious pursuits towards the maximization of usefulness, while the said practice may simultaneously be subject to economic logic. Likewise, these practices have their own economy, their own immanent rationale that is not brought down to economic rationale as the economy of practices infinitely defines many functions and aims).

Transferring this notion to an axiological level facilitates the awareness of the functioning of the multiplicity of the various "economies of practices", while also in the sphere of axiology and in the management of economic value. This enables not only the better perception of the real transformation occurring in the processes of management, but also increases the possibilities of forming their desired directions. It is not possible to forget that one of the fundamental tasks of humanist and social sciences is not only to create descriptions with it and more or less accurate interpretations of the reality. Their mission is also to illustrate the cause and effect analysis of the relations and co-dependencies, while also to propose efficient ways of influencing changes in the desired cultural, social and economic directions.

A significant inspiration for these changes, while also their verification is that of values, as well as legislative and ethical norms. Some of them were formulated a long time ago and still exert a significant impact on humanity, on their lives, way of thinking and procedure, economic activity and social ties. This may be exemplified by the biblical Ten Commandments, which were formulated approximately 1,300 B.C. Of the multitude of others, it is

---

[18] P. Bourdieu, L.J.D. Wacquant, *Zaproszenie do socjologii refleksyjnej*, Oficyna Naukowa, Warszawa 2001, p. 105.

worth mentioning the earlier Code of Hammurabi, which was formulated 1,800 B.C., which registered the regulations of the Penal Law, Civil Law and Economic Law (to utilize modern terms), in which a high level of importance was given to the issue of the quality of work and products. The Declaration of the Rights of Man and Citizen in 1789 that was passed in France during the Great Revolution signified the beginning of the end of the feudal era in the world and the inauguration of the rights of menthe first modern-day constitutions in the world – in the USA in1789 and the Konstytucja 3 Maja (Constitution of 3 May) in Poland in 1791, placed emphasis on the foundations of contemporary parliamentary democracy and civic society.

Economic value that is viewed from a broad perspective requires a significantly more profound overview that transgresses outside of economics and its preferred historically shaped values of the given moment, which are most frequently of a utilitarian nature. The wisdom and notions included in other fields of humanist and social science, while also in various religions and philosophies may be of great use in such a profound view of economic value.

Economics, just as any other science is by the nature of things, fragmentary and incomplete. It cannot develop in isolation and without the aid of other social sciences as the market is only one of the elements of a wide social environment and people operating there. Together with these changes that are taking place in this environment, there are also changes in the systems of values and aims, as well as the applied ethical norms of the management entities. As the market is not the only institution by means of and thanks to which the people may satisfy their needs, the aforesaid changes also have a significant impact on all the other non-market institutions that participate in the social processes of management. The social nature of economics is once again appearing in this sphere.

The pace of the occurring changes and the associated lack of durability of everything places the theory and practices of economics in an extremely difficult situation as it is expected to provide effectiveness in terms of the implemented solutions in a situation of growing uncertainty, which even relates to the near future. The hitherto and rather commonly accepted academic assumption, according to which it is assumed that in conditions of a fully transparent market and symmetrical access to information, business entities operate in a fully rational manner, which is simply not true. The mass human behaviour significantly diverges from the conventional assumptions of neoclassical economics and the neoliberal doctrine based on it. The concept of economic rationality and the theory of national expectations viewed on a macro-scale may be of a completely different nature, sense and social effects than one which is restricted to individual decisions and actions. This is also one of the reasons why such a substantial dichotomy arises between the micro and macro-levels of activities.

The lack of a sufficient application of the interdisciplinary approach in economics would not be replaced by its multidisciplinary development, while its cognitive tool functions, utilitarian and most frequently replicative level of economic engineering exist. For these very reasons, it is worth undertaking attempts at new ways to understand the nature of economic values with the aid of introducing the meta-philosophical language into deliberations on this issue.

Reflection of this kind is also necessary as the hitherto forecasts and hopes associated with the optimistic predictions that resulted from the assumptions of neoliberal capitalism of the 20th century and the first decade of the 21st century have not borne fruition. This fact is indicated by an increasing number of researchers such as, among others, U. Beck, F. Fukujama, S. Hunttington, J. Naisbitt, G. Sorman, J.E. Stigler, W. Szymański and L. Zacher. These excessively optimistic predictions were derived from various sources. They were based on among spects, the theory of progress, modernization, the theory of equalizing the levels of development, cultural unity of the world, the theory of the network, the information society, the economy based on knowledge, etc.

An extreme example was the theory of Francis Fukuyama, who declared the slogan of the "end of history", with regard to which the conviction of the indivisible, following the fall of the USSR, liberal democracy and the free market economy.[19] However, it has turned out that the world develops in various directions and with relation to this, it is necessary for it to have a "reset" in terms of the hitherto thinking about the occurring changes and development models that were to reflect these changes. On the one hand, we are dealing with the multiplicity of solutions to the issue of the needs and various types of development that are created by the concept of sustainable and long-term growth. On the other hand, the real processes of change taking place indicate something completely in contrast – the intensifying and increasing types of dysfunctions, inequality, disintegration and social and technological disproportion, unemployment, forced emigration on a mass scale, poverty, emergence of new and increasing areas of exclusion, climatic disasters caused by human activity, war, etc.

The vision of the world as an integrated global and universal civilization is in contemporary times nothing more than having no chance of being fulfilled in the near future, as well as being a romantic dream and in itself utopia. The development of the world takes place in conditions of a rapidly increasing pluralism of values. This gives rise to the questions which were asked almost a quarter of a century ago by the outstanding Polish scholar Bogdan Suchodolski: "w jaki sposób zachować w zmiennym świecie różnorodność wartości nie niszcząc wartości trwałych? Jak umacniać uniwersalne wartości

---

[19] F. Fukuyama, *The End of History and the Last Men*, Free Press, New York 1992.

życia poprzez rozwój i poszanowanie różnorodności i odmienności?"[20] (In what way should the variety of values be preserved in a changing world so as not to destroy the fixed values? How to strengthen the universal values of life by means of development and respect for variety and diversity?).

From the viewpoint of the activity of the researchers who not only become involved in the description and mapping of these phenomena, but also have ambitions to influence the control of them, which is difficult to over-state. The subject matter of the mainstream public debate on these issues is also important, as well as what the most important problems are that have attracted the attention of the researchers. In fact, in crisis and breakthrough development moments, the most important appears to be the power of the impact of the created and promoted notions and visions of the future states of the world, their accuracy or its lacking.

It is becoming increasingly clear that the contemporary economy is not only developing in conditions of incomplete knowledge, but also the fact that the significance of the factors of uncertainty and risk are growing within it, which it constantly accompanies. Rapid acceleration of changes in the contemporary socio-economic systems has led to the case whereby the *status quo* is constantly being questioned. In such situations, the increasing power of the relation between the created and dominating theories of the so-called main trends and politics is becoming the area for their realization. Economic and management sciences when viewed from this perspective bear a particular type of social responsibility for what it deals with and what priorities it adopts, what great growth of knowledge is in the context of the occurrence of threats, dilemmas and development barriers, while also in what way and in what areas the adequate solutions are searched for.

Economization and financialization, the pursuit of the commodification of everything, while also the desire to make the world economy and social life "one big supermarket", leads to nothing more than the hitherto view of the essence of the economic values created and the associated processes of the accumulation of capital. They also lead to encompassing the accompanying processes of destruction of economic values and various types of dysfunctions and pathologies associated with them.

Various expectations are formulated at various stages of economic development with regard to economic values that have different tasks to fulfil. Under the influence of the rapidly emerging changes in the world economy the theory of management is significantly expanding and the area of its interests is intensifying. This has its own advantages, but is also a large threat in itself as it may lead to the blurring of its essence. It is not permissible to lose the

---

[20] *Trwałe wartości i zmienny świat. Zbiór studiów z konferencji* w Śródborowie 20–22 listopada 1990, red. B. Suchodolski, Dom Wydawniczy Elipsa, Warszawa 1995.

historical perspective in all of this and be little what was primary and the most important.

In the context of the emerging changes, this requires a clear display of the main elements and their composition in the new relationship. For sure, further forms of the development of the theory of management of values shall first and foremost depend on the cultural conditioning, as well as the differences in the applied practices ("economies of practices").

The contemporary world economy is developing within a hugely diverse cultural space. Within its environs, we are dealing with the growing number of differentiated societies, within the framework of which the processes of convergence accompany the phenomenon of divergence. The challenge of the upcoming decades of the 21st century is thus becoming the crossing of the borders of our own culture, whatever that may be. Various historical traditions lead to different ways of thinking about the most significant economic values and about such ways of realization that would render it possible to remain in agreement with different cultural practices.

We may adopt two different approaches to all values, including economic ones: hermeneutic and phenomenological. The first one is based on the specific practices interpreting the sense and significance of the given values. The basis of the latter is that of an eidetic analysis, which is oriented towards grasping the essence of things (in this case, values), in terms of what is the most important and the most characteristic, while also the phenomenological reduction (*epoche*), resignation from all types of adopted a priori assumptions. With the aid of these two different approaches, attempts may be made to decipher and understand values once more with the use of the meta-philosophical language.

Together with the passing of time in the theory of the management of values in an enterprise and in broader terms contemporary organizations, various trends are becoming distinctive. As already well-known, their origins may be searched for in the concepts of value for shareholders. However, does the first trend penetrate and connect with the new ones to a sufficient extent, in which the aim of the new trends is to eliminate the lack of completeness of the theory on one joint foundation, which gives rise to doubts at present. There is currently a selection and search for solutions in such "areas–bonds", such as sustainable growth, corporate social responsibility, or management via values. Thanks to this fact, an increasingly complete structure of the management of economic value is emerging. However, whether and to what extent this is a real common foundation or merely a temporary measure whose aim is to ease the crisis phenomena taking place in modern times shall be shown in the future.

In economic-based literature, there is no singular or universal definition of an enterprise. Depending on who and what aim it serves, it is possible to encounter various ways to define it. **From the viewpoint of the management of values of a firm, it would seem that the most practical is first and foremost such a perception of an enterprise that treats it as an economic organization, which is capable of exchanging values.** These values may of course take on various forms, as they may be goods and services, capital, but also more and more frequently intellectual capital, information and knowledge.

In this context, it is worth remembering that since the times of Jean Baptiste Say, the way of defining and interpreting economic value has become widespread by identifying it with the price on the market. Hence, it is also necessary to search for the monetary source in terms of the logic of the development of the market economy, together with the development of the forms of money, including virtual money and the acceleration of the circulation of the exchange of economic value. Nevertheless, it has been well-known for some time that the assumption that economic entities operate in a fully rational way in conditions that are perfectly transparent and symmetrical access to information is a utopia. The same conviction that the market price reflects the economic value does not match the reality.

It is worth knowing about this as the exchange based on the actual contribution of value never took place. The exchange of value has always accompanied the desire by someone to grasp some value, but who is not its creator, which is coupled by speculation and increasing greed. This phenomenon is more or less visible in terms of the entire world history of trade, while in contemporary times it has multiplied in intensity under the impact of financialization.

4. Directions of supplementing the incompleteness of the theory of management of economic value

The theory of the management of value in an enterprise as a separate research trend in the theory of management was formed and has been developing intensively around the world for over thirty years. The bases of this theory were created by Alfred Rappaport and Tom Copeland. In Poland this trend in management and the associated techniques of management have existed for almost twenty years. From the perspective of slightly more than a hundred years (management as a theoretical discipline has existed for so long), the period of the theory of the management of values in an enterprise is not very short.

This is a circumstance that justifies the undertaking of attempts at reflection on the state of development of this theoretical concept. Not only numerous crisis phenomena lead to this, but also the new areas of uncertainty associated with them and the fast growing levels of risk. As usual in extreme conditions, the weakest elements of each economic theory most quickly become apparent. This is the situation we have at present. It is possible to note the missing elements of these theories more clearly than in previous years and put forward the question with regard to the direction and possibilities of their completion. It would seem that it is worth initially considering the expansion of the area of interest with regard to the theory of management of value with an indication of the issues listed below:

- realities of new geo-economics;
- relations with culture and organization;
- relations of the processes of management with new drivers which determine the creation of economic value, while first and foremost the management of knowledge as the new creative factor;
- taking account of the needs of all the main stakeholders of the organization;
- strengthening the role of corporate regulation and supervision;
- making attempts at the synthesis of the management of economic value by means of the "hard" elements with the "soft" elements, namely management via values.

In the briefly outlined context above, it is worth drawing attention to the **ten key areas of incompletion of the theories of management of economic value**, which require supplementing. Together, they realise the multi-dimensionality of the categories of economic values and the necessity of their formulation in a significantly broader scope and more profound sense than up to now in terms of economic sciences, in such a manner as to take account of the social nature of contemporary economics more broadly.

The choice made is of course to a large extent of an arbitral nature. Nevertheless, it would appear that this does not lessen its significance. The primary aim here is the attempt to initiate a broader scientific, interdisciplinary and problem-related discussion on this subject matter. Such a one, whose category of economic values would enrich and make more complete, as well as more useful from a social and practical viewpoint.

4.1. Weak relations between managing economic value and the management of risk and uncertainty

Although both the theories of the management of economic value and the management of risk and uncertainty are rather well-developed, it is their contacts and mutual influences that are less frequently analysed and poorly described. The factors of surprise and unpredictability, the expanding sphere of uncertainty and risk associated with the realities of geo-economics as a new form of geopolitics would seem to be underestimated.

The beginning of the 21st century in the world economy is associated with the initiation of long-term global processes of change in its structure. An increasing amount of various analyses and reports have emerged on this subject, which diverge not only outside the horizon of the year 2030, but even touch on the year 2050. Nevertheless, we are not more certain because of outlining the shape of the future. For instance, we do not know if we are correctly defining the coefficients of risk by calculating the levels of leverage in terms of the planned developmental intentions and the associated investment projects. Economists, alongside fortune-tellers, belong to the social group that most frequently tries to tell the truth, while most frequently with poor results.

Long-term undertakings, which are created by means of future scenarios usually transgress the horizon of responsibility of those who define them. In conditions of an economy based on uncertain knowledge, it is very difficult to predict the course of these processes, or even to be more certain of their main trends. Likewise, it is also difficult to specify who their beneficiary shall be and who shall lose out. As the certainty of getting to know the future is impossible, then it is necessary to first and foremost focus on revealing the visible co-dependencies that shape the future in order to try to define the degree of the risk undertaken with regard to the possible activities of the future. Risk adopts a form that is more or less an accurately objectified form of uncertainty which relates to future events.

With reference to the growth in the pace of change and the factor of surprise, the role of the factor of uncertainty shall undoubtedly also increase. Doubtless to say, this process shall simultaneously accompany the emergence of new and previously unknown types of risk that shall translate to the efficiency and competitiveness of the process of management. Thus, the implementation of economic value into the theories of management in terms of merely various improvements, primarily of a "technical" nature, shall do little to improve the situation in the sphere of the possibilities of the increase in the predictability and better control of events that may take place in the future.

This phenomenon captures the attention of a multitude of researchers at present, who emphasize that there is an increasingly visible lack of control on the directions taken by the changes implemented. This is so, due to the fact that in contemporary society not only is the structural transformation being radically accelerated, but their continuity is being broken. This relates to both the economic processes, as well as the social and cultural processes. The constant questioning of the status quo has become the norm in such a situation.

The scope and impact of these changes on social and everyday behaviour are subject to the simultaneous impact of the processes of globalization. As a result, the phenomenon of the lack of longevity of everything is evident, which also affects the institutions that functioned up to now. This in turn, requires the search for and implementation of other forms of control than the existing ones associated with the growing risk.

4.2. Slim relations between the theory of managing economic value and the management of culture

There is no such thing as a singular universal model of civilization that is accompanied by one model of development that is appropriate for it. An increasingly large role in the civilizational transformation processes is played by the socio-cultural and cyber-cultural conditioning that is of a non-economic nature. Macro and micro-economic stability thus depends not only on the market criteria, but also on a multitude of other factors, of which a particular role is played by cultural, religious and demographic circumstances.

Events that are viewed from this perspective once again undermine the genuineness of the theory which was announced a short time ago by Francis Fukujama relating to the end of history accompanied by a great media commotion. This theory is understood as the final victory of the universal and timeless western formula of the market economy and the only appropriate ways of its realization. Once again, it turned out to be impossible as it does not depend on economics, but first and foremost on the broad cultural context in terms of the effectiveness of the institutional solutions and social norms applied. This signifies that the model of society and the resultant pattern of the economy that is appropriate in a given time in a given place in the world, need not be appropriate and desirable in another place, the more so in another time. There is no such thing as a "universal market standard", which ensures everyone of development, tranquillity and social stabilization. Not only the world of Islam rejects such a thought process and adoption of the accompanying cultural values of the western world as this has been exemplified by China for a long time. A similar policy of development was applied successfully many years ago by the following: the long-standing Premier Mohamad Mahatir in Malaysia, while also Premier Lee Kuan Yew of Singapore, as well as prior to them by the authorities of Taiwan and South Korea. At present, they are applied with at least partial success by among others, the authorities of Vietnam, Kazakhstan, Venezuela and Brazil. They are striving towards a balance between modernization and tradition, without which it would lead to chaos and various types of social and political upheavals.

In all of these countries there is a search for their own original developmental solutions, which are to be applied to their history and cultural traditions, as well as the resultant social expectations to the maximum extent. This is the fundamental assumption for the strategies of the development of entrepreneurship created there at the macro and micro-economic levels. Thanks to this fact, favourable conditions for the market success of indigenous entrepreneurs are created in those countries.

The wide use of the instruments and mechanisms of the market economy is of course applied there, but their basis for the application in practice is in fact the culture and the resultant systems of values. These are systems of values that are rather commonly accepted in social terms, thanks to which the development of the vibe of trust and predictable behaviour between entrepreneurs is possible. Nowadays, we may observe how Islam and Confucianism are to an increasing extent these systems of values, thanks to which in many regions of the world it is possible to create social trust and where people are not dragged down to the role of human capital as a particular factor of production.

In search of answers to the questions of how to internationalize the activities of an enterprise and in what way to strive towards becoming a global firm, require the expansion of knowledge on the issue of cultural divergence and the differences in the values accepted by business partners. Without this, it would be difficult or impossible to build long-lasting business relations. In particular, a great weakness is the limitation to solely the American or Europocentric viewpoint of the processes of increasing economic value and attempts to impose western systems of values, while also the pursuit of the unification of the cultural identity of the societies of the countries outside the Euro-Atlantic zone.

Standardization of the world may also not be successfully completed in the sphere of the management of economic values. In as much as the economic values themselves are the same in different cultures and may signify the same, the management of them, their relations with other groups of values and hierarchies in different cultures are, and no doubt in the foreseeable future shall be at least partly divergent. The failure to note this fact must lead to the weakening of the application nature of the theories of the management of values of an enterprise. Likewise, this also leads to various and culturally different approaches to the evaluation of risk. Thus, it is not possible to create economic values by viewing them in isolation from a specific culture in a specific place and time.

4.3. Divergence in the theories with the realities of contemporary capital markets that are to an increasing extent not only creating but are seizing economic values

The economic values, such as efficiency, profitability, viability, competitiveness, entrepreneurship, innovativeness and others, are the expression of sound enterprises and a sound economy, as well as the fact that they share this "soundness". Albeit very important, these are not autotelic values, nor are they paramount from the viewpoint of the criteria of the aim, both individual and social by nature. We are dealing with the double alienation as follows: economic values from the total number of values of capital markets and from the economy; both of which are usurping their overvalued positions. Grzegorz Kołodko writes of a systemic crisis, as well as structural and institutional crises of contemporary capitalism, which "ewidentnie preferuje mało produktywny na długą metę kapitalizm spekulacyjny ponad twórczy kapitalizm przedsiębiorców. A tylko ten drugi – i to też nie bezwarunkowo – może mieć dobrą przyszłość"[21] (clearly prefers speculative capitalism that is not very productive in the long term over the creative capitalism of entrepreneurs. And only the latter – and this is not unconditional – may have a good future).

4.4. Incoherence in knowledge management and economic value, as well as atrophy of accounting records

Intellect and its associated knowledge has always been present in economic activity. In contemporary times, not only the new sources, but first and foremost the most important sources of growth in the value of enterprises and competitiveness of national economies are however becoming increasingly clearer. The accuracy of the theoretical and practical way of interpreting their place in the processes of management thus counts for a lot.

In accordance with the well-known maxim, such a theory is always better that enables the undertaking of effective practical activities, particularly when it becomes a guide to the activities of a strategic nature. With relation to this assertion on the problematic issues of knowledge as the new source of development, this has its own far-reaching methodological and practical implications. This leads to the formulation of a multitude of new questions and the search for new interpretations and research sources.

The hitherto criteria of assessing the actual value of an enterprise has undergone universal change. The place of accounting value has been completely taken over by the market value. Thus, the search for the causes and sources of such significant differences between them was commenced. At present, this signifies the necessity to depart from the hitherto different indicators commonly applied in economic practice by Polish enterprises, whose fundamental weakness and simultaneously common feature is directed towards analysis that refers to the past. Such a feature is characteristic of all accounting indicators that are associated with the balance of an enterprise. They reflect time in a static and short-term manner and not what is most important from

---

[21] G. Kołodko, *Zanim nadejdzie jeszcze większy kryzys*, [w:] *Globalizacja, kryzys i co dalej?*, red. G. Kołodko, Poltext, Warszawa 2010, p. 13.

the viewpoint of the owners of the firms, namely the future and expected value and the rate of return on the capital invested by them.

Analysis of the barriers to implementing the methods of managing the value of an enterprise reveal a multitude of different types of weaknesses of the traditional system of financial accounting that are binding in the Polish economy. A significant proportion of these barriers relate to the information entered into the annual reports of enterprises, which most frequently does not respond to the demand relating to managerial information and new challenges for strategic management in enterprises. Glaring gaps in the sphere of information capital do not facilitate the identification of the actual state and possibilities of the increase in value, which is increasingly hidden in the intangible resources of enterprises.

The traditional financial accounting of enterprises, in order to fulfil the contemporary market challenges must yield to the radical changes itself. This means that in its case of among others, there is a necessity for the expansion of the applied conceptual apparatus and tools of analysis in such a way as to reflect not only the condition of the functioning of the current industrial economy, but first and foremost the conditions creating the "new" market of services, which is based on knowledge.

There is no singular model of knowledge management in an enterprise. Its specific form depends on what sector a firm functions in, what type of organizational culture it functions in, while also what professional and leadership levels its managerial staff represent.

4.5. Insufficient consideration of *behavioural economics* and *new institutional economics* including the context of the management of value

Behavioural economics enriches neoclassical economics by means of taking account of the point of view and results of the sociological and psychological research on the areas and issues that are interesting and promising for the economy. The new institutional economy makes up for the longer period of the lack of interest of economists of the theory of institutions, which after all also exert influence on the economic reality as such an influence is not only exerted by the market.

Albeit, both these economies are present and have been developing for several decades now, their sufficient integration with the mainstream economy has not occurred yet, which among other aspects, leads to the case whereby the theory of economic values has also availed of them to an insufficient degree. This is a pity, as human behaviour frequently has little in common with the traditional perception of the principle of rationality. Man is a *homo oeconomicus* but only to a certain extent, and the dichotomy between the micro and macro-economic analysis should decrease and not increase.

4.6. Underestimating the development of the sphere of Webonomics and its impact on economic value

The growth in the significance of economic activities of knowledge and the advanced IT technologies reduces not only the time and spatial restrictions in economic processes, as well as leading to the development of globalization processes. New business models are also being created more rapidly, which radically transforms the competitive strategies of firms. Thanks to the dynamic development of IT, a new area of studies has emerged with relation to production, distribution and the consumption of goods, services and notions in the World Wide Web, which Evan I. Schwartz defined by the term Webonomics.

In contemporary times, we are dealing with a new universal phenomenon, which is also becoming characteristic for a multitude of various fields of economic life. Its essence is the change in the ways of perceiving and methods of increasing the dimensions of the constructions built. "From a constructor's point of view, there are two ways to increase something. The first one is to increase the physical dimensions and people have devoted a lot of time to making bigger things by learning how to supply more energy to specific systems, building bigger houses, increasing the size of their own territory at the cost of others…but there is another method– it is possible to make something bigger by making it smaller! The size of any system actually does not depend on the physical dimensions, size in reality is the relation between the largest and the smallest element of the system–it is an issue of which of the smallest elements we can use…" These are the words of Moore's Law and this is the historical reality of the new technologies.[22]

The driving force and source of divergence in terms of the contemporary breakthrough technologies result from the revelation of the two regularities in economics that had not been noted until recently. The first one arose from the existence of the afore-mentioned Moore's Law, while the latter from Metcalfe's Law. Nowadays, Moore's Law is the basis for understanding what is being done within the framework of the third global socio-economic revolution. When G. Moore formulated his theory in 1965, nobody realised the importance of it. Currently, it is the key to the perception of the transformation that is taking place in the sphere of the new breakthrough technologies.

In turn, Metcalfe's Law is nothing more than the observation that value rises together with the growth of the number of participants. As a result of the

---

[22] *Nowy renesans*, red. J. Brockman, CIS, Warszawa 2005, p. 271.

revelation of the activities of these two new regularities, an unprecedented level of progress took place in the development of the economy and the information society. Simultaneously, it turned out that the restrictions in terms of advancement and calculative possibilities of the computer hardware are not becoming a barrier, but rather the issue of keeping pace with the development of the software systems. Hence, it is actually this field that is above all worth searching for the sources of the future competitive advantages in.

Simultaneous to the rapid growth of the sphere of Webonomics, there is also growth in the significance of the cultural sphere and the mutation occurring within it. New systems of signs and symbols are appearing there, as well as ways of exercising economic power, while also other ways of symbolic communication of the entities operating on the market. Unfortunately, at the same time manipulation of symbols and their abuse for the purpose of influencing and manipulating human behaviour also occurs there. The growing uncertainty and the accompanying types of risks lead to the case whereby there is rising anxiety that causes the creation of varied marketing strategies of firms on its basis, while also strategies that enable the application of social engineering on a macro-economic scale. Zygmunt Bauman illustrates this phenomenon as the emergence of the "kapitał lęku" (anxiety capital) and the pursuit of managing anxiety whose aim is to transform it to profit.

4.7. Insufficient consideration of the needs of all the stakeholders of the organization and concentration mainly on the interests of the owners / shareholders

An excessively one-sided concentration on the interests of the owners (on shareholders in listed companies), advocated in the 1970s and 1980s, particularly by Milton Friedman, may have an impact on the narrowing down of values that serve an organization and are at conflict with the good of the other stakeholders. The necessity to take account of the needs and justified expectations of all stakeholders was called on by entrepreneurs and management personnel in among others, the Manifest of Davos (1973), the Round Table of Caux (1994) and Global Compact (2001). At the level of values, this means the purposefulness of aiming towards both the honest and dignified profit for the owners / dividends for shareholders, as well as the good quality of products, conditions of sales and guarantees for clients, work and fair remuneration for employees, cooperation in terms of the realization of the common goals with local communities, respecting and protecting the natural environment, while also responsibility for the fate of future generations (what kind of world we leave behind).[23] It is worth noting that the interests of the owners

---

[23] Erich Fromm defined this by the term "love of the future."

and shareholders, as well as other stakeholders are at least partly convergent; thus, they should be perceived as (or perhaps primarily) antagonistic. Ethical postulates of taking account of the good of all the stakeholders does not have to be at conflict with the interests of the owners, particularly over a longer time perspective, albeit there are various areas of conflict.

4.8. Weakness of supranational market regulations and corporate supervision

For some time, convictions have been expressed with regard to the necessity of implementing greater rationality, harmonization and honesty in the economic and political mechanisms of globalization. These have been advocated by among others, G. Kołodko, J. Sachs, J. Schumpeter, J.E. Stiglitz, W. Szymański and R. Zoellick.

Globalization is commonly acknowledged to be incomplete. Władysław Szymański was in favour of "koordynacją transnarodową, w pierwszym okresie ograniczoną do niewielu ważnych, ale stosunkowo łatwych do uzgodnienia i nie budzących wątpliwości spraw"[24] (transnational coordination, which in the first period is restricted to a few important issues, but relatively easy to settle and without arousing doubt in the matter).

He adds that no doubt "najbardziej wstydliwym zjawiskiem dla elit intelektualnych jest unikanie jednoczesnego i kompleksowego wyciągania wniosków z kryzysów ekonomicznego i ekologicznego (…). Gdy [bowiem] szansą i postulatem warunkującym wyjście z kryzysu gospodarczego jest dynamiczny wzrost popytu i aktywności gospodarczej, obecna dynamika produkcji z punktu widzenia ekologii jest ślepym pędem do absorbowania coraz bardziej ograniczonych zasobów Ziemi"[25] (the most shameful phenomenon for the intellectual elite is the avoidance of the simultaneous and complex conclusions to be drawn from the economic and ecological crises […]. If the opportunity and postulate which conditions the exit from the economic crisis is the dynamic growth of demand and economic activity, the current dynamics of production from the viewpoint of the ecology is a blind stampede to absorbing the increasingly limited resources of the Earth).

G. Kołodko claims that "klucz do przyszłości tkwi w reinstytucjonalizacji gospodarki (…), przy czym teraz idzie o zmiany zasad funkcjonowania gospodarki światowej"[26] (the key to the future lies in the reinstitutionalization

---

[24] W. Szymański, *Jakie wnioski wyciągniemy z kryzysu*, [w:] *Globalizacja, kryzys i co dalej?*, red. G. Kołodko, Poltext, Warszawa 2010.

[25] Ibidem.

[26] G. Kołodko, *Świat na wyciągnięcie myśli*, Prószyński i S-ka, Warszawa 2010, p. 157.

of the market [...] whereby it now relates to the changes in the principles of the functioning of the world market).

However, he also perceives this as a longer process timewise, which is calculated over generations, in which the world shall not be divided by almost two hundred national economies, but rather "będzie się składał z kilkunastu wielkich regionalnych ugrupowań integracyjnych" (shall consist of great regional integration groups). Thus, this would mean regulations at the level of macro-regions, rather than the world as a whole, which would not match the range of significant and urgent needs relating to the principles and fundamental regulations that the demand has already revealed on a global scale. Certain regulations are essential on a macro-scale, as, in the words of J.E. Stiglitz in the aftermath of the last crisis, no-one shall claim [for a long time] that "rynki same potrafią naprawiać swoje błędy, a my możemy po prostu zdać się na egoistyczne zachowania uczestników rynku mając pewność, że wszystko będzie działać jak należy"[27](the markets themselves can fix their own mistakes, while we may simply count on the egoistic behaviour of the market participants with the certainty that everything shall work as it should).By claiming that there is a need for more regulation than prior to the crisis, he particularly sees this need in the financial sector, especially with relation to the problem of the representative bodies (entities operating on behalf of the owners of financial centres), as well as *externalities*; which relates to the effects of specified transactions that affect third parties, which are sometimes so numerous that they threaten the entire system.[28] It is almost certain that financial leverages shall be shortened.

J.E. Stiglitz also draws attention to the fact that the problems requiring solutions on a supranational scale are not restricted to merely financial issues. One of them is the fact that impoverished states are not able to support their enterprises effectively as wealthy countries are. They perceive the risk that accrues from the badly managed globalization, but there is a long way to changing this state of affairs and it is not yet known how this would look.[29] There are narrow political issues and the question of what specific system would replace neoliberalism. It does not appear to be realistic for this to be a common system for the world as a whole, also in terms of the sphere of global corporate supervision. In turn, if they are significantly different systems, it would be justified to ask the question relating to the possibilities of integration and restriction of global regulations. Nowadays, nobody can provide answers to these questions, nor indeed to other key questions.

---

[27] J.E. Stiglitz, *Freefall, jazda bez trzymanki. Ameryka, wolne rynki i tonięcie gospodarki światowej*, Polskie Towarzystwo Ekonomiczne, Warszawa 2010, p. XVIII.

[28] Ibidem, p. 15.

[29] Ibidem, p. 340.

4.9. Relations between economic values and consumption and threat of consumerism

Such values as economic growth and development, efficiency, profitability / viability, competitiveness, innovativeness and other economic aspects may be important and grow in terms of significance thanks to the material aspirations of people. The economy is of key importance for contemporary societies, while the efficient demand and consumption are the driving forces that provide employment, economic development, while also increased prosperity. The high level of consumption that is stimulated in various ways by producers and sellers, brings however both benefits, as well as threats. The threats are particularly associated with the lack of moderation and greed, civilizational illnesses ("prosperity illness"), devastation of the natural environment, aggressive forms of competing for resources (wars, neo-colonialism), maintaining the proportion between the spiritual and cultural dimensions and the material life of man, the insufficient civic and social activities of the people that are excessively concentrated on earning money and consumption, social disintegration against the background of excessive differences in the material status and lifestyles. It is of course obvious to separate consumption and consumerism. In as much as the former may be perceived mainly as a necessary and desirable category, the latter as the attachment of excessive importance to intangible goods[30] is difficult to say anything positive about. Consumerism is also termed as hedonistic materialism and is associated with the identification of values / quality of life with the level of consumption and accumulation of material goods.[31]

Activities associated with the promotion of products, particularly including aggressive marketing, while also the *effect of demonstration*, the human pursuit of imitating icons of abundance and prosperity, as well as imitating attractive lifestyles that favour both the increase in consumption, which is generally a benefit to the economy and workplace, as well as developing consumerism in societies that is generally non-beneficial from the viewpoint of the universal development and health of man and the capacity of the natural environment.

4.10. Problem of apparent values fetishization of money

The outstanding postmodernist French sociologist and philosopher, Jean Baudrillard, who is interested in the transformations occurring in the systems of values in contemporary times, draws attention to, what is in his opin-

---

[30] *Słownik języka polskiego*, Wydawnictwo Naukowe PWN, Warszawa 2007.
[31] *Konsumpcjonizm*, http://pl.wikipedia.org/wiki/Konsumpcjonizm.

ion the very dangerous phenomenon of replacing actual reality (physical, actual) with an artificial and virtual reality. This is accompanied by the emergence of the illusory and apparent values that have very little or rather nothing in common with the world of real values. They are merely their substitute, which facilitates various manipulation and speculation that is a threat to society. By drawing on the notion of ersatz created by J.E. Stiglitz, it is possible to acknowledge these artificial values as composite elements of capitalism.

To a certain extent, moving from real values to virtual values also relates to the highest entity in the temple of capitalism, namely financial capital. In contemporary form, in the theories of managing the values of an enterprise, the assumption is held that enterprises create economic values first and foremost by means of the capital acquired from investors. The principal aim is becoming the creation of such financial/cash flows that facilitate the acquisition of the expected rate of return from the invested capital. Enterprises by essence compete with each other, thus the attractiveness of the rate of return from the acquired capital is significant.

This way of life in terms of economic values is therefore connected with the life of money. Together with the reallocation of money, regardless of the extent of its current symbolic, virtual and intangible nature, the movement of economic values also occurs, or in other words, its migration.

The growth of economic values is in this way viewed as constantly very narrow and mainly through the prism of financial engineering, or in other words, the rate of return on the invested capital with relation to the costs of its acquisition (ROIC). Such a reduction in the manner of viewing the principal aim of assessing the efficiency of the activities of the enterprise, bringing it down to financial flows has its own far-reaching negative consequences. It does not take account of the changes that occurred in the social nature and life of money, as well as the associated changes in the ways of realizing values.

It is worth referring to Baudrillard here again, who avails of the example of the changes that take place in the functions that contemporary money fulfils, "niebędący już równowartością niczego" (without being equal to anything). Since the moment when the sphere of the real economy ceased to be reflected in the symbolic sphere, namely since capital flows in the global economy have nothing in common with real trade, as the function of money has been connected with the development of the virtual economy. In this way, money has ceased to be a gauge of real exchange value and value in use and has become a tool that is purely speculative and commonly fetish. This is associated with the artificial reality whose most complete reflection is to be found in the definition of the reality by the term Matrix ("virtual sleep"). This is already creating the mere illusion of a gauge of real values of anything and initiation of the process of self-destruction, which is becoming increasingly visible on the financial markets worldwide.

Money is becoming greater in the sense of its importance, while also increasingly a more doubtful substitute for the real values that leads to the metaphysics of economics by creating the illusion of existence. The virtual world, which is a world of information, symbols and signs, is becoming independent of the real economy, by creating its own set of values. This is very close to a simulacra, namely something that only simulates reality. In this actual area, it is necessary to search for the principal reasons for the growing lack of relation between the realities of the capital markets and the real economic value. As a result of this threatening phenomenon, the shortening of the cycle between the subsequent economic crises, the expansion of their geographical range, as well as the spreading of the moral hazard- both corporate and individual by nature are occurring. It is not possible to forget about the fundamental truth that the economic value is derived not from money, but is created by entrepreneurial people.

5. Management via values on the way to sustainable growth

For the past several decades, there has been growing interest in the concept of sustainability worldwide, which in Poland is better known by the term sustainable growth. This takes account of not only economic reason and values, while also respecting the economic needs and other values too, especially the necessity of respecting and protecting the natural environment, as well as the need to ensure living standards for the future generations. Thus, it is assumed that economic development should not be associated with the over-exploitation of raw materials, particularly non-renewable ones. The greenhouse effect, which is partly associated with human activity should be stopped, while forests, the air, water resources and the land should be protected better. There should be a change in the approach to flora and fauna, as it is not possible to continue the destruction of tens of thousands species annually as has been the case on this planet for many decades. These are ambitious and very difficult assumptions to execute. Nevertheless, they are essential. Our planet is becoming increasingly devastated by human activity and has lost its capacity of self-renewal to a significant extent.

Some remarks have been presented below that are formulated as a thesis with reference to the relations of management of values and sustainable growth as follows:

(1) Sustainable growth would seem to be the only concept that is safe for the future, rather an objective necessity than a variant of choice.

(2) Sustainable growth is not possible without changing the paradigm of management, while also without the strong sense of respect and promotion of values, which are not only economic ones.

(3) The continuously prevalent neoliberal doctrine does not serve sustainable growth; in some issues it is neutral, while in others, no doubt more numerous ones, it is with regard to them in opposition.

(4) Sustainable growth and the associated "good governing" by respecting and promoting values may make management more humanistic. Simultaneously, they are already becoming an important zone in practical terms, while also metalanguage (integrator) in the area of social sciences.

(5) Management, of which we speak, should be concentrated on the most important for the organization and society of values, which are shared by their stakeholders that are associated with these values not only in a tangible way, by means of their varied needs and interests, but also emotionally.

(6) Contemporary management should increasingly take account of the public values and the area of public values, within the framework of which every stakeholder is simultaneously perceived to be a social player and dissident.

(7) Implementing values and systems in such a space may play both the role of the bond that connects people in various types of communities, as well as the catalyst of transformation.

(8) In theory and practice, such a perceived sustainable growth and the resultant "good governing" of the connection of the material sphere and the symbolic sphere is becoming increasingly necessary, as well as the search for new forms for executing power.

(9) The necessity of the greater integration of the research run in the area of the theories of economics with that of research is growing, which relates to the sphere of management of the enterprise. Management that respects and promotes values may become a good integrator.

(10) The interdisciplinary and problem-related approaches are indicated. This points to the need for closer ties between the economists, sociologists, social psychologists, ecologists, anthropologists of culture, lawyers and other representatives of the other social and humanistic sciences in such a way as to be able to counteract the excessive fragmentation of the research field of theories and practice of the management of economic value.

Bibliography

Bauman Z., *Etyka ponowoczesna*, Wydawnictwo Aletheia, Warszawa 2012.

Bourdieu P., Wacquant L.J.D., *Zaproszenie do socjologii refleksyjnej*, Oficyna Naukowa, Warszawa 2001.

Brockman J. (ed.), *Nowy renesans*, CIS, Warszawa 2005.

Dowbor L., *Demokracja ekonomiczna*, Instytut Wydawniczy Książka i Prasa, Warszawa 2008.

Fukuyama F., *The End of History and the Last Men*, Free Press, New York 1992.

Kołodko G., *Świat na wyciągnięcie myśli*, Prószyński i S-ka, Warszawa 2010.

Kołodko G., *Zanim nadejdzie jeszcze większy kryzys*, [w:] *Globalizacja, kryzys i co dalej?*, red. G. Kołodko, Poltext, Warszawa 2010.

Oleksyn T. (red.), *Filozofia a zarządzanie*, Wolters Kluwer Business, Warszawa 2013.

Patel R., *Wartość niczego. Jak przekształcić społeczeństwo rynkowe i na nowo zdefiniować demokrację*, Muza S.A., Warszawa 2010.

Piketty T., *Capital in the Twenty-First Century*, Belknap Press World, Cambridge Massachusetts 2014.

Sedlacek T., *Ekonomia dobra i zła. W poszukiwaniu istoty ekonomii od Gilgamesza do Wall Street*, Audiobook 2012.

Suchodolski B. (red.), *Trwałe wartości i zmienny świat. Zbiór studiów z konferencji w Śródborowie 20–22 listopada 1990*, Dom Wydawniczy Elipsa, Warszawa 1995.

Stiglitz J.E., *Freefall, jazda bez trzymanki. Ameryka, wolne rynki i tonięcie gospodarki światowej*, Polskie Towarzystwo Ekonomiczne, Warszawa 2010.

Sztumski W., *Transformacja nowym paradygmatem ewolucji społecznej*, „Transformacje. Pismo Interdyscyplinarne", Centrum Badań Ewaluacyjnych, Akademia Leona Koźmińskiego, Warszawa 2013.

Szymański W., *Jakie wnioski wyciągniemy z kryzysu*, [w:] *Globalizacja, kryzys i co dalej?*, red. G. Kołodko, Poltext, Warszawa 2010.

Szyszkowska M., *Każdy bywa pacjentem. Zarys filozofii farmacji*, Dom Wydawniczy Elipsa, Warszawa 2010.

Tatarkiewicz W., *Historia filozofii*, PWN, Warszawa 1982.

Teichman J., *Etyka społeczna*, Oficyna Wydawnicza, Warszawa 2002.

Urbański J., *Prekariat i nowa walka klas*, Książka i Prasa, Warszawa 2014.

Tadeusz Oleksyn

2. NATURE OF VALUES AND CATALOGUE OF VALUES IN MANAGEMENT

1. Nature of values

There is no singular definition of values. The assumption adopted here is closer to the perception of *social values*, in that **value is a general abstract principle that marks out the patterns of behaviour in a given organization / community / society which, as a result of the process of socialization – the members of a given community value highly and around which the integration of individual and social aims are executed.**[32]

The prototype of values was that of virtue (Greek *arete*, Latin *virtus*). Two and a half thousand years ago during the times of the sophists and Socrates, five of them were known: wisdom, prudence, valour, moderation and piety. Two hundred years later, Aristotle described 18 virtues in total.[33] Nowadays, the term *virtue* is more seldom utilized and has been pushed out by *values*, whose number is enormous and impossible to establish precisely.

The purpose of this paper is adopted to a significant extent from Nicolai Hartmann (1882–1950), Władysław Tatarkiewicz (1886–1980) and Hans Joasem (born in 1948), in terms of the following assumptions:

- Philosophy, while also morality and ethics have certain constant achievements of a transhistorical significance, which also include virtues and values, while also being the universal trophy of these sciences.
- Values exist in an objective way,[34] while the ideal entity from the other types, for instance mathematics, in which it is distinguished by the fact that they do not express necessity, but obligation is a significant feature of values.
- Each value that is excessively one-sided and displayed may be a threat to other values and for mankind itself. Hartmann termed this the "tyranny of value". As we know from the experience of the 20th century, such values became a threat in the form of social justice, the happiness of future generations, the good of Germans (in the Third Reich), pa-

---

[32] On the basis of A.S. Reber, *Słownik psychologii*, Wydawnictwo Naukowe Scholar, Warszawa 2002, p. 810.

[33] Arystoteles, *Etyka wielka*, Polskie Wydawnictwo Naukowe PWN, Warszawa 2010.

[34] This is the view of among others, I. Kant and N. Hartmann. W. Tatarkiewicz was inclined to hold the conviction that values are neither objective, nor subjective, but rational while also manifold and varied.

triotism and courage. Contemporary threats are becoming values such as freedom, efficiency and competitiveness, while doubtless to say the good of the Russians, albeit by itself, without the excessive and pathological display they are, as in the previous cases, positive notions. As regards freedom, at least we know that the limits of the freedom of an individual is the violation of the freedom of others. Unfortunately, we do not know where the borderline of efficiency is (or where it should be), as well as competitiveness and practically every other kind of economic value which leads to the case whereby the phenomenon of the tyranny of economic values is already strongly advanced, at least in the most highly advanced countries.

- Exuberant relativism is rejected as a false concept. In this light, not only values, but all others may be blurred and questioned.[35]
- The aim is not the promotion of ethical perfectionism. As stated by W. Tatarkiewicz, "Przypisywać komuś, by dążył do doskonałości wydaje się tak niesłuszne, jak ganić go za to, że do niej nie dąży. Wedle różnych zasad można dobrze żyć, a nie każda każdemu odpowiada."[36] Ponadto, „dążenie do doskonałości łatwo budzi poczucie wyższości i zadowolenia z siebie (…). Często jest to dążenie egocentryczne i daje gorsze wyniki moralne i społeczne, niż postępowanie ekstrawertyczne, oparte nie na doskonałości własnej, lecz na dobroci i życzliwości dla innych" (Assigning someone to pursue perfection would seem to be improper as chiding him for not pursuing it. According to various principles it is possible to live well and this does not suit everyone. Furthermore, pursuing perfection easily arouses the feeling of superiority and self-satisfaction […]. This is frequently a egocentric pursuit and provides worse moral and social results than extroverted behaviour that is not based on self-perfection, but on kindness and goodwill towards others).
- All forms of the ideologization of values are rejected.
- The view of Hans Jonas is shared, namely that the operationalization of [a multitude] of values is very difficult, if possible at all.
- The existence of autotelic and fundamental values is acknowledged, whose realization is good in itself, which is not dimensioned and assessed from a praxeological point of view with the use of the methods, techniques and tools that are appropriate for economics, praxeology, psychology, sociology and other sciences.

---

[35] Consistent and absolutized relativism falls victim to its own convictions: as everything is relative and doubtful, then relativism is too (J. Teichman, *Etyka społeczna*, Oficyna Naukowa, Warszawa 2002, p. 23).

[36] W. Tatarkiewicz, *Historia filozofii*, PWN, Warszawa 1982.

– It is deemed to be a worthy form of support for the concept of *sustainability*, which is most frequently termed sustainable growth in Poland. It is also accepted that sustainable growth is only possible in the case of balancing economic and non-economic values; whereas in conditions of dictatorship the economic values of sustainable growth are not possible.

2. Two approaches to values in management

It is possible to distinguish two approaches to values in management as follows: (1) respecting; (2) promoting. In the first case, this relates to how to avoid non-conformities with the generally accepted values and norms while managing as this gives rise to conflicts and discomfort among our partners (employees, clients and trading partners, etc.) and shapes our negative image. In the latter case, this relates to taking account of specific values during the course of shaping the mission of the organization, while also the recruitment and selection of personnel, integrating, motivating, promoting, leading and shaping organizational identity and culture, etc. This refers to the promotion of the values that are important for the organization among the people it co-operates with and deals with. Likewise, it also relates to the active utilization of values as the driving force of the development of enterprises and their efficiency, entrepreneurship, level of involvement and social cohesion. Management that is embedded in the professed values develops people and becomes the source of greater satisfaction and conviction that people are involved in proper things and just causes (if that is the case).

By both respecting and promoting values, it is necessary to go beyond economic values that are insufficient, albeit very important. In contemporary times, a multitude of people are of the conviction that professional work and earning money have excessively dominated their lives. The managers and employees of many corporations are often extremely exhausted, not only in Japan where the image of a person in an expensive suit and wearing an expensive watch, while falling asleep anywhere, even on a footpath is of no surprise to anyone.[37]

New definitions of poverty have emerged which do not only take account of the lack of tangible goods, but also spiritual and cultural, feelings and emotions, the lack of time for recreation, relations with close ones and other people. In this new and broader notion, a poor man may also be a multimillionaire.

---

[37] *Po zmroku*, „Wysokie Obcasy", 29.11.2014. Interview by Anna Maziuk with photographer Paweł Jaszczuk, who for many years lived and created work in Japan.

3. What is and what could be useful in managing the catalogue of values

As a multitude of different groups of values exists, as well as an enormous number of particular values, of which many of them are of partially or significantly similar meaning, there is an objective need for the choice of values that are the most significant from the viewpoint of managing the organization, as well as its transformation and development. It is not possible to *work on the basis of thousands of values.* A huge number of values of course continues to exist and has a greater or lesser impact on us. This refers to the concentration on those values, which from the viewpoint of management are of the greatest significance.

The catalogue of values is helpful material in the choice of values that are deemed to be important in a given organization, while simultaneously an explanation of the significance and way of understanding the catalogued values. The catalogue of values is of authorial nature, thus subjective.

A good catalogue of values may fulfil several useful functions as follows:

(1) facilitating the choice of common values in an organization or organizational / corporate entity of the expected and consolidating people associated with it; easing certain balancing between excessively low *organizational / corporate values* as is most often the case,[38] while also an excessively large number, which would be dysfunctional;

(2) facilitating the similar perception of values, particularly those that are to be the binding force connecting people and in the same manner enabling communication in the organization;

(3) constitute a certain clue and facilitation for management that respects and promotes values;

(4) constitutes aid in terms of social and professional development of people in an organization in the field of the so-called soft competences. There is often a fine line between values and competences;

(5) be an inspiration for the preparation of professiograms / profiles of positions, facilitating recruitment and shrewd selection of people for work positions;

(6) guiding the management of the culture of an organization to constitute one of its determinants;

(7) constitute one of the elements of the motivational system.

---

[38] The average number of organizational /corporate values amounts to 4.7 (see: *Corporate Value Index 2009*, Ecco International Communications Network, http://www.biznespolska.pl/ files/reports/ raportecco.pdf).

The catalogue of values is a certain proposition that is possible to adopt as a whole, or reject it. Likewise, it also displays a certain way of thinking and exploring.

2. Catalogues / lists of values in the notion of the chosen authors

Catalogues or lists of values (which amounts to the same thing) have been prepared only of late. Although reaching all of them is impossible, it would seem that there are not many of them. Hence, we are rather dealing with the problem of a shortage and not a surplus. This is not relating to several chosen values that are usually illustrated as *corporate* values, but values that are useful in the broad perception of management, which constitutes more than just a few.

Steve Pavlina prepared an extensive list of 418 values (formulated in alphabetical order). These values were set out and explained from the viewpoint of their significance in the life of man, thus the aim was different to the one that is of interest to us. The author emphasizes that only some values on the list are of significant meaning in the life of a specific person; the majority of which are of little or marginal significance. There is no explanation of the significance of these values.[39]

C. Roberts offers a list of 79 values, which he proposes to add values to that are not stipulated, but are significant for a specific person, while subsequently choosing 10 of the most important and then gradually reducing them in such a way as to choose the most important one. This is a specific exercise aimed at reflection on the values and their hierarchy. Nevertheless, the author does not display interest in management by values from the viewpoint of the organization and their management, but rather their significance for the particular employees.[40]

Roy Posner presents his own list of 134 personal values, which, in his opinion, exert influence on the aims, pursuits and behaviour of people in a conscious manner or not.[41]

The Values Center of Australia prepared a catalogue of business and managerial values, which shall be therefore presented in a more extensive way here.

---

[39] See: http://www.stevepavlina.com/articles/list-of-values.htm. See also: www.stevepavlina.com/articles/living-your-values.1.htm.

[40] C. Roberts, *Checklist for Personal Values*, http://www.selfcounselling.com/help/personalsucces/personalvalues.html.

[41] R. Posner, *The Power of Personal Values*, http://www.gurusoftware.com/GuruNet/Personal/Topics/Values.htm.

The Values Center distinguishes 31 **business values**,[42] which it divides up into three groups as follows: (1) Physical values; (2) Organizational values; (3) Psychological values.

Physical values encompass 11 values, which include the following:
- Precision / accuracy;
- Cleanliness / neatness;
- Maximum Utilization of Resources – time, money, equipment, materials, space, people, etc.;[43]
- Orderliness – in offices, studies, on the shelves, in documents, in files, in phone numbers, priorities at work, daily and weekly plans, etc.;[44]
- Punctuality and Timeliness; this is perceived in a broad sense and encompasses among other aspects, the timely settlement of financial obligations;
- Quality of products and services;
- Regularity: meetings, reports, sales, interviews, etc.;
- Reliability / consistency – this also encompasses the ability to acquire the same features and results of activities;
- Responsiveness – the way in which people, an organization, or systems, etc. react to the needs that appear both externally and internally;
- Safety – of products, clients, employees, other;
- Speed of operations – the ability to act sufficiently fast over time.

Organizational values encompass 7 elements:
- Cooperation and teamwork – within and outside the organization;
- Coordination;
- Discipline – this has a broad perception, which also includes the executive discipline (in the sphere of the realization of plans, principles, systems, procedures, plans, standards, ethical norms, etc.);
- Freedom for Activity and Initiative of Employees – expressing suggestions, developing plans, making decisions, submitting propositions and modifying activities and other similar areas;
- Integration – integrating activities between different levels of an organization in the field of plans, priorities and decisions;
- Standardization – relating to the forms, files, procedures, reports, evaluation of performance, equipment, training, recruitment, orientation, communication, etc.;
- Systemization – relating to sales, marketing, services for clients, accounting, research, production, engineering, forecasts, recruitment, training, promotion, communication, coordination, reporting, etc.

---

[42] *List of Business Values*, The Values Center, http://gurusoftware.com/GuruNet/Business/Values.htm. The names of the authors of this list have not been provided.

[43] These have been enumerated in orders according to the authors of this list of values.

[44] As in reference 11.

Psychological values encompass 13 elements:
- Continuous Improvement – the ability and tendency of an organization to constantly improve everything;
- Creativity – in the sphere of new products and production methods, notions, systems, technologies, ways of financing, marketing strategies, etc.;
- Customer Delight – attempting to evoke positive emotions and joy among clients / consumers that is associated with interactions with our people, products and services;
- Resoluteness / decisiveness – in terms of resolving problems, planning and the realization of plans, speed of activities, etc.;
- Development of people – the desire and ability to develop people in an organization;
- Harmony – a generally favourable atmosphere and good relations between people, departments, divisions, systems, activities, principles and policies within the organization, as well as the external environment;
- Innovation – the desire and ability of an organization to become involved in novelties in various areas;
- Integrity – encompassing employees, clients, traders, the government, etc.;
- Loyalty – mutual loyalty of suppliers, clients and employees (it is also possible to add the owners and the management staff);
- Ingenuity, resourcefulness – ability to initiate creativity and imagination to resolve problems, including untypical and difficult ones, while also in unfavourable circumstances.;
- Respect for Individual – expressed in terms of running policies, setting out principles, projects and systems, taking decisions, etc., while also expressed in terms of care for health, safety, listening to and taking account of opinions, etc.;
- Service to Society – associated with the common good of people in an organization, protected working environment, satisfaction of the actual needs of people in an organization associated with the tangible conditions of the working environment;
- The will to succeed – in all aspects associated with work.
- The list of business values presented above has been prepared by The Values Center and its concise explanation is both interesting and inspiring, albeit arousing certain reservations. Firstly, their division into three groups of values: physical, organizational and psychological, is blurred, while the allocation in certain cases is inappropriate. For instance, the maximum utilization of resources should not be assigned to "physical values". Secondly, not all the categories termed values can be

deemed to be values. This is exemplified by precision / exactness which is rather a requirement set by some types of work (also competence no doubt), than value. Social servicing is a function of HRM rather than a value. Nevertheless, it is necessary to take account of the fact that the perception of values may be different, while the notion itself is ambiguous and defined in different ways; thus this type of accusation needs to be formulated in a careful way. Thirdly, some of these values may be combined to avoid excessive fragmentation, for example cleanliness / neatness with that of order, coordination with that of integration and creativity with that of ingenuity. Fourthly, some very important values (of interest to us) are not mentioned here, for example responsibility, efficiency, courage and the ability to take permissible levels of risk. There is also no mention of the business orientation, albeit its significant elements are stipulated, such as the maximum utilization of resources, customer delight, the will to succeed (no doubt economic one too, although it is not stated). Sixthly, the catalogue prepared by The Values Center is geared towards values of a pragmatic nature, which however omit the values of a philosophical and ethical nature that are important for the management of an organization, such as justice, responsibility, honesty, kindness and trust.

5. Proposition of self-catalogue of organizational values particularly useful in management

The list proposed below is a list of values that is useful in management, whose acceptance, application and development are recommended by its insight into both the individual and collective good.[45] This may be a starting point for the definition of corporate values, after adding or deducting the number presented below appropriately to the autonomous decisions of the particular entities.

The values in this catalogue have been set out in alphabetical order (in the English language). Hence, it is not a ranking, nor does it take account of the degree of their importance, which may actually be perceived in different organizations in different ways that are variable over time.

---

[45] By way of intention, this list puts up with, or at least mitigates the conflict between the values required in an organization and those that are important for man and society, accruing from the asymmetry of values (commonly occurring in the case of the display of only several values acknowledged to be important for the organization, while ignoring some that are important for man and society).

The number of distinguished competences is always a controversial issue, of which there has already been a reference to. They may be adopted to a greater or lesser degree. There are hundreds, if not thousands of important values of varying degrees for people. Some of them are of significance for the management of organizations, their credibility, efficiency, the realization of the mission, integration, development and satisfaction. Such values exceed the number quoted in the catalogue. Nevertheless, it is difficult to work with all of them and promote them, which is why self-restriction has been adopted. The simultaneous distinction of a group of 34 competences is significantly greater than the ones adopted as corporate values and due to this fact they may be acknowledged as (excessively) large. The author of this catalogue opines that the number of corporate values is insufficient and not an excessive number of values in the catalogue. However, opinions may be varied.

(1) Auxiliarity / Subsidiarity

The notion of subsidiarity is derived from ancient times (Greece, Rome) and is one of the fundamental principles adopted in the EU.

Subsidiarity, in its contemporary perception involves priority, while in terms of activity and the resolution of problems it should have individuals (citizens, employees). If they are incapable of dealing with this, the following should be initiated: family / colleagues, superiors – management of the highest level in an organization-local authorities – regional authorities – the state – the European Union. Each level of authority executes only the tasks and resolves only these problems that the lower level is incapable of dealing with. The higher level is initiated only when it is absolutely necessary or when it obvious that the problem exceeds the competences of the lower level. The state should allow free-flowing activity and development in terms of the activities of citizens, families, local self-government, civic society and the free market, and should only intervene in extraordinary circumstances in a manner that is not in capacitating and not destructive for the activity, creativity and the previously mentioned resourcefulness.

Subsidiarity constitutes the panaceum for the omnipotence and paternalism of the state, which are always a threat to citizens and democracy itself, albeit the problem currently lies more frequently in the fact that such omnipotence and paternalism are demanded by a significant proportion of contemporary societies that are tantalized by populist politicians that are prevalent in the majority of countries and parliaments. Likewise, subsidiarity, civic societies and democracy are also at threat.

In the sector of enterprises, subsidiarity has acquired a new dimension since it began in the 1980s in the Silicon Valley. The numerous firms forming there (mainly small and medium sized firms in the sector of ITC) dealt with everything directly, in terms of what they could do and what they could cope with. What they could not deal with was ceded to the external environment in the form of services, including managerial ones. Nevertheless, they did not lose their sovereignty, nor did they become subordinate with regard to this; but rather the relations of equal entities, while the mutual obligation was stipulated in the appropriate agreements. Such a model works well.

After a certain period of time, the practices of the Silicon Valley began to be adopted by large and indeed very large organizations and the **reverse delegation** was formed. In smooches the "management lights" shared power and ceded their authority "downwards", which was regarded as the pinnacle of achievements, at present the autonomous entities themselves are taking on as many competences as they can muster, while only passing on what they are incapable of doing well (including some managerial services); thus, the notion of "upwards" and "downwards" is losing out in terms of importance. The experience of the Silicon Valley also points to the knowledge of how large the autonomous entities should be in order to operate in the best and most effective way (up to 120–160 people).[46]

Such a perception of subsidiarity is a great challenge in Poland and simultaneously an opportunity to overcome bureaucracy and inefficiency faster. There are no shorter synonyms or antonyms for subsidiarity.

(2) Business orientation[47]

Business orientation is the ability and tendency to do business, while also make such contacts and relations with other entities that lead to the achievement of profits. This term is associated with the positive approach to business activity and earning money, as well as the readiness to cooperate and even significant effort. This signifies the particular interest in their clients and partners in terms of business, their needs and expectations that are treated as priorities. Business orientation is accompanied by the awareness of the social nature of interactions occurring in business, as well as the skill of observation, the feeling of place and time, in which activities are undertaken (timing). Some opportunities and possibilities arise only once and for a fleeting moment. Nevertheless, business orientation usually signifies the necessity of a long-lasting and consistent pursuit of the designated and constantly updated aims.

---

[46] Ch. Handy, *Wiek Paradoksu. W poszukiwaniu sensu przyszłości*, Dom Wydawniczy ABC, Warszawa 1996, rozdział 7: Subsydiarność (*The Empty Raincoat: Making Sense of the Future*, 1994).

[47] T. Oleksyn, *Zarządzanie kompetencjami. Teoria i praktyka*, Oficyna Ekonomiczna, Kraków 2006, pp. 68–69.

Business orientation is both a value and a competence that is highly valued in the sector of enterprises. Konosuke Matsushita underlined the social aspect of business orientation by stating the following: "Actually, it does refer to the needs of society – and that is the reason for entering business. If people who are involved in business do not understand this, then I would not call their business real. I am of the opinion that the sale of products and the profit which accrues from these sales are secondary. In business both the seller and the buyer must be satisfied with the result of the transaction. The buyer must be pleased that he has made a good purchase, enriched his life and improved its quality. The seller, apart from the feeling of pleasure that he has made the buyer happy, should also feel satisfaction from making a good product and selling it at a profit."[48]

Business orientation is the perception that an enterprise is a place whereby money is earned as a result of satisfying the specific needs of clients by offering them products of properties that are expected by them (or better than those expected), while also pursuing the gaining and maintenance of clients, perceiving sales and profits as the necessary conditions for the existence and development of enterprises. Business orientation is the capability and readiness for the personal and conspicuous involvement in the realization of the economic aims of the business activities of firms, while also supporting other areas and people that are directly involved in this by treating them as internal clients.

Business orientation favours entrepreneurial attitudes that are also associated with the *internal entrepreneurship*.

Similar term: business acumen. Antonym: reluctance towards business / business activities.

(3) Confidence

Trust – this is the conviction that it is possible to rely on someone or something, count on his/its reliability (people, product, system, etc.), count on the genuineness of the sources, facts, dependability, etc. Trust is easier in the case of good familiarity of a given entity and the hitherto positive experience with it. Trust is also conditioned by personality and environmental factors. Indeed, it is particularly important and necessary in crisis situations.

Trust is not only a value, but also one of the fundamental interpersonal ties. Nevertheless, trust is often mistaken for hope.

With relation to some institutions, trust is so strong and conditions their very existence that they are termed institutions of public trust.

---

[48] *Zarządzanie z pasją czyli rozmowy z Konosuke Matsushitą*, oprac. PHP Institute Inc., Matsushita Group, Medium, Poznań 2004, pp. 162–163.

The technique of *management by trust* exists, which is based on the 18 principles of creating trust. "In management by trust, it is not about trusting or not trusting, but to know how and to what extent to trust and build trust professionally."[49]

Here are several statements by famous people on the issue of trust:

- "Trust is courage" (Marie von Ebner-Eschenbach).
- "Trust is not something you possess. It is something that you bestow" (Eric E. Schmitt).
- "Experience has proven that if someone never trusts, he shall be cheated" (Leonardo da Vinci).

Synonyms: entrustment, confidence. Antonyms: lack of trust, distrust, suspicion.

(4) Cooperation

Cooperation/co-working – is the pursuit of aims and execution of tasks together with other people. This should take place in a manner that is effective and efficient, harmonious, consensual and peaceful, free of dictatorship possible, coercion and pressure, while taking account of the realistic competences, possibilities and interests of the particular partners.

Cooperation is frequently listed among corporate values, which is no wonder as not much can be done individually and cooperation is the common objective necessity.

More and more frequently cooperation is being carried out within the framework of mono or inter-disciplinary teams. This frequently requires greater competences than in the work executed individually in the spheres of flexibility, communication, mutual tolerance, synchronization and coordination of activities, openness, trust, comradeship and solidarity.

Without common and skilful cooperation of people, the development of the human civilization or great achievements would not have been possible. The same may be said about organizations.

Cooperation may be carried out within the organization and with external entities. The feature of contemporary times is the increase in terms of openness in this area that is particularly visible in network organizations where employees quite often work with their partners from other firms within the framework of networks/clusters in a constant and almost uninhibited fashion by exchanging information, mutually inspiring and realizing joint projects.

Cooperation has a favourable impact on the social and professional development, as well as integration, friendship, resolution of problems and coping with difficult situations.

---

[49] See: http://pl.wikipedia.org/Wiki/Zarządzanie_przez_zaufanie.

Synonyms of cooperation: cooperation, co-working, partnership, co-participation. Antonyms: lack of cooperation, rivalry.

(5) Courage (moral courage)

Napoleon claimed that courage was the only virtue that cannot be faked. Courage is the ability to control anxiety and take action associated with personal risk that must be realized in the name of higher goals and values despite the fears felt. In accordance with Aristotle, courage lies between cowardice and foolhardiness. The failure to feel anxiety and taking excessive risk is not courage, but the lack of common sense, the lack of knowledge relating to the nature of the threat or lack of imagination.

In peaceful times, courage most frequently appears (or should appear) in the so-called *civil courage*.

There is an array of different types of situations that occurs in organizations, in which courage is required. This particularly relates to the managerial staff that take the most important decisions that are usually associated with greater or lesser business risks and other risks that translate to the personal responsibility for the success and effects of the aforesaid decisions. Fear of responsibility should not objectively speaking, paralyse the actions that are necessary to undertake. Civil courage is also needed in order to correct the inappropriate attitudes and behaviour of the people associated with the organization (not only its employees), as well as fighting against various types of pathology and abuse.

Courage is also sometimes necessary to set out the requirements associated with the work, demand good quality and efficient work, good cooperation, adherence to norms of community life, as well as the culture of work and manner. It should be a factor taken into consideration when making appointments for at least some work positions.

Civil courage conditions the declaration of and defence of arguments, views and interests, which is associated with assertiveness. This is particularly necessary in the case whereby (real) views and (necessary) actions are unpopular and are not in conformance with political correctness. It is also the foundation of freedom and civil society, which are values that require constant activity and defence, as they are not given forever.

Synonymous term: bravery. Antonymous term: cowardice. Partially antonymous terms: procrastination, opportunism.

(6) Creativity

Creativity is the ability to create new or improved states: notions, paradigms, theories, hypotheses, scientific work, books and articles, works of art, methods, techniques, tools, products (goods or services), processors, etc. Historically speaking, the term *creativity* was for many centuries associated with art and artism. This encompasses scientific and technical creativity only after the second half of the 19th century.

Creativity is the most important competence of artists, designers, engineers and scientific employees. The range of its usefulness is continuing to grow. Managers, leaders, specialists and more and more frequently the executive employees should all be creative. Creativity refers to new ideas, but also improvements that are sometimes tiny, but whose significant number may lead to the saltatory qualitative change (which is the essence of *kaizen*). The mistake which is quite often made involves the expectation of great innovations – new ideas, theories, concepts, patents, utility models, etc. with the simultaneous neglect of improvements. Consequently, there is frequently neither the former, nor the latter.

Since several decades ago, creativity in a multitude of organizations was the subject matter of methodological work executed in specially appointed teams for this purpose to resolve specific problems (*problem-solving teams*), or also to generate new products or their elements with the aid of the method of heuristic/creative resolutions of problems. Apart from the most well-known methods of brainstorming and analysis of the values, the following methods are also applied: decision trees, Delphi method, morphological, the devil's advocate, 635, synectics, the six thinking hats (De Bono), black boxes, discovery matrix, the rest method, teratological, transfer of notions, definitions and many others.

Creativity should not be required from all the employees. In many areas the greatest advantage is the strictly adhered to binding procedures, methodicalness and diligence of work, mindfulness, timeliness and precision. This relates to services of maintenance, repairs and renovation, serving the production processes and an array of others. No-one would probably want to employ a creative cashier, while "creative accounting" would end in high-profile scandals, bankruptcies and court verdicts.

P.F. Drucker observed that "innovative activity that draws firms away from their current operations rarely end in success."[50]

Synonym of creativity: creativity. Similar terms: innovativeness, ingenuity, originality, *creative vein*. Antonyms: emptiness, malaise, stagnation.

---

[50] P.F. Drucker, *Myśli przewodnie Druckera*, MT Biznes, Warszawa 2002, pp. 215–216.

(7) Development

Development – the process of change associated with the transition from simple forms to more intricate and improved forms. This is associated with progress,[51] particularly in terms of knowledge and its implementation.

Development may be perceived as autotelic value. Development is commonly appreciated value, both in terms of the development of an organization, as well as the people connected with it, while also products, technologies, market value of the firm, etc. The work on offer and the possibilities of developing competences are significant values for work candidates, employees and local communities, while also for employers if they can develop their firms, thereby increasing their competitiveness and attaining economic benefits. Development and economic growth are states that are generally desirable in the economy.

However, it is possible to encounter the view that development is not merely a value (autonomous), but the consequence of other values such as: competence, entrepreneurship, activity, positive thinking, health and good psycho-physical condition, etc.

The term development is most frequently utilized with reference to the particular fields and areas. There are references made to economic development, professional development, development of science and art, development of a person and his personality, etc.

The term *development* and *growth* are similar in meaning, while the states associated with them are most frequently set out as the goals of economics and management. Nevertheless, the representatives of other professions may perceive it differently. For instance, biologists emphasize the necessity to control development and growth from the viewpoint of preserving balance in nature, which in healthy and unspoilt eco-systems takes place in a natural and spontaneous manner; various species of plants and animals mutually regulate their numerical amount, whilst not allowing for excessive expansion that would threaten the whole environment. In economics the growing awareness of threats arising from the unrestricted economic development is paving the way for the concept of sustainable development. Nevertheless, in many organizations there are significant possibilities for generating the growth of production, services, as well as sales, particularly completely new products, in which the participation of raw materials is slight or even none at all, thus the burden on the environment is minimal, while the most significant are the innovative products, human thought, inventions and opening up of completely new possibilities.

---

[51] *Wielki słownik języka polskiego*, red. E. Polański, Krakowskie Wydawnictwo Naukowe, Kraków 2008, p. 724.

Similar terms: growth, rise. Antonyms (of varying significance): stagnation, recession, depreciation, degradation.

(8) Dignity

Dignity – the feeling and awareness of your own value for yourself, honour, as well as pride.[52] Dignity has two different meanings as follows: (1) honourable position, office, title, function, as well as (2) the feeling of your own dignity and the expectation of dignified treatment. According to Aristotle, dignity is the balance between conceit and subservience. Immanuel Kant associated dignity with the subjective treatment of man who should be a goal, yet not the means to this goal for others.[53]

In the Polish Constitution, dignity is given special importance (preamble, art. 30), by describing it as the source of all freedom and rights of man and citizen, while constitutionalists perceive dignity as a legislative *meta clause*, the primary one with regard to the constitution and consequently indelible. Dignity also has a high level of importance and total protection in EU and international law.

In Christianity, the *dignity of human beings* is the independent state of man as the *child of God*, due to the *redemption at a high cost* and the *final destiny of man*; which is of a *transcendental dimension*.[54] This is also the foundation of the Canon Law. Likewise, in other great religions the dignity of man is of particular importance: in Judaism it is acknowledged that man receives his dignity from God. "Whoever violates human dignity – by mocking, ridiculing or humiliating also directs his behaviour towards God." In the Talmud there is the following reference: "Whoever raises his status by means of humiliating others shall not participate in the world that is to come" (Chagiga 2:1).[55] A similar view is to be found in Islam.[56]

Orientations (philosophy, anthropology) of both naturalist and atheistic nature are opposed to the perception of the dignity of man as that of value commanded by God, but perceive this as an acquired feature and refer to the law established by people.

Dignity appears in two meanings: as personal dignity and personality dignity. Personal dignity is something that every man is deserving of for the very fact of being a human being. Personality dignity belongs to those people who have deserved it due to their advantages, behaviour and achievements.[57]

---

[52] *Słownik języka polskiego*, PWN, Warszawa 1978, t. 1, p. 673.
[53] Arystoteles, *op. cit.*, p. 46.
[54] *Katechizm Kościoła Katolickiego*, Pallotinum, Poznań 1994, p. 446.
[55] See: http://the614thcs.com/40.1111.0.0.1.0.phtml.
[56] Koran, Sura Komnaty, 11–12.
[57] See: http://pl.wikipedia.org/wiki/Godno%C5%9B%C4%87_cz%C5%82owieka.

A term which is similar in meaning to dignity is that of **respect.** Respect is a reference to esteem, respect for self-dignity and towards another person, avoiding offence and causing distress. The opposite to respect would be as follows: slander (saying untrue things that place a person in an unfavourable light) defamation (saying things that are true, but placing a person in an unfavourable light without cause), arrogance, contempt, offending, while also conviction of superiority. Respect for yourself and for others is a significant element of personal culture, as well as the proper development of man and society.

Treating clients with respect and kindness, as well as superiors, employees, work colleagues, shareholders, local communities and other entities with whom the organization has contact and cooperates should be the canon of procedure in all organizations. This is of business, cultural and motivational importance. This is required by both business interests, as well as good practices.

There is a multitude of situations in the workplace where the temptation of a terse expression of disapproval exist, e.g. in cases of the lack of effects, inappropriate attitudes and behaviour, violation of the law and good practices, violation of the business interests of individuals or groups, unjustified accusations and suspicions, impertinence or arrogance displayed by bosses, employees, clients, or others. People may be guided by bad emotions. It is worth shaping the culture of the organization, the styles of leadership and management of the whole organization in order to limit these situations to a maximum extent in which emotional, impulsive and adamant reactions lead to the violation of the dignity of man, even by behaving and proceeding in an improper way. To a certain degree, it is possible to learn this during the course of training workshops and training for those professional groups that are more exposed to situations which provoke uncontrolled behaviour and reactions (sellers, employees of customer service, stewards and stewardesses, employees of ZUS (Social Insurance Office), the police, security guards, etc.).

Synonyms of dignity: respect, esteem. Antonyms: lack of dignity, belittlement, disdain, contempt.

(9) Discipline

Discipline is the readiness and ability to adhere to the specified social, ethical and organizational principles. It is the adherence to the rules of behaviour, procedure, instructions, yet also the discipline and the execution of orders from superiors. In the industrial era, discipline was deemed to be very important and was absolutely required. In the army and paramilitary organizations, while also in the church, monasteries, hospitals and a multitude of other organizations, it is still one of the most important values. In other organizations, it has generally lost its significance in comparison with the past to that of creativity, innovativeness, freedom, freedom of choice and action, while also other values. In some environments it is perceived to be a certain anachronism, or display of asymmetry in terms of internal relations, sometimes even as humiliation. Nevertheless, in a multitude of collective entities and many types of activities its significance is upheld and sometimes even increasing in places where it is essential to rigorously adhere to procedures, technologies, assigned treatment, safety: personal safety and that of other people, micro-biological and ecological safety, etc. Likewise, the extension of the sphere of work on your own account where it is easy to experience laxity and the loss of self-control lead to the case whereby internal discipline is one of the significant conditions of the existence and success of a firm.

The necessity of *conscious discipline* has been indicated for a long time. Its adherence not (only) due to the fact that the superior demands it, but (mainly) as a result of understanding the reasons, usually of higher order, for which it is necessary. K. Blanchard and M. O'Connor claim, no doubt slightly excessively that "in a firm that is really managed in conformance with values, the only boss is the values professed by the firm."[58] Hence, discipline and self-discipline.

Traditionally, great importance is attributed to the discipline of **work** in many organizations, and a significant proportion of the work regulations is devoted to these problematic issues. In education, therapeutics, trade, public administration and many other types of activities, especially in the broad perception of services, the constant presence of the employee (teacher, doctor, official, sellers, etc.) is prevalent in an established place and time. A specified time scale is of great significance for the realization of the mission of the organization, as well as opinions about it and its employees, the feeling of comfort or discomfort of its clients (students and listeners, patients, etc.). During the course of teamwork, the absence or lateness of one or several employees may render the work of the others impossible and lead to significant losses.

In business and indeed business meetings, great emphasis is placed on punctuality, not only because of the saying that *time is money*, but also in its perception as an expression of respect for the participants of a meeting, or indeed its lacking in the case of lateness.

On the other hand, wherever possible various forms of organization and working time are made commonplace by taking account of the needs and preferences of both the employers, as well as the employees.

---

[58] K. Blanchard, M. O'Connor, *Zarządzanie poprzez wartości*, Wydawnictwo Studio Emka, Warszawa 1998, p. 119.

Discipline should not be brought down to only the formal discipline of work. In the system of 5S that was initiated in Japan and already applied in many countries worldwide, there are five mutually connected elements in evidence as follows: *seito* (order), *shitsuke* (discipline), *seiri* (organization), *seiketsu* (standardization) and *seiso* (cleanliness), which mutually condition and strengthen each other. Cleanliness in many sectors constitutes an important element in the technological discipline (the regime of the technological process) in the food sector, as well as the pharmaceutical, cosmetics, chemical goods and the arms sectors, etc.

Similar terms: order, regime (e.g. technological). Antonym: disorder.

(10) Effectiveness

Effectiveness is the skill of achieving aims and results despite the existing adversities, difficulties and restrictions. This requires the possession of and initiation of an array of competences as follows: abilities and predisposition, knowledge, skills, experience, activity and involvement, cooperation, sometimes even courage and intransigence, determination in terms of operations, while also expending mental energy. Sometimes external support is necessary, which also requires skill in terms of its acquisition.

The effectiveness of operations is a value whose significance is usually appreciated in cases of its shortage, the reliability of operations and not the skills of attaining the accepted targets. This is featured by a well-organized society and state of a high level of civilizational development, high standard of living, as well as organizations that achieve success.

Effectiveness is very closely connected with the efficiency of operations, which in turn is the main subject matter of interest of praxeology.[59] Perhaps it would be better to perceive it as a combined form by referring to it as *efficiency and effectiveness*.

The efficiency and effectiveness of operations are surely the most important features of managers and in a broader sense the management staff as a whole. This is at least what P.F. Drucker thought.[60] It is possible to and it is necessary to learn them as nobody is born with them. Developing skills in this field is mainly carried out by good practices, albeit there are also highly useful principles in this sphere, particularly prepared by the theories and practices of management, as well as praxeology.

---

[59] Praxeology was initiated in 1890 by the French philosopher Alfred Espinas. This was transposed to the field of economics by Ludwig von Mises. A significant role in the development of praxeology was played by the Polish philosopher Tadeusz Kotarbiński.

[60] Effectiveness is the keynote of his acclaimed book entitled *Effective Executive* from 1967, known in Poland as *Menedżer skuteczny*, MT Busines, Warszawa, 2009.

The efficiency and effectiveness of operations are values that are extraordinarily significant for all organizations and their leaders. On the other hand, these values require supplementation in the form of ethical procedure. Effectiveness alone, without morality or amorality, merely raises the scale of abuse and unhappiness.

The efficiency and effectiveness of operations should be taken into consideration in the case of entrusting the majority of work positions, not only managerial ones. This generally speaking, points to the promotion of people that turn out to be effective in their hitherto work. People who are educated and eloquent, while also creating a good impression are not always efficient and effective in their activities as the managerial craft and everyday reality make them bored and they display little interest in this. As stated by J. Kotter, business is mundane and involves a great sense of originality, novel strategies and brilliant ideas to only a slight extent. Success in the execution of tasks most frequently relate to "hardworking, persistent and tireless grumblers."[61]

Similar terms: efficiency, effectiveness, functionality. Antonyms: ineffectiveness, inefficiency, dysfunctionality.

(11) Efficiency

Economic efficiency is the relation between the acquired effects and the increased outlays. Efficiency also signifies the utilization of resources in a way that is the most effective and rational. Efficiency increases when the effects rise and / or the costs reduce. They are significant not only as the absolute levels of effects and outlays, but also in terms of how many relations exist between them. Outlays in terms of the level and structure should be such as to achieve the maximum effects. An alternative approach is to strive towards achieving the given goal (business like and economic) with minimal outlays. Such an approach entails an advantage only when the target it is heading towards is clearly stipulated and cannot be greater, which is not the prevalent case. Wherever effects can grow rapidly, it is usually not worth focusing mainly on the restriction of outlays. On the contrary, it is usually worth increasing the outlays in order to gain even better effects.

Efficiency is one of the most important values in the market economy. It usually strives towards the maximization of economic efficiency, nevertheless sometimes **optimization** is more appropriate from the viewpoint of various significant variables (in specific cases), while also sensible assumptions of the strategic policies.

---

[61] J. Kotter, *Co właściwie robią przywódcy?*, "Harvard Business Review Polska", June 2005.

Global efficiency only occurs when the economy is to be found at the limits of its production capacity.[62] From the viewpoint of individual enterprises, the situation which is generally optimal is one that avails of the production capacity available to the fullest, by finding markets for their products (goods or services). However, this is not easy.

Economic efficiency depends on various factors: the quality and attractiveness of products, prices, market saturation, the technological processes applied and others, the level of sales, the quality of management and the competences of the management staff and the employees, the competitive position, cooperation / outsourcing and many other aspects.

Efficiency has the advantage that it is possible to gauge and express in numerical form. Likewise, it is possible to research and analyse in a structural notion, as well as a dynamic notion, compare with the efficiency of various organizations, market leaders, etc. It is easy to define it at the level of enterprises and at the lower levels (to a certain degree), where centres of costs and profits are created. Defining the economic efficiency with relation to one group of employees is easy, whereas difficult in the case of others, if at all possible (without the appropriate preparation). The same relates to individual employees. Analogically speaking, the specification of the impact of singular areas, teams and individual employees in terms of the value of the organization is simpler, whereas in other cases more difficult, particularly when they work on behalf of its future.

Efficiency is deemed to be a value from the set of economic categories. However, it is possible to acknowledge it as a moral requirement, especially with relation to the management staff; the lack of economic efficiency, the loss making, the waste of resources (frequently non-renewable or rare) which are all in essence immoral, at least in the opinion of Konosuke Matsushita, not only one of the greatest entrepreneurs of the 20th century, but also a brilliant philosopher of management. The same may be most frequently said of the lack of effectiveness.

Synonym: lack. Similar terms: effectiveness, efficiency. Antonym: inefficiency.

(12) Entrepreneurship

Entrepreneurship is a value and at the same time an intricate competence that is associated with the ability to generate from the possible to the profitable realization of ideas, mainly business ones, the effective creation of contacts and cooperation, conviction of the appropriate people towards activity and

---

[62] P.A. Samuelson, W.D. Nordhaus, *Ekonomia 2*, Wydawnictwo Naukowe PWN, Warszawa 1996, p. 510.

involvement, the acquisition of resources, as well as organizing the necessary processes and activities. Primarily understood as the features that are appropriate for entrepreneurs, for the past several decades this has also developed into the form of the so-called internal entrepreneurship, particularly within the framework of corporations among the managers of various levels and the majority of employees.

Entrepreneurship has always been associated with risk, thus this requires the skills of calculating and taking risk, as well as coping with uncertainty. Likewise, entrepreneurship is associated with creativity, flexibility and adaptiveness, while also as opined by R. Vesga and D. Norde – *the obsession of seizing the opportunity*. Entrepreneurship is an important factor that has an impact on the creation of added value. Indeed, entrepreneurship is not only a value and intricate competence, but also a process whose coordination requires organizational abilities and skills. A significant form has become intellectual entrepreneurship. As perceived by S. Kwiatkowski, this involves "the creation of tangible wealth with intangible knowledge."[63] This is particularly connected with the *knowledge employees*, whose significance is constantly rising.

P.F. Drucker acknowledged that the society of the 21st century is in the phase of transformation in the direction of *entrepreneurial society*, thus such a one where entrepreneurship shall exist on a widespread scale and become the foundation of development. It is worth remembering that A. Marshall deemed entrepreneurship as the fourth factor of production (1924), which has been adopted on a rather widespread scale.

Entrepreneurship is particularly associated with enterprises, which already suggests the linguistic similarity between these two words in other languages too. It is frequently acknowledged as the corporate value and advocated in various ways, ranging from the recruitment and selection of personnel while taking account of their competences, through the frequently adopted entrepreneurial strategies, techniques of management and motivational systems developing the entrepreneurship of the management staff and employees, to the entrepreneurial culture of an organization.

Similar terms: initiativeness, enterprise, resourcefulness. Antonyms: lack of entrepreneurship, helplessness.

(13) Generosity

Generosity is a value and also a feature that is associated with noble thinking and behaviour, magnanimity, forbearance, the lack of pettiness, readiness to forgive and transitioning from the daily order of things to the issues of

---

[63] S. Kwiatkowski, *Przedsiębiorczość intelektualna*, Wydawnictwo Naukowe PWN, Warszawa 2000, p. 8.

lesser importance, namely in cases whereby a co-worker has understood his mistake and does not want to repeat it. Generosity is also a precious value as it facilitates taking and realizing all the aims and concentration on them, whereas motivation is not in general an insight into the personal benefits and accolades. As the opposite to generosity, pettiness is defined by St. Thomas as *false humility*, which leads to the case whereby people reject promotions or the execution of more ambitious tasks, albeit they have the qualifications for this work, but due to laziness, the fear of failure or excessive servilism, this camouflages the lack of discernment in terms of their own possibilities.

Alexandre Havard[64] is of the opinion that generosity is the most important of the virtues, binding the remaining ones together.

There may also be superficial generosity and forbearance, which result from the features and reasons whose advantages are not the following: indifference, laziness and comfort, exaggerated tolerance, insufficient civil courage, lack of awareness of risks and threats, as well as others. The shortage of generosity, or its deficit may in turn result in the excessive explosion of pettiness, meticulousness, aggression and conflicts. Pettiness causes a stifling atmosphere and creates the grounds for mobbing.

Synonyms and similar words: magnanimity, goodwill, forbearance, clemency. Antonyms: pusillanimity, pettiness, unfavourableness.

(14) Health

A new broad and holistic definition of health has been assumed here as defined by the World Health Organization (WHO), according to whom "health is not the total absence of illness or invalidity, but also the state of a full physical, mental and social well-being and frame of mind."[65] In accordance with this definition, the condition of being healthy is not only the treatment of illnesses, availing of the aid of the health care services and pharmaceutical industry. The active pursuit of a good frame of mind, as well as a good psycho-physical condition is also necessary, which requires the appropriate nutrition, physical exercise, avoidance of factors and substances that are damaging to the health, such as overburdening stress, narcotics (including alcohol), coping with your own emotions, positive thinking and good relations with others as "gdy dusza choruje to i ciało niedomaga" (if the soul is sick, then the body ails).[66]

---

[64] A lawyer and expert in the field of leadership, the author of a book translated into 13 languages entitled *Etyka przywódcy* (*Virtuous Leadership*, New York 2007), basing on the ancient Greek virtues, recently extended by the virtue of goodwill; founder of the European Centre for Leadership Development.

[65] See: http://www.seremet.org/who_zdrowie.html [16.01.2015].

[66] Ibidem.

To be healthy, social well-being is also necessary, thus socially isolated people for instance are not healthy in accordance with this definition.

Particularly in wealthy societies, health has become one of the most important values. Simultaneously, health, including a good psycho-physical condition is perceived as a significant personal and employee competence. Likewise, it also constitutes an important element of human capital.[67]

Organizations influence the health of people that are associated with them in a twofold manner as follows:

- by means of the type and intensity of work and conditions in which it is executed, which in turn has an impact on the health condition of employees, whether favourably or unfavourably;
- by means of involvement (or lack of) of employers in health prophylactics, as well as organizing and financing or co-financing the treatment of employees, rest and recreation.

In some types of business activities there are threats to the health and lives of employees, thus significant importance is attached to those activities that improve the conditions of health and safety, restrict stress and professional burnout by means of the appropriate medical tests, organizational and technical forms of the humanization of work, rotation of people in terms of work positions, particularly where longer working hours exposes employees to occupational illnesses, which is to all lead to the creation of the culture of the organization and work that is friendly to the employees.

Synonym: shortage. Similar term: well-being. Antonyms: illness, lack of health.

(15) Honesty

Honesty is a value and also a personal competence that is important in business and in management, as well as interpersonal relations. Honesty is associated with responsibility, good intentions, sincerity, respect for the truth and being guided by it, respect for yourself and for others, dignity and dignified behaviour. Generally speaking, honesty favours the developed empathy, thus facilitating the imagination of the effects of the lack of health and what a person affected by this may experience. A positive role is played by the "good upbringing", which is taken from home. In pathological environments and certain sub-cultures, honesty arouses aversion and ironic comments among sociopaths.

However, it is not so simple. Even among people who have the opinion of being honest in their own eyes and in the eyes of other people, dishonest behaviour can happen. The reasons for this are temptations, including con-

---

[67] The broad perception of competences are in essence identified with human capital.

sideration of the material benefits. With great surprise we may sometimes hear of criminal scandals in which the negative heroes involved are people who are well-known and who up to recently had been respected, i.e. The premiers of Japan, South Korea, outstanding businessmen (as it had appeared), etc. The world is not black and white. As stated by M. Kosewski, "ludzie uczciwi czasami kradną, a złodzieje [niekiedy] ujmują się honorem i zachowują przyzwoicie"[68] (honest people sometimes steal, while thieves [sometimes] behave with honour).

There can be no doubts that in organizations it is possible and is even necessary to commonly demand honesty from everyone and the fact is that it is a value without which it is not feasible to work together and run business.

Law and order and honesty (and to a certain extent justice) are associated with not only what the individuals think and do, nor what happens in various mini-communities and in particular organizations, but also with the quality of law and the effectiveness of its execution, habits and customs, professed religions and the power of their impact, the socio-economic structure of the state and the quality of its institutions, including the law enforcement bodies and the judicature, the general level of morality and international relations.

The research carried out by J. Szczupaczyński in Poland reveals that among other aspects, "instytucjonalne niedopasowanie, jako cecha systemu prawno-politycznego, ma wyraźny wpływ na proces kształtowania się moralnego etosu ludzi biznesu. Wiąże się to ze szczególną dualizacją ładu aksjonormatywnego (...), z rozchodzeniem się porządku prawnego i więzi moralnych, postrzeganiem prawa jako systemu norm pozbawionych moralnych odniesień. W efekcie nieprzestrzeganie prawa stosunkowo rzadko budzi moralne refleksje. [Inną konsekwencją jest] oddzielenie sfery ideałów moralnych od praktyki kierowania przedsiębiorstwem"[69] (institutional misfits as a feature of the legislative and political system have a clear impact on the process of shaping the moral ethos of the people of business. This is associated with the particular dualization of the axionormative order [...] with the divergence of the legislative order and moral ties, adherence to the law as a system of norms deprived of moral references. In effect, the failure to adhere to the law relatively seldom arouses moral reflection. Another consequence is the separation of the moral ideals from the practices of managing an enterprise). Simultaneously, as the author notes in terms of the same source, this instability is greater in the case of entrepreneurs than in the case of managers as entrepreneurs are more affected by the aforesaid "institutional misfits".

---

[68] M. Kosewski, *Układy. Dlaczego uczciwi ludzie czasami kradną, a złodzieje ujmują się honorem*, Wydanie na prawach rękopisu, Warszawa 2007.

[69] J. Szczupaczyński, *Władza a moralny wymiar przywództwa*. Dom Wydawniczy Elipsa, Warszawa 2013, p. 408.

There are no short synonyms for the word honesty. Similar terms: integrity, reliability. Antonym: dishonesty.

(16) Innovation

The notion of *innovation* is derived from the Latin word *innovare*, which signifies the creation of something new and was introduced into economic science by J.A. Schumpeter.[70]

The value of innovations involves the fact that they develop the human civilization, resolve various problems, create improved and new products, new demand and places of work, bring in revenue-albeit innovations may also be associated with the increased risk and sometimes bring losses instead of profits.

Innovativeness is strongly supported by the EU, particularly via running pro-innovative policies. It is supported by among other things, the Single European Act of 1986, as well as the Treaty of Lisbon of 2007, where the *European Research Area* was created to promote research in which the area of scientific knowledge and technologies involve the free flowing exchange, while the aim is to have faster development and the growth of the competitiveness of the EU. Although the Treaty of Lisbon is criticized with regard to many issues (also with relation to innovations), as well as the reality of the assumptions, it nevertheless, as claimed by Ewa Okoń-Horodyńska, constitutes "pierwszy całościowy program rozwoju UE o charakterze ofensywnym na wejściu, zakładający radykalną transformację gospodarki UE" (the first complete program of development of the EU of an offensive nature from the outset, by assuming the radical transformation of the EU economies), whereas in terms of the feasibility it is counting on the accepted formula of the "open policy of innovation" that shall make it flexible and facilitate thefeasibility that is to be treated as a process.[71]

For several years now, the notion of (or phenomenon in the opinions of some) *Open Innovation* has been spreading rapidly, which is interesting both from the practical, as well as the theoretical point of view by basing on several assumptions as follows:

- in contemporary times, no-one is capable of completely independent execution of significant innovations without availing of the support of science, other firms from the sector, creative clients, licences, patents, utility models, etc.: it is necessary to combine the external innovations

---

[70] See: http://mfiles.pl/pl/index.php/Innowacja [16.01.2015].

[71] E. Okoń-Horodyńska, *Polityka innowacji w UE: Przerost formy nad treścią?*, Referat na IX Kongres Ekonomistów Polskich, Kraków 2012.

and outsourcing with the internal innovations carried out in a given organization;

- availing of the generally rich internal resources facilitates the shortening of the time period of innovative cycles;
- the result of the compilation of external ideas and technologies with your own innovations is becoming the subject of commercialization and launching of external market offer, preferably on a global scale. The aim is that of commercial success, which requires activities to be run on an appropriate scale.[72]

Innovativeness is/should be developed both at an individual level (particular people and particular organizations), as well as network organizations geared towards innovativeness and the systemic activities on an even wider scale.[73]

(17) Integrity

Integrity is the nobleness and honesty of intentions and activities, as well as their legality, while also the adequateness of behaviour, adherence to the legislative and ethical norms and good customs, carrying out morally correct choices and decisions, while also helping the poor. Integrity is both the value, as well as the feature of the character. Likewise, integrity excludes such features, attitudes and behaviour as injustice, dishonesty, pusillanimity / pettiness, spitefulness, insidiousness, aggressiveness, parsimony, as well as looking after your own interests while showing indifference to the fate of others.

According to Prof. Tadeusz Niwiński, "dignity may be enumerated among virtues. It is life in accordance with the highest standards. It facilitates listening to your own conscience, doing what is necessary and keeping to the truth. Dignity provides us with the feeling of respect for ourselves and a calm conscience."[74]

Several claims that are associated with dignity have been taken from *mahajana* of Buddhism as follows:

- "it is not through issuing arbitral decisions that a man becomes dignified";
- "a man is not noble who hurts other creatures; a noble man is someone who does not harm other living creatures";

---

[72] O. Gassman, E. Enkel, *Towards a Theory of Open Innovation: Three Core Process Archetypes*, https://www.google.pl/?gws_rd=ssl#q=Gassman+O.%2C+Enkel+E.%2C+Towards+a+t heory+of+Open+Innovation.

[73] W. Vanhaverbeke, M. Cloodt, *Open innovation in value networks*, Chapter 13 in *Open Innovation: Researching a New Paradigm*, Oxford University Press, 2006.

[74] See: http://niwinski.blog.onet.pl/28-Prawosc,2,ID427846507,n [16.01.2015].

– "we do not call a monk a Worthy Elder just because his hair is grey; if he is only mature by age, he is a man who got old for nothing."[75]

The word *dignity* may be perceived in modern times as a certain archaism, or as a slightly old-fashioned term, which is similar to the case of the word *nobleness*. Nevertheless, it expresses consequential issues, thus it has been kept in this catalogue. Its direct use however, may be hindered due to its slightly archaic sounding. An alternative to this would be its break-up into the composite values – honesty, justice, respect for the law and good customs, etc., instead of using the forms of aggregated dignity.

Similar terms: nobleness, benchmarking, honourability. Antonyms: iniquity, dishonour ability, unworthiness.

The dignity of procedures is one of the significant conditions of being an authority, or at least acknowledged as one. Dignified people enjoy acknowledgement and respect (in non-pathological environments).

Similar terms: nobleness, decorum, respectability, chastity, decency, straightforwardness. Antonym: iniquity.

(18) Justice

Justice is behaviour that is based on the truth and righteousness, which are adequate to the events and situations, as well as the generally adopted and accepted norms of procedure and behaviour, as well as legislative, customary, etc. – neither excessively liberal (mild), nor excessively severe, while taking account of the intentions and context. Plato deemed justice to be the most important of all virtues.

Just – proceeds in accordance with the ethical principles, while also objective in terms of management, as well as respecting the rights of others.[76] It is possible to add the following: also respecting their rightful expectations.

Although almost everyone plays the role of proponents and protagonists of justice, in essence many people (probably the majority of people in fact) do not desire justice at all, but rather preferential and privileged treatment. This would explain the fierce defence of the various sectoral and occupational privileges that most frequently do not have any substantive justification when viewed from a broader perspective. People want justice "as a last resort", when attempts to find a privileged situation fails. A great challenge is the credible and convincing stipulation of what is just and what the measures of justice are.

The perception of justice has altered over the passing of time. It is visible that, especially in the areas of European culture, there is a mitigation of law, namely there is no (generally speaking) torture or capital punishment, while

---

[75] See: http://mahajana.net/mb3s/publikacje/dhammapada/prawosc.html [16.01.2015].

[76] *Wielki słownik języka polskiego, op. cit.,* p. 774.

everyone has the right to a lawyer and a fair trial, as well as the fact that in a multitude of European countries the conditions of imprisonment are much more bearable than in the past. Justice and fair treatment are guaranteed by the rights of man, the constitutions, the codes of law, norms and procedures. From a formal and legislative viewpoint, people within our cultural environs have the right to a fair wage, can count on help in finding employment and social welfare when they find themselves in a difficult situation. By virtue of the law, practices of discrimination, mobbing, sexual harassment are prosecuted. The principle of equal remuneration for the same work, as well as social solidarism are binding. However, in practice it appears to be much worse.

Maintaining such important values as justice encounters all types of difficulties. Apart from bad will, it is frequently extraordinarily difficult to establish and agree on what is fair and what is not. This is exemplified by the tax system, where all ideas and drafts are criticized whatever they may be. The differentiation of remuneration is equally controversial and to a broader extent incomes. The majority of specialists are of the opinion that excessively egalitarian systems, as well as excessively elitist are unfair. Likewise, they are also inefficient. Nevertheless, there is no way to agree on what the word "excessively" specifically means and what differentiation would be deemed appropriate. We do not have any credible methods, techniques or tools at our disposal; while the methods of evaluating work are also subjective and controversial.

The management staff of organizations are in a difficult situation as they must be fair, proceed in a fair way and create fair systems, although no-one entirely knows what that specifically means. In this situation a certain minimum is determined by the binding law, good practices, social consensus, experience, benchmarking, good will and intuition. Likewise, good IT systems are also good, as well as efficient communication, openness, effectiveness (while also a certain flexibility) in terms of the implementation of the necessary changes. It is sometimes worth availing of the aid of external experts, as it is generally speaking cheaper than conflicts and costly strikes.

Similar terms: dignity, objectivity, respect for the law and rightful expectations of others, honesty in judgement. Antonym: injustice.

(19) Kindness

Kindness is a competence and attitude, as well as a way of life that is featured by a positive, favourable and friendly attitude to another person. It is associated with affection, positive thoughts and emotions, altruistic well-wishing for others. The tendency to take action that lie in the interests of people appears, as well as resolving or mitigating their problems, shortages, inconveniences, eliminating or restrict ingdistress and suffering due to altruistic motives. This is facilitated by empathy- the developed ability to show compassion for the reactions and emotions of others.

Kindness, due to its very nature is a precious value that is desirable in organizations as it improves the atmosphere at work, mitigates stress, facilitates the social and occupational adaptation of new employees, favours creativity and initiativeness, consolidates and integrates people in an organization. It improves communication, mitigates attitudes of anxiety and resistance and favours development.

The convictions are expressed that a person who is by his very nature malevolent, should not hold a managerial position, nor should be promoted as this would signify the lack of competence that is so important in leadership.

Synonyms: cordiality, friendliness, good will. Antonyms: malevolence, antipathy, bad will, hostility.

(20) Leadership

The essence of leadership is the exertion of a strong influence on people, which in turn creates the premise for their effective organization around the mission and vision of the organization, while integrating and effectively achieving the aims and execution of tasks. In a more narrow perception of leadership, this constitutes one of the four classic functions of management, alongside planning, organizing and controlling. Likewise, leadership is also an intricate competence which consists of the specific abilities and predisposition, knowledge and experience associated with the management of people, as well as the specific skills and technical and social capabilities.

In a broader and less technical perspective, clever and efficient leadership is also a significant value that is desired in organizations of all types, from a team in an enterprise, various formations in an army to political parties and the highest positions of the state and international organizations.

The value of leadership is frequently expressed by such adjectives as "strong", "conspicuous", "effective", "charismatic", which is often necessary and expected. The relations between leadership and charisma are particularly embedded in the consciousness, which was heavily influenced by Max Weber who also initiated the institutional notion of leadership. This notion and concept was subsequently developed by Philip Selznick by displaying the cultural significance of the identity of an organization and its distinctive competences and roles in their creation that may be played by a charismatic leader. In the concept of the New Leadership, by referring to Weber and Selznick this indicates the usefulness of charismatic leaders particularly in three types of situations as follows:

– in the creation of the expansive and inspiring visions of development;
– in the initiation and implementation of great and difficult changes;
– in conditions of crisis and great dangers.[77]

However, charismatic leadership is not always the optimal solution. In an array of cases, transactional leaders are more required and useful than charismatic ones, while in other cases it is better to have "leadership without leadership", in which a leader makes discreet suggestions as to the course of activities and cheers people up when necessary. Henry Mintzberg states ironically that in the 20th century there were three outstanding charismatic leaders – Stalin, Hitler and Mao. He also acknowledged that the excessive advocation of leaders leads to the demotivation of all the others.[78] Jack Welch at the turn of the 21st century implemented the notion of the "paradoxical leader" in GE , by applying the maxim of "manage less, manage better."[79] Prior to this, a similar model of leadership (naturally speaking, not the only one for every organization and situation) was advocated by Fred Fiedler within the framework of his "fourth level of managing".

P.F. Drucker claimed that we should not create an organization whose existence depends on heroic leaders, as it is too risky and drives the organization into trouble when such a leader is lacking.[80]

Nevertheless, leadership should be developed as it is generally speaking necessary, which is first and foremost revealed in crisis situations. This is not very possible to effectively execute by means of academic teaching, particularly in the case of full-time students, thus this challenge must be first and foremost taken on by the organizations themselves.

The value and usefulness of leadership is associated with among other aspects, the differentiation of its models and styles, as well as intelligence, flexibility and other features of leaders that facilitate taking account of the various situations which organizations find themselves in at various phases of their development and various situations that function in various cultures, while having people working in cooperation at your disposal of very different characteristics.

(21) Liberty

The freedom of activity, while remaining on the level of the organization is to allow people to realize their own notions, projects and ideas, as well as activities in a way that is preferred by them, while also the free-flowing exchange

---

[77] J. Szczupaczyński, *op. cit.*, pp. 123–124.
[78] H. Mintzberg, *Zarządzanie*, Wolters Kluwer Business, Warszawa 2012, p. 272.
[79] J.A. Krames, *Jacka Welcha leksykon przywództwa*, Studio Emka, Warszawa 2003, p. 249.
[80] H. Mintzberg, *op. cit.*, p. 271.

of information and contact with others, as well as cooperation in such a large scope as possible without violating the rightful interests of the organization, quality, economicality, the law and good practices, as well as a favourable image of this organization. The freedom of activity may be perceived as a significant element of freedom, albeit freedom is obviously a broader notion.

People of a high level of competences and a strong professional position usually remain in the given organization when the occupational role suits them, namely a satisfying position and a broad perception of remuneration, as well as the possibility of realizing their notions and ideas. Thus, the freedom of activity is a highly rated value, albeit not by everyone.

The freedom of activity in an organization depends on an array of factors as follows: the philosophy and style of management of the whole organization, the styles of leadership of the particular managers, systems of management (including IT), the competences of the management staff and employees, the type of activities, the type of products, the types of threats associated with the activities run, the technological processes and many others. Hence, it is not solely the issue of good will or bad will of the owners, management staff and employees.

The fact that the freedom of activity is appreciated by people in an organization of value, generally points to its expansion, albeit competences, credibility of people and the level of trust are significant here.

Synonyms: *free hand*, authorization / authorizing the right to undertake activity. Antonyms: shortage of /restriction of the freedom of activity; addiction; dependence.

(22) Loyalty

Loyalty is perceived as honesty in terms of mutual ties, faithfulness, as well as a necessary element of trust. As written by Prof. Maria Szyszkowska, "loyalty is associated with the cautious treatment of another person, with sensitivity leading to the correction of our own egotistical nature. Being loyal is by not cheating, especially for benefits. Loyalty requires keeping promises, keeping entrusted secrets confidential, as well as the unequivocal attitude in which there is no place for «talking behind backs». The obligation to defend a given person from the negative judgements, as well as the deeds of other people stems from loyalty. Hence, loyalty is much more than the passive attitude of not causing harm. The perfect state would be commonplace with the mutual state of loyalty, which is worth pursuing. In the meantime, the unquestioned obligation of each of us is that ofloyalty restricted at least to a group of familiar people. This also includes loyalty with regard to yourself.

In brief terms, I would define loyalty as one of the features of the character of a decent man."[81]

The multi-sided loyalty of owners – management staff – employees – clients – suppliers / cooperating partners – local communities increases the chances of survival and development of the organization and people associated with it. Likewise, it also leads to better international relations. Loyalty is perceived as the honesty of mutual relations, faithfulness andnecessary element of trust. The surplus and misunderstood loyalty ceases to be an advantage if it leads to breaking the law, good practices, cliquishness and remaining in a state of error.

Synonyms: faithfulness, devotion. Similar terms: reliability and honesty (in relations with people, authorities, the state). Antonyms: disloyalty, treachery.

(23) Moderation

Moderation is the maintenance of sensible proportions, avoidance of excessive and surprising activities, extreme behaviour; while alsothe *noble restraint*. Moderation is associated with that of optimization. What is characteristic for modernity (especially in economics), namely the pursuit of maximization and minimization, while also the under-estimation of optimization **maybe** associated with the lack of moderation and even provoke it. Moderation works well with the concept of sustainable development. Indeed, all the philosophical and religious systems exhort moderation.

On the other hand, moderation may be associated with mediocrity, the incomplete utilization of the opportunities that arise, the lack of ambition or what could lead to that. An equal rhythm of work is generally speaking an advantage, but in reality work is not like that as in some periods of life a person works a lot and treats professional work as a priority, whereas in other periods he may (and sometimes even should) change the set of priorities. Hence, it is worth maintaining *moderation in moderation*.

In organizations, pursuit of moderation could result in various activities. A common problem not only in Poland is that of the unequal workload. A multitude of research results indicate that we are dealing with the Pareto principle / imbalance: approximately 20% of employees in white-collar positions are constantly over-burdened, whereas the remaining 80% work significantly below their capabilities and the needs of the firm, frequently with the lowest level of efficiency tolerated. The former group constitutes competent, ambitious and reliable people who work well, who frequently come to work early and leave later than required, while also constantly receiving additional urgent tasks from their superiors as they can always be relied on. The latter

---

[81] See: http://szyszkowska.bloog.pl/id,329253164,title,LOJALNOSC,index.html?ticaid=6ef4c.

group is more difficult to stimulate towards more efficient work and transgression over the minimum standards. Everyone, including the managers, become accustomed to this kind of "working landscape" and treat it as a natural thing. The pursuit of moderation would signify the discontinuance of the constant overloading of some employees and burdening (or replacement) of the latter group.

Another frequently encountered symptoms of the lack of moderation is the imposition of excessively high targets and tasks that are impossible to achieve. This spoils the good practices, results in stress and professional burnout.

The lack of moderation is also charging horrendous fees on the part of top managers that are not justified by either the performance of the firm, or the personal contribution of the top manager in the result achieved in comparison with the contribution in terms of work by the other managers and employees, as well as their earnings. Likewise, it is also unjustifiable in terms of the level of risk as they are usually hired managers who do not risk their own personal fortune, but rather the money of another person – the owner. This is not only a Polish problem, although Poland has adopted the British and American model of an excessively large income bracket surprisingly quickly, while ignoring the practice of continental Europe, the Scandinavian states, Japan and many others where these relations are more dignified. This of course does not mean that solutions such as the "public sector salary cap" make sense and should be continued. Nevertheless, there are no reasons for which a hired manager that does not risk his own wealth in the case of poor financial performance of the firm would receive an annual salary in millions of zloty, while non-income deferred over time (shares of the company); may be deemed to be immoral. This is also socially dangerous as this man feels obliged to undertake excessively risky activities and in essence anti-social activities in order to illustrate his own extraordinariness and effects that he brings to his owners / shareholders: the mass reduction of employment in the firms that had not been threatened by bankruptcy, insufficiently justified mergers, over-exploitation calculated over a short timescale, financial gambles, etc.

Synonyms: moderation, sustainability, balance. Antonym: lack of moderation.

(24) Openness

Openness is on the one hand cognitive curiosity, readiness to become familiar with and adopt new ideas, views and solutions if they are acknowledged to be more true, better and developmental. On the other hand, openness is the readiness to operate and function with a "raised curtain" in a clear and honest way that is in the eyes of the public by demonstrating the integrity of aims, sincerity of intentions, lack of insidiousness and intrigue, availability, readiness for talks and cooperation without harming anything.

Openness and transparency are the features of democracy and civil society. Thus, they should penetrate into all organizations, without restricting this to only political and executive powers. In the realities of the organization, openness and transparency signify the following:

- equality of opportunities in terms of the accessibility to employment, professional development and promotions; the actual competences and features of the candidate should decide and not some type of "arrangement" and connections;
- the common availability of information, without which it is not possible to work / operate; only some information should be deemed to be secret and confidential, on the basis of well-known and accepted criteria;
- familiarity with aims, results, situation of the organization, challenges and problems for solving, criteria of evaluation, system of motivating and promoting, as well as other important issues for the management staff and employees;
- control over whether the people running the organization operate for the good of the interested parties and not for himself (solely or mainly);
- clarity, articulateness and acceptability of the system of management, the principles of procedure and assessment;
- good formal communication; and when this does not work informal communication appears and expands on the basis of frequently confabulation, rumours and slander.

Openness and transparency are the safety valves that facilitate the control of (all) authorities[82] and counteract various types of pathologies. The system is open, if it is capable and willing to adopt new facts, knowledge and inspiration, as well as rational modifications. In terms of communication, this system is acknowledged to be open if it facilitates the execution of every given order.[83]

Synonyms: transparency. Similar terms: expansive horizons, acumen. Antonyms: secrecy, unavailability, non-transparency, mysteriousness, impenetrability / murkiness, "glass ceiling."

---

[82] See: http://www.demokraci.pl/slownik/t/181-transparentno- [16.01.2015].

[83] A.S. Reber, *Słownik psychologii*, Wydawnictwo Naukowe Scholar, Warszawa 2002, p. 473.

(25) Positive thinking

These are values and predisposition, as well as competences favourable towards the creation and development of both the organization, as well as on a personal level. Criticism, even, without bad intentions often work destructively, by weakening and discouraging, while sometimes even frightening by nature. There is a well-known saying that says only optimists create new things and renew even the world, while pessimists are of the opinion that it shall not succeed or is not worth it.

Positive thinking increases creativity and facilitates operations. Optimists are more determined, more patient, capable of greater effort, while also do not give up. It is easier for them to get up after a failure and undertake new activities by drawing conclusions from the aforesaid failure. They do not feel that they have suffered a failure and claim that they acquired valuable experience. Optimists are healthier and feel better.[84]

Remez Sasson claims that "positive thinking is a mental attitude that favours the acquisition by the mind of thoughts, words and imagination that lead to growth, expansion and success. It is a mental attitude that favours good and beneficial results. Positive thinking anticipates happiness, joy, health and efficient activities."[85]

It is not however commonplace, nor does it meet with common acknowledgement. Positive thinking varies in various countries. Americans are particularly known for this, whereas in Poland other countries of our region this depends, albeit it would seem to be generally changing for the better.

Positive thinking is important and indeed expected both in professional life, as well as in personal life. People are eager to be in the environment of people with positive thinking, rather than negative thinking, as the latter group are perceived to be "toxic". Such bosses acquire worse results, enjoy less respect and fondness, while there is also a worse atmosphere among the teams run by them.

Positive thinking also has a second context, namely it has a positive impact on another value which is health.

In contemporary slang terms of the youth, optimism and positive thinking which is accompanied by the joy of life are frequently defined as *good energy*, or *power*.

Synonyms: realistic and sensible optimism. Antonyms: negative thinking, pessimism.

---

[84] See: http://www.pozytywne.com/artykuly/25/Korzysci-z-bycia-optymista [16.01.2015].

[85] R. Sasson, *The Power of Positive Thinking*, http://www.successconsciousness.com/index_000009.htm.

(26) Professionalism

Professionalism is the ability and predisposition, knowledge, experience, principles of behaviour and habits, while also adherence to the ethics and dignity of the profession, as well as other frequently barely perceptible features facilitating the qualitatively good, safe, economic and pro-ecological execution of work in accordance with the principles of the professional art with that of good practices.

Professionalism is frequently perceived as the opposite to amateurism or amateurishness. This is associated with activities that are competent, fast, effective and efficient, while also free of unnecessary emotions and unnecessary absorption of the attention of the environment, together with the high standard of work.

Professionalism is associated with the broader range of knowledge and professional skills. An employee who has gained a perfect command of a narrow range of several or umpteen operations on a production line shall not be described as a professional. A professional follows the progress taking place in his field, learns new technologies, ways and methods of executing work, while also eagerly broadening his work content and develops himself from a professional viewpoint.

A professional knows his own value (which is sometimes overly-displayed). If he does not find the opportunities to operate or professional fulfilment in the given professional environment, or when he is allocated impossible or even unethical tasks, or if he finds himself in an inappropriate environment that he is not able to change, then he shall leave without regard for the money or the possible difficulties of finding subsequent employment. If he is a real professional, then these difficulties shall be merely temporary, while the crisis situation which he solved in such a manner shall become an opportunity and may open up new and more interesting perspectives.

Professionalism, as in the case of everything may have its negative sides. Professionals, by availing of the differences in the levels of knowledge between himself and the environment, may succumb to the temptation of the specific use of power that he possesses and abuses (doctors with relation to patients, lawyers with relation to their clients, etc.) by imposing their will by deciding for patients and clients, thus exposing them to various risks and expenses. Quite often, while wanting to maintain and strengthen their privileged position, they aim towards the restriction of access of new apprentices to the practicing of the profession by means of special formal authorization, which is deliberate terms very difficult to acquire (licences, certificates, authorization of assessor, etc.), while also striving towards the organization of a compulsory professional association and corporation.

Synonymous terms: professionalism, expertise. Antonyms: amateurism, amateurship.

(27) Profit

Profit in terms of the accounting of sales revenue minus the costs of the appropriately entered goods sold. In the theories of economics, profit is understood as the difference between the sales revenue and the entire cost of the lost opportunities associated with the production of the given product.[86]

A multitude of people have been displaying distrust (some until this very day) for a long time and would have a problem with the acknowledgement of profit as a value that has been achieved honestly and without running over-exploitation, while also large value, not only economic, but social ones too. This facilitates the existence and development of the enterprises, maintenance and increase in employment, contributing to the state budget and the satisfaction of the social needs, for which money from taxes and tax-like charge rates are required. As once stipulated by Konosuke Matsushita, profit is moral; what is immoral is its shortage caused by incompetence. An enterprise that is unable to achieve profit, wastes the resources, of which too many are non-renewable and should terminate business and give an opportunity to someone else who can.[87]

This was and still is the subject of controversy of whether the maximization of profits over a long period of time is universal and the most important aim of the enterprise, similarly to an array of other issues associated with profit: the way of sharing profit (including the participation of employees in the financial results), the privileged position of shareholders, the orientation towards first and foremost the satisfaction of clients, the corporate social responsibility and the costs of this responsibility, the level of financial involvement on behalf of environmental protection, charity activities, while also an array of others. In terms of such issues, there are various views and practices.

According to J.K. Galbraith, in contemporary times, the fundamental fields of battle are no longer associated with the conflict between capital and work, as well as in the past, but rather between entrepreneurs and the state. State power is to be found under pressure from various environments and groups of the electorate: the municipal and rural poverty, the proponents of the social housing construction, subsidized transport, environmental protection, while also various programs of aid. The election promises and concessions on behalf of all the demands are carried out at the cost of the private

---

[86] P.A. Samuelson, W.D. Nordhaus, *op. cit.*, p. 553.

[87] *Słynni przedsiębiorcy – Konosuke Matsushita, pionier nowoczesnego biznesu*, „Zarządzanie na Świecie" 1997, no. 6.

entrepreneur, as well as the profits and development of his firm. No-one asks the aforesaid entrepreneur for his opinion or consent, while the resources taken from him are frequently wasted.[88]

Synonym: surplus financial outcome. Antonym: shortage.

(28) Quality

The good quality of a product (goods or services) is surely the most important, while also the ethical obligation of an organization. Likewise, it is one of the most significant values for clients, thus also for enterprises. The quality of a product is decided on by an array of its features, particularly the following:
- usefulness;
- safety of utilization;
- reliability of activities;
- pattern designing and aesthetics;
- durability;
- costs of utilization;
- guarantee conditions;
- servicing (availability, quality, costs);
- speed of moral wear and tear.[89]

Although it is acknowledged that the expectation of the high quality of products is a feature that only became characteristic of contemporary times, in the Code of Hammurabi (Babylon, 18th century B.C.) there was an entry relating to penalties for the poor quality of goods.[90] In the Middle Ages corporal punishment, as well as pecuniary penalties and confiscation of property were applied in the case of the poor quality of goods.

It is acknowledged that the high quality of goods is not possible without the high level of competences of employees and management staff, proper realization of the total processes in an enterprise and its pro-qualitative culture. This is served in a particular way by the Total Quality Management (TQM), which is no longer a system, as for example the ISO norms, but the philosophy of the management of an enterprise in which quality takes on the main significance and is placed ahead of quantity and profit.

There is no singular theory relating to quality, nor one culture of quality. Various concepts wear each other down, particularly relating to the require-

---

[88] J.K. Galbraith, *Perspektywy ekonomii – krytyka historyczna*, PWE, Warszawa 1991, pp. 299–300.

[89] This term in economics is defined by a decrease in values regardless of the physical wear and tear, which is particularly associated with the emergence of new and better products of a new generation. The product in possession is still capable of being used, but clients no longer want it and replace it for the new one.

[90] This code was based on the significantly older Sumerian.

ment of good quality, as well as in the cases of cheap products and contrasting concepts in terms of quality as a function of price. Nevertheless, it is expected that even cheap products shall fulfil certain fundamental standards of quality. Simultaneously, a market of luxury goods exists with very high qualitative and expensive goods, having its own clients who do not purchase cheap products at all.

The orientation towards low costs and transfer of production associated with globalization has had an unfavourable impact on the quality products in general.[91] Maintaining at least an average level of quality in terms of articles produced in some countries (with very low remuneration and a weak level of motivation of employees) requires a return to the rigorous control as a way of influencing quality, which means returning to the period of time prior to the formulation of the "Deming's 14 Principles"; one of which declares that it is not quality control that constitutes the quality of a product, but rather competences, motivations and the awareness of contractors (as well as the quality of the project and technologies of its production naturally speaking).

Quality as a value is not restricted to products, but is also of a universal value. Good quality should be related to every job, project, management, working conditions, etc.

Although a multitude of people are proud of their perfectionism, which they also require of others, it is a positive value only in some cases, in terms of both people and their produce. Perfectionism brings with it a significant increase in terms of time consumption and costs. Hence, from a social and economic viewpoint, in the majority of cases it should be sufficient if the quality is good.

Similar terms: class, value, type. Antonyms: mediocrity, worthlessness.

(29) Responsibility

Responsibility is the perception of the necessity and readiness to bear the consequences of the effects of self-deeds and negligence. This is associated with the mental maturity, knowledge, experience, as well as imagination. It should be accompanied by freedom (*the more freedom, the more responsibility*).

There is a multitude of the types of responsibilities such as: professional, disciplinarian, legislative (civil, penal, contractual, liability, other), moral /

---

[91] This is not a rule. For instance, cars produced in the Czech Republic and Slovakia by the Volkswagen Group have in many respects better quality than the ones manufactured in Germany. The quality of cars manufactured in Fiat Auto Poland in Tychy is the highest level attained by the whole FIAT Group.

ethical, individual and collective, joint and several liability, administrative, auxiliary, political and many others.

Value is not merely responsibility, but the **feeling of responsibility**, which is associated with the defined state of knowledge and awareness. The developed feeling of responsibility is the result of upbringing, knowledge, experience, imagination, intuition, as well as higher emotions. Emotional ties such as friendship and kindness have a favourable impact on this.

The feeling of responsibility is generally speaking developed in the working environment. Both the management team, as well as the employees are guided by them in the majority of cases. Likewise, the ethics of duty and responsibility, namely deontology, is in general terms close to working people and is understood by them.

As in the case of everything in excess, such a feeling of duty may bring negative effects: over-protection with all its known consequences, relieving others of duties, overloading of work and duties of management staff, as well as professional burnout.

Various work types are associated with various types of responsibilities: for the results and effects of work (also unintended effects), for the safety of other people, for the natural environment, for the resources and the subjects of work (often of significant values). In some positions there is a material responsibility or co-responsibility. Responsibility is borne not for the activities and their effects, but also for negligence of activities that should have been undertaken.

Deontology, which concentrates mainly on the issues of responsibility is an important area of philosophy and ethics, which is fortunately close to practitioners dealing with management and the majority of employees.

Similar terms: dutifulness, maturity, reliability. Antonyms: irresponsibility, undutifulness, unreliability.

(30) Safety

Value, which is what safety is, has a multitude of meanings. They are most frequently within the environs of work safety, including commuting to work and return journeys home as in accordance with Labour Law accidents connected with commuting to work are qualified as accidents at work, in terms of all the legislative and financial effects involved.

Life and health are commonly acknowledged to be the highest good. Hence, the most important duty of an employer is to ensure safety in the working environment to the people employed, but also all others to be found, such as suppliers, clients, people visiting the company, etc. This not only relates to technical aspects, the safety of constructions, the technological processes, security, etc., but also the responsibility of people, their mindfulness, intolerance of flippancy, breaking the rules and regulations of health and safety, road traffic, while also the requirement of sobriety, etc.

The safety of the products on offer is still significant, thus primarily the safety of clients and users. Certain products are by their very nature dangerous, for instance cars or motorcycles and the point is for the designers and producers to ensure as much safety as possible. Others, due to their type and designation, should not be dangerous, but may become so as a result of applying the inappropriate materials and ingredients, e.g. in the production of food or toys. A separate topic is that of the safety of deposit accounts whereby clients themselves choose between safer and less safe firms taking account of the interest rates, while also the forms of activities and reputations. The scandal of Amber Gold after all illustrated that even deposits not guaranteed by the state may be the reason for blame to be aimed at it.

The third dimension of safety relates to the security of work/employment, as well as social security. Following the oil crisis of the 1970s, this type of safety radically reduced and in practice the old unwritten agreement ceased to be binding: the security of employment in exchange for good work and loyalty with regard to the employer.

Various employers and various employees attach varying levels of attention to this third type of safety. This is associated with not only the real possibilities of the further existence of the given organization and offering of employment, but also in terms of the age and competences of the employees and their position on the labour market in the perception of loyalty, the law and good practices, as well as other factors. Likewise, the custom is becoming widespread, at least in the EU of making senior staff redundant due to reasons on the part of the company, which is done under the guise of high severance payments.[92] This certifies to the fact that the employers (albeit not all of them) feel a certain discomfort in such situations and try to ease the material and psychological effects in terms of the redundancies of employees due to reasons on the part of the company, to put it in legal terms. Such a practice is also the expression of the awareness that redundancies cause people to feel disappointment and violate their economic security. The severance payment thus becomes a form of compensation or damages for the redundancy.

Similar terms: security, guarantee. Antonyms: lack of security, danger.

---

[92] Likewise, in Poland there is a spread of the custom that was implemented several decades ago in Germany that this type of severance payment constitutes the equivalent of 18 months of remuneration, while sometimes even more (this does not relate to small firms, or the so-called budgetary sphere in general).

(31) Solidarity

Solidarity is the care for the common good, the feeling of ties and common fate with others, the readiness to act for the common good, giving up on *main* favour of *us*. This may become intensely associated with the philosophy of communitarianism, which results from this philosophy and may also strengthen it.

Solidarity supports people, particularly the weaker individuals and social and professional groups, by helping them to survive the difficult moments, being useful and active, counteracting social exclusion or at least restricting it. This occurs in among other areas, the voluntary practices of *job sharing*, which enables a more effective fight for fair rights and more just regulations. In turn, solidarity occurs at various levels – individual, group, departmental, local, regional, national, international and worldwide. There is a multitude of examples where it is actually human solidarity that radically altered the realities and brought change for the better.

Solidarity is connected with altruism, empathy, as well as higher emotions. On the other hand, solidarity in a bad matter, solidarity is restricted to political correctness or excessively motivated by particular interests that may be contraindications.

In the majority of organizations, there is a prevalence of the aspects of positive solidarity: together, jointly, easier to get through difficult moments, overcome difficulties, create various communities, compete effectively, support the weaker and less capable, create a good atmosphere at work.

Synonyms: social cohesion, common / collective activity. Antonyms: lack of solidarity, lack of social cohesion, *the rat race, social Darwinism.*

(32) Sustainable development

Sustainable development does not signify the same aspects at global, macro-economic and micro-economic levels.[93] On a global and macro-scale, this relates to the harmonization of economic growth with social needs (which are not restricted to the economy) and with the limited capacity of the natural environment, as well as the needs of the future generations; our current production and consumption that is rampant in many countries and social groups should not render the normal existence of our children and grandchildren and even further generations impossible. In an enterprise, this relates to the harmonization of economic goals with activities that are usually

---

[93] *Zrównoważony rozwój przedsiębiorstw – moda czy konieczność?*, dyskusja redakcyjna, prowadzona przez A. Hermana z udziałem K. Jaskuły, K. Kucińskiego, W. Kulpy, J.S. Zegara, „Kwartalnik Nauk o Przedsiębiorstwie" 2011, no. 1.

associated with the corporate social responsibility. This particularly refers to balancing the professional roles with the family and civil roles, as well as a responsible approach to the natural environment. However, an enterprise operates on a different scale and does not feel (it cannot feel) responsible for the sustainable development on a global or national scale. Nevertheless, it has its own important role to play. Sustainable development is a great value: the owners, the management staff and the employees should not devote themselves exclusively to professional work as they must also have the time and strength to fulfil their family and civil duties as without this, there shall be no future and they themselves shall experience burnout early. Without care for the environment on a micro-scale, there shall not be economies of scale on a wider scale.

At the level of the general formulations of the afore-mentioned aims, they are commonly accepted, albeit sometimes it is possible to hear the opinion that the crisis situation of enterprises may bear the possibility of the sufficient care for non-economic dimensions ad hoc. Nevertheless, it is possible to share the hope of A. Herman that "an enterprise is more and more commonly ceasing to be identified [only] with a machine for making profit."[94]

The problem mainly involves the answer to the question as to in what way should sustainable development be run. The general answer to this is that with this aim in mind, it is necessary to harmonize the legislative solutions, economic impact, as well as managerial, administrative and social impact. Destroying the environment should not only be banned, but also economically unprofitable by means of a system of higher pecuniary penalties than in the case of the costs of less onerous technologies and installations which effectively protect the environment.

Synonyms: sustainability, responsible growth. Antonym: over-exploitation.

(33) Wisdom (including knowledge)

Socrates deemed wisdom to be the most important of virtues. In his opinion, all other virtues stemmed from this.[95] A man who was really wise therefore, could not be either rash, or insensible, cowardly or audacious, miserly or profligate, greedy, petty, cruel or malicious, deprived of moderation, lazy, or "killing oneself with work", etc. thus, wisdom is generally associated with moderation. Likewise, this is connected with knowledge and experience.

---

[94] Ibidem.

[95] In terms of philosophy, this problem is granted the title of "unity of virtues". Not all philosophers accept the thesis that virtue is in essence singular.

Of the Buddhist stipulations, in the "Noble Eightfold Path", the appropriate view and appropriate intention are mentioned, which when combined constitute *prajna* (wisdom). These require a change in the manner of perceiving the world and condition the entering of this path.[96]

Wisdom is something more than information, or even knowledge or experience. It is also the skill of making the right choices, as well as applying knowledge and experience in practice, including in your own life. There is a multitude of people who have extensive knowledge, but are not perceived to be wise. Wisdom also occurs in what we do and how we do it, as well as what we do not get involved in.

Wisdom is a virtue/value that is constantly developed, which requires work and is worthwhile. This develops over a long process, essentially all through life.

Wisdom is relatively frequently associated with kindness, the skill of controlling negative emotions and caution. This is particularly expressed in difficult situations and is associated with intelligence, albeit it is not identified with this.

Wisdom may be perceived not only as a virtue/value, but also as an intricate competence, which encompasses an array of elementary competences. Although it is important in the management by values also, it is rarely taken into consideration in contemporary times due to its intricate nature that is difficult to measure and evaluate.[97] The emphasis on the significance of only one of the elements of wisdom, namely knowledge, creating an economy based on knowledge (more seldom) in the knowledge society. Nevertheless, apart from the aforesaid aspects, wisdom is not only knowledge, but also the experience and the skills of their application.

It would be deliberate evolution from the economy based on the knowledge, via the knowledge society in the direction of the society of wisdom. It is possible to suppose that such an evolution is taking place, despite all the scoldings. This is favoured by the following: widespread education, impact of the cause and effect rule, the pressure of the surroundings and external forces, whims and actually everything.

Although wisdom is a precious value, it is not clear whether this is sufficient to become part of the catalogue of values that is realistically operating in organizations. Firstly, it is difficult to discredit wisdom (although in many cases we expect and even demand most frequently in an indirect manner). Secondly, it is easier to perceive and assess its measureable symptoms

---

[96] J. Powers, *Szlachetna ośmioraka ścieżka*, „Świat Buddyzmu", http://www.buddzym.com.pl; http://www.buddyzm.com.pl/?k=&e=&s=&app=1&menu=all&pos=46 [16.01.2015].

[97] All complex values and competences are difficult to evaluate due to their intricate nature.

– effectiveness, efficiency, achievement of aims, resolving problems, taking good decisions, etc. than me who stands behind them.

Similar terms: maturity, mindfulness, sensibility. Antonyms: stupidity, immaturity.

6. Grouping values in the catalogue

The values mentioned above may be divided up into three different groups as follows:

(1) economic-managerial values (13), encompassing the following in accordance with the aforesaid catalogue in alphabetical order as follows:
  – safety;
  – discipline;
  – efficiency;
  – innovativeness;
  – quality;
  – business orientation;
  – entrepreneurship;
  – effectiveness;
  – subsidiarity;
  – cooperation;
  – sustainable development (including environmental protection);
  – profit (long-term and short-term); it is possible to use the term profitability here;

(2) social competence values (8), encompassing the following:
  – creativity;
  – wisdom (including knowledge);
  – courage;
  – positive thinking;
  – professionalism;
  – leadership;
  – development;
  – psycho-physical health and condition;

(3) ethical-cultural values (12), encompassing the following:
  – dignity, respect;
  – loyalty;
  – responsibility;
  – openness;
  – integrity;
  – solidarity;

- justice;
- honesty;
- moderation;
- generosity;
- trust;
- kindness.

The name of the group of values is debatable, however it would seem to be appropriate for the needs of an organization, associated with management. Values and their group may be further developed whatever the distinctions, nevertheless this relates to more than diversification by moving away from the issue of whether management should be a discipline within the framework of the area of science about management, how it is in Poland at present, or whether it has finally emancipated, as exemplified by the USA.

The qualifications of certain values for the particular groups may be debatable. In particular, the responsibility could also be founding a group of economic and managerial competences, while solidarity in the group of ethical and cultural values, as in the case of subsidiarity. Sustainable development has been enumerated among the competence values – both developmental and social by nature, albeit it could also be added to the economic and managerial, as well as civil an social issues. However, it does not have great practical significance.

7. Personal remarks on the catalogue of values

1) The nature of values is complex, while the notion itself has a multitude of meanings and is blurred. The values in philosophy may be understood differently, while also different in psychology, in economics and other sciences. In this work, the main values in the context of management have been considered.

2) The prototypes of value are ancient Greek virtues (initially five of them were distinguished), while also the old Chinese moral determinants, also amounting to five. They were formulated at more or less the same time, no doubt at the turn of the 5th century, regardless of each other. Over time, the term *values* partly replaced and displaced *virtues*, while the number of values grew enormously, in such a way that there are thousands of them at present. It is difficult to calculate them as among other things, with relation to the fact that without their definition, while assuming what is called in practice in various countries and organizations, the divisions are very blurred and the values are strongly overlapping. In such a way (without defining the values and relying on their individual perception), the major-

ity of research is approached, which in fact has little in common with the subject matter raised here.

3) A significant proportion of the afore-mentioned values is convergent with the broad perception of human competences in an organization. The broadly perceived human competences are to be precise, human capital.

4) In respecting and advocating the values and competences, it is worth having the awareness that there are no people in this world who would have them all and be capable of achieving at a high level. Thus, this rather relates to a long-term and consistent pursuit of specified goals, which is the task for the whole professional life, rather than the rigoristic execution today. As was appropriately put by Zygmunt Bauman, with relation to ethical values "być istotą moralną jest boleśnie trudno" (being a moral creature is painstakingly difficult).[98] Nevertheless, it is worth trying for.

5) As revealed by research, in Polish enterprises the highest rated are those of economic values, albeit the level of importance of the others is usually greater than we expected as researchers. Greater interest in non-economic values is also indicated due to the fact that in the majority of cases they strengthen the values and economic results indirectly. For instance, paying more attention to honesty shall have a positive impact on the economic results of enterprises, in which there shall be fewer thefts and fraud, while furthermore shall be better for their image among clients and local communities, which shall surely have an impact on the greater loyalty of clients on the increase in sales. It is not stated here that the current level of honesty is low, but merely expressed that the assumption thanks to the strongest promotion of values in management and the values in management could be even higher. It is possible to make the same statement about many other values.

Bibliography

Bauman Z., *Etyka ponowoczesna*, Wydawnictwo Aletheia, Warszawa 2012.

Blanchard K., O'Connor M., *Zarządzanie poprzez wartości*, Wydawnictwo Studio Emka, Warszawa 1998.

Corporate Value Index 2009, Ecco International Communications Network, http://www.biznespolska.pl/files/reports/ raportecco.pdf.

Drucker P.F., *Menedżer skuteczny*, Nowoczesność, Akademia Ekonomiczna w Krakowie, Czytelnik, Warszawa 1994.

Drucker P.F., *Myśli przewodnie Druckera*, MT Biznes, Warszawa 2002.

Drucker P.F., *Zawód menedżer*, MT Biznes, Warszawa 2004.

Encyklopedia Zarządzania, http://mfiles.pl/pl/index.php/Innowacja.

---

[98] Z. Bauman, *Etyka ponowoczesna*, Wydawnictwo Aletheia, Warszawa 2012, p. 386.

Galbraith J.K., *Perspektywy ekonomii – krytyka historyczna*, PWE, Warszawa 1991.

Gassman O., Enkel E., *Towards a Theory of Open Innovation: Three Core Process Archetypes*, https://www.google.pl/?gws_rd=ssl#q=Gassman+O.%2C+Enkel+E.%2 C+Towards+a+theory+of+Open+Innovation.

Handy Ch., *Wiek paradoksu. W poszukiwaniu sensu przyszłości*, Dom Wydawniczy ABC, Warszawa 1996, rozdział 7: *Subsydiarność* (pp. 114–118).

Katechizm Kościoła Katolickiego, Pallotinum, Poznań 1994.

Havard A., *Virtuous Leadership*, Scepter, New York 2007.

Kosewski M., *Układy. Dlaczego uczciwi ludzie czasami kradną, a złodzieje ujmują się honorem*, Wydanie na prawach rękopisu, Warszawa 2007.

Kotter J., *Co właściwie robią przywódcy?*, "Harvard Business Review Polska", czerwiec 2005.

Koza-Granosz M., *Tyrania wartości N. Hartmanna*, Internetowy Magazyn Filozoficzny „Hybris" 2009, no. 9.

Krames J.A., *Jacka Welcha leksykon przywództwa*, Studio Emka, Warszawa 2003.

Kwiatkowski S., *Przedsiębiorczość intelektualna*, Wydawnictwo Naukowe PWN, Warszawa 2000.

Mintzberg H., *Zarządzanie*, Wolters Kluwer Business, Warszawa 2012.

http://niwinski.blog. onet.pl/28-Prawosc,2,ID427846507,n.

Oleksyn T., *Zarządzanie kompetencjami. Teoria i praktyka*, wyd. 2 rozszerzone i zaktualizowane, Wolters Kluwer Polska, Warszawa 2010.

Posner R., *The Power of Personal Values*, http://www.gurusoftware.com/GuruNet/Personal/Topics/ Values.htm.

Posner R., *Business: Utilizing Business Values*, http://www.gurusoftware.com/GuruNet/KnowledgeBase/ Business/Values.htm.

Powers J., *Szlachetna ośmioraka ścieżka*, „Świat Buddyzmu", http://www.buddyzm. com.pl/?k=&e=&s=&app=1&menu=all&pos=46.

Reber A.S., *Słownik psychologii*, Wydawnictwo Naukowe Scholar, Warszawa 2002.

Roberts C., *Checklist for Personal Values*, http://www.selfcounselling.com/help/personalsucces/personalvalues.html.

Samuelson P.A., Nordhaus W.D., *Ekonomia 2*, Wydawnictwo Naukowe PWN, Warszawa 1996.

Sasson R., *The Power of Positive Thinking*, http://www.successconsciousness.com/index_000009.htm.

Słynni przedsiębiorcy – Konosuke Matsushita, pionier nowoczesnego biznesu, „Zarządzanie na Świecie" 1997, no. 6.

Szczupaczyński J., *Władza a moralny wymiar przywództwa*, Dom Wydawniczy Elipsa, Warszawa 2013.

Tatarkiewicz W., *Dzieje sześciu pojęć*, Wydawnictwo Naukowe PWN, wyd. 5, Warszawa 2011.

Tatarkiewicz W., *O szczęściu*, Wydawnictwo Naukowe PWN, wyd. 11, Warszawa 2012.

Teichman J., *Etyka społeczna*, Oficyna Naukowa, Warszawa 2002.

Vanhaverbeke W., Cloodt M., *Open Innovation in Value Networks*, Chapter 13 in *Open Innovation: Researching a New Paradigm*, Oxford University Press, 2006.

Zarządzanie z pasją czyli rozmowy z Konosuke Matsushitą, oprac. PHP Institute Inc., Matsushita Group. Medium, Poznań 2004.

Zrównoważony rozwój przedsiębiorstw – moda czy konieczność?, dyskusja redakcyjna prowadzona przez A. Hermana z udziałem K. Jaskuły, K. Kucińskiego, W. Kulpy, J.S. Zegara. „Kwartalnik Nauk o Przedsiębiorstwie" 2011, no. 1.

http://www.seremet.org/who_zdrowie.html.
http://mahajana.net/mb3s/publikacje/dhammapada/prawosc.html.
http://pl.wikipedia.org/Wiki/Zarządzanie_przez_zaufanie.
http://www.demokraci.pl/slownik/t/181-transparentno-.
http://www.pozytywne.com/artykuly/25/Korzysci-z-bycia-optymista.
http://szyszkowska.bloog.pl/id,329253164,title,LOJALNOSC,index.html?ticaid=6ef4c.
http://www.stevepavlina.com/articles/living-your-values.1.htm.
http://www.stevepavlina.com/articles/list-of-values.htm.

Andrzej Herman
Tadeusz Oleksyn

3. FINAL REFLECTIONS

1. The inspiration for research was the conviction that management may be more accepted, effective and efficient, while the management team more credible, the co-workers more strongly motivated and convinced of the sense of what they do if it is based on the acknowledged values. It has been assumed that management in harmony with values shall be better adopted and proceed more easily than management with the violation of the respected values or disregarding their existence and ignoring these values. Such assumptions would seem to be common sense and rather obvious, albeit only in a world where values and principles have survived and defended themselves and in which there is still room for values. As a multitude of varying opinions have been voiced on the issue of the nature of the contemporary world in this very context, this thesis need not have been so obvious.[99]

2. We have analysed a certain small section of the world – the representatives of only some enterprises functioning in Poland. One of the aims of

---

[99] Some social philosophers, sociologists and psychologists claim that in the realities of the strong influences of the philosophies of utilitarianism, relativism and post-modernism in the hedonistic society of consumerism of the Atlantic civilization, while also the domination of situational ethics and fetishization of money in the turbo-capitalism of the turn of the 21st century, the traditional values significantly lost out in terms of their previously held credibility and power of influence, as in the case of moral principles. The phrase utilized here, namely "significantly lost out" is very circumspect. Zygmunt Bauman, who with relation to these changes expressed it in terms of the metaphor of "liquid modernity" by suggesting that the condition of the contemporary "liberation of power" is not entirely known in terms of what power and in what direction it can go is the melting of everything that has been preserved as a "solid", albeit not much has been preserved (Z. Bauman, *Płynna nowoczesność*, Wydawnictwo Literackie, Kraków 2006, Foreword, Chapter 1). Herbert Marcuse also used the formulation of "liberation" in a certain absurd sense which was what the "liberation" of the thirty years of post-war times were for him in terms of the "unprecedented growth of wealth and economic security in the wealthy countries of the Western World" (Z. Bauman, *op. cit.*, p. 26). This notion has been more intensely undertaken by Charles Handy by comparing the "liberation from traditions and the relative control of time", as well as the excessive acceleration and congestion of changes over needs and the human measure of progeria, the genetic disease as a result of which the transformation of human matter undergoes acceleration, which in effect means that a child at the age of ten or a little older may die as a decrepit old man (Ch. Handy, *The Empty Raincoat: Making Sense of the Future*, 1994). This is naturally speaking, an open question as to what extent these visions are true and to what extent they are the result of over-sensitivity and the self-suggestions of the authors themselves. Nevertheless, it would not seem that they would be worth completely ignoring.

the research was to become familiar with the opinions of managers and specialists in organizations of varying types with relation to values, their significance and validity / rank of importance in organizations functioning in Poland in which they are employed. In a manner of speaking, this therefore also related to testing whether and to what extent we are dealing with "post-modernity" and how "fluid" in terms of professional and organizational environments.

The results of research have turned out to be in general optimistic and uplifting. The decisive majority of the managers and specialists surveyed expressed the conviction in a variety of ways that values are currently fulfilling a significant role in the management of their organizations. A similar case applies to the enterprises described within the framework of case studies. These results have been rather extensively described in sections I and II of the herein report on the research, thus there is no need to refer to them once more. At the same time, the acquired results in general do not confirm the rather catastrophic image painted by Zygmunt Bauman in his work – whilst taking nothing away from the creativity, incisiveness of analysis and merits of the aforesaid author in terms of exploring the issue undertaken. We must emphasize that our research related to only a small fragment of the subject matter that was undertaken by Z. Bauman – the significance of values in management in certain organizations functioning in Poland.

3. Greater interest in terms of values and the pursuit of their recognition in management would also seem to be justified with regard to the change in th enature and course of a multitude of works, which have either already been executed, or are being executed at present. The direct contact characteristic of the industrial era[100]– including eye contact of the "superior" and "subordinate", while also the "work of hired employees that is subject to and executed under the management of the employer"[101] are no longer so prevalent as in the past, while in many organizations and types of activities they practically do not exist anymore. More and more frequently, independent specialists actually work completely independently away from the headquarters of the firm and away from the possibilities of being controlled by their bosses – if they have any. Even if they do not have

---

[100] It is worth noting that in as much as the industrial era that is perceived to have been a certain set of paradigms and as an ideology belongs to the past, the perception of the high ranking in importance of industry does not belong to the past. Never before has industry been so important as at present, while never before has such challenges been undertaken, nor such great projects realized as at present. Without industry, maintaining and satisfying the material needs of over 7 billion people on our planet would obviously be impossible.

[101] This sanctified and antipathic formula still remains the favourite hypallage of a multitude of Polish lawyers, especially those specializing in Labour Law.

such, then very often it is them and not the bosses that have the higher qualifications in a given specific field. Sensible bosses know this and give them a free hand as the negative alternative is to direct people that are substantively stronger by those who are substantively weaker, which of course does not make sense at all. Hence, a new bond is necessary, a new integrating factor in place of the omnipotent boss of the past. This bond may be the mission and vision of the organization – if they are authentic and treated seriously, as well as the values which after all frequently constitute an element of the mission.

4. A further reason to support values is that of a certain crisis of leadership that is also expressed in the questioning of the bases, the sources and scope of the organizational power of the managers. This questioning is by no means unjustified: essentially, the legislative basis and organizational determination of the power of managers are rather fragile, particularly in entities that have departed from stipulations of the "bureaucratic / administrative school" of Max Weber almost 100 years previously, or have never applied them and where there are no organizational regulations that are described in detail and constantly updated in terms of the scope of activities, authorization and responsibilities for each position and described with detail in terms of the mutual ties and obligations of the "superiors" and the "subordinates". In this situation, it is better to become refocused in the direction of communities of people that are connected by common goals and commonly shared values and who realize their dreams and projects together, while also earn money together rather than persisting with the "conferred power", "power of coercion" and "power of punishment", which were referred to in the types of power as written by R.L. Katz half a century ago.

5. One of the aims of the research was to establish to what extent the values are actually present in management and what causative power they have, even if this very fact is well-perceived. We were rather convinced that it is not possible to manage only "via values", as such management would resemble a not very professional "management by appeal", however we wanted to check this from an empirical viewpoint. Likewise, we thought that the aim should rather be "management that respects and promotes values" than "management by values", albeit it is already known under the latter name, to a significant extent due to the creators and propagators of this method of management, Ken Blanchard and Michael O'Connor.[102]

6. There is a good vibe and a good time to spread the word of management that respects and promotes values, at least in Poland. We have encountered

---

[102] Polskie wydanie: K. Blanchard, M. O'Connor, *Zarządzanie poprzez wartości*, Studio Emka, Warszawa 1998.

approval and authentic interest among our respondents with relation to the subject matter at hand, while the responses received and opinions expressed entirely empower us to make this very statement. We feel that this is good news, the more so as mainly negative and critical opinions of reprehensible deeds that are not in accordance with the law or good practices find their way into the public opinion. Likewise, we are of the view that this is first and foremost the fact that evil is more media worthy and attractive than as material for *news* than positive information about good practices, the appropriate attitudes and activities. It is also our opinion that the majority of entrepreneurs and managers run their businesses in a honest manner and manage in accordance with values.

7. Professional work, particularly in the sector of enterprises, displays the significance of the economic and managerial values in a somewhat natural way, such as in particular, efficiency, effectiveness, entrepreneurship, profitability and viability of business activities, competitiveness, quality and business orientation. The self-financing and competing enterprises must clearly concentrate on the creation of good products, high quality of everything they do / make and (goods and services), as well as their sales. The management team must focus the attention of co-workers and integrate the activities around the business aims. Likewise, they must take care of the good opinion and trust among clients and on a broader scale, society itself. Research, of both survey type and case studies have illustrated that the facts are commonly perceived, both among managers of various levels and leaders, as well as among specialists (the opinions of operational and auxiliary employees were not analysed).

8. We did not encounter any cases of contesting the economic values, nor were we informed in anonymous research, or in conversations of any critical opinions on the subject of the excessive display of the aforesaid values, setting excessive requirements, or even worse the exploitation of employees.[103] This certifies to the fact that the owners and managers generally speaking can set people requirements in such a manner that does not arouse protests, nor evoke their resistance. In truth, the research was not particularly oriented towards conflict situations arising out of managerial activities associated with the realization of business goals, however it would undoubtedly have revealed this as this had been a significant and frequent problem.

9. Apart from the (1) economic and managerial values, other groups of values exist, including the following (as the subject matter of our interest in the research carried out); (2) competence, developmental and social, as

---

[103] However, we encountered on Internet blogs, albeit not very common but anonymous responses, including the spirit of employees in terms of two of the analysed enterprises.

well as (3) ethical and cultural. The question of whether, why and to what extent the organizations (including enterprises) are to take account of the non-economic values in their systems of management is valid in the broad perception of the term "are to" and what it signifies.

The answer to this is partially simple and does not arouse any doubts: it is necessary for obvious reasons to adhere to the law and good practices. Such values as honesty, responsibility, trust and loyalty are supported by business and economic values, while respecting them wins clients and serves to maintain them. Justice is essential in terms of shaping all the principles and interpersonal relations, particularly in the cases of the superiors and subordinates, as well as in personnel decisions, while also the lack of justice evokes tension and conflicts, while also being demotivational, destroying trust and cooperation. Solidarity is associated with trust and loyalty, cooperation, while also facilitating (sometimes conditioning) the achievement of difficult aims and counteracting injustices, as well as enabling the defence of the fight for variousjust causes and endeavours for necessary changes. Similarly, it is possibleto justify the need to respect and support a multitude of in organizations and illustrate that the non-economic values are in essence supporting the economic values, albeit not always immediately as sometimes it happens over a medium and long-term time perspective.

10. Nevertheless, in as much as the pronouncement is rather easy at the phase of a great level of generality and we are inclined towards the thesis that almost all values that have been presented in the aforesaid catalogue of values may be acknowledged to be significant,[104] the difficulties appear, which are large in the subsequent phases of the analytical and diagnostic processes, which are necessary to get through in search for the answers to the following questions, among others:

(1) What choices would be necessary to make and according to what criteria in the cases of conflicts of values as exemplified by the conflict between personal freedom and freedom of choice, while also the good of the natural environment and future generations and also personal state of health. In this example, there may be conflict caused by the penchant for lavish lifestyle or the psychological addiction to shopping (*shopaholism*), which even in its morbid intensity is not after all subject to forced therapy, nor legislative or administrative restraining orders. Without doubt, the choices mentioned here would be very different depending on the specific situation, degree of real freedom of the particular entities, their bargaining power, etc.

---

[104] This thesis would be worth analysing in a more profound way.

(2) Should we measure and how to measure non-economic values; at least some, if not the majority of which are impossible to gauge. Should we specify and how to specify the level of fulfilment of needs, not only material ones? What would specifically arise from that?

(3) What are the real decision dilemmas associated with values and what is the real margin of the freedom of choice? In reality, no doubt the entire free choices in conditions of the conflict of values cannot be executed by anyone. Nevertheless, the freedom of choice for a private entrepreneur is significantly greater than the manager hired by him, or (the more so) a hired employee. How is this to be analysed and evaluated?

11. The research of management that respects and promotes values in organizations is significant, necessary and in our view should be continued. It would be possible, within the framework of their continuation, to analyse the possibilities, ways and limits of operationalization of such management, including an attempt to design compilatory techniques of management, for instance combining the technique of MBO (Management by Objectives), MBR (Management by Results) or TQM (Total Quality Management) with the technique of MBV (Management by Values) or its elements. It would also be worth undertaking research on the situation in which conflicts of values appear, which happen when these conflicts are resolved as the analytical and decision-making processes look and what decisions are taken.

12. Restricting research on the values to only micro-economic entities would seem to be insufficient, the more so as **what is rational at a micro-economic level, need not be at such "high" levels of the structure and broader point of view**. Expansion of the research to also include management that respects and promotes values at other levels than the micro-economic one would be essential, thus at themes and macro-economic levels, while in the case of creating the appropriate international cooperation and acquisition of funds to muster up theoretical reflection and at least research in a global sense.

13. Hope and necessity are stronger and have a more widespread orientation towards sustainability. This is already a fact in an array of countries, particularly in the Scandinavian countries of Europe (Denmark), while also Germany and Holland. Sustainability is also an intellectual concept and increasingly a practice that is extremely necessary in the realities of the dangers to our planet partially evoked by the irresponsibilities of man, as well as being a great value.

The second convergent challenge is to learn the method that is possibly devoid of the shocks of functioning in conditions of the lack of the growth of GDP, or slight growth. Up to recently, no economist or politician wanted to hear about this as it was acknowledged that it must lead to the growth of unemployment, worsening of social moods, the loss of power, stagnation or the decrease in incomes. However, particularly in wealthy countries the constant economic growth calculated at present may be counteracted both due to the depleting resources of our planet and the necessity of their costly renewal, as well as the inexpediency and incapacity to replicate the way of development of the wealthy countries by the other countries that also display aspirations of wealth, in which this wealth may however be unrealistic for them.

The continuation of the current road to development (and its hitherto perception) may not only be practically impossible, but also lead to large local and international conflicts, as well as wars over resources. A way-out would be to at least partially distract individual and social attention away from material matters and attract their attention to issues of the natural environment and areas of greenery, clean rivers and seas, clean air, reduction of the burden connected with work and "job sharing", the total development of man (not only consumption of material goods), greater spiritual and cultural development, greater involvement on behalf of the family and local communities, the beauty and aesthetics of the environment, improvement of the collective transportation, better organization of life and an array of other activities which bring satisfaction and a higher quality of life for people without the further development of individual consumption, frequently to excess and the feeling of indecency, while damaging the state of health.

14. A significant problem associated with values and their ranking in importance is associated with the increasingly anachronical and excessive impoverishment of the method of expressing the development of a country by means of the indicator of the Gross National Product (Gross Domestic Product, GDP). This indicator does not fully gauge even the economic development of the country, not to mention the civilizational level, quality of life, or (the more so) happiness. Nevertheless, its common use and abuse creates the illusion that this is a "total" indicator, which is the most significant not only in terms of the assessment of economic development, but also the measurement of the standard of living, quality of life and civilizational level that the particular countries and societies have attained.

For some time now a multitude of excellent scientists, among others – laureates of the Noble Prize Joseph E. Stiglitz, Gary Becker, Amartya Sena, while also Jean Paul Fitosoussi, Ezry J. Mishan, Daniel Bell, Alvin Toffler, including scientists from Poland: Jerzy Chłopecki, Jan Danecki, Andrzej Hodoły, Grzegorz W. Kołodko, Andrzej K. Koźmiński, Tadeusz Kowalik, Elżbieta Mączyńska, Adam Noga, Maksymilian Pohorille, Krystyna Świderska, Władysław Szymański (in alphabetical order), have all been very critical of GDP and postulate over the necessity of its profound modification by taking account of among other aspects, prosumption, thus the contribution of households towards economic growth, which is unfortunately generally not counted. It is not good when the aspirations change, while the catalogue of precious values is expanded, but the indicators of development and progress remain the same, one-dimensional and excessively weak.[105]

Bibliography

Bauman Z., *Płynna nowoczesność*, Wydawnictwo Literackie, Kraków 2006.

Blanchard K., O'Connor M., *Zarządzanie poprzez wartości*, Studio Emka, Warszawa 1998.

Handy Ch., *The Empty Raincoat: Making Sense of the Future*, 1994.

Herman A., *PKB i poszukiwanie szczęścia,*"Kwartalnik Nauk o Przedsiębiorstwie" 2015, no. 1.

---

[105] A. Herman, *PKB i poszukiwanie szczęścia*, "Kwartalnik Nauk o Przedsiębiorstwie" 2015, no. 1.

TECHNICAL EDITOR
Renata Włodek

PROOFREADER
Małgorzata Szul

TYPESETTER
Wojciech Wojewoda

Jagiellonian University Press
Editorial Offices: Michałowskiego St. 9/2, 31-271 Kraków
Phone: +48 12 663 23 81, +48 12 663 23 82, Fax: +48 12 663 23 83